C000314892

Cavendish
Publishing
Limited

CONSTITUTIONAL

&

ADMINISTRATIVE LAW

TITLES IN THE SERIES

Administrative Law

Business Law

Child Law

Civil Liberties

Commercial Law

Company Law

Conflict of Laws

Constitutional & Administrative Law

Contract Law

Criminal Law

Criminal Litigation and Sentencing

Criminology

Employment Law

English Legal System

Equity & Trusts

European Community Law

Evidence

Family Law

Intellectual Property Law

International Trade Law

Jurisprudence

Land Law

Law of Tort

Public International Law

Revenue Law

Succession, Wills & Probate

'A' Level Law - Paper I

'A' Level Law - Paper II

Cavendish
Publishing
Limited

CONSTITUTIONAL

&

ADMINISTRATIVE LAW

AP Le Sueur, LLB, Barrister
Lecturer in Laws
University College London

&

JW Herberg, LLB, BCL
Barrister
London

First published in Great Britain 1995 by Cavendish Publishing Limited, The Glass House, Wharton Street, London WC1X 9PX.
Telephone: 0171-278 8000 Facsimile: 0171-278 8080

British Library Cataloguing in Publication Data

Le Sueur, AP and Herberg, JW
Constitutional & Administrative Law – (Lecture Notes Series)
I Title II Series
344.202

ISBN 1-874241 67 8
Cover photograph by Jerome Yeats
Printed and bound in Great Britain

Preface and Acknowledgments

This book was written over the summer, autumn and winter of 1994 and we have stated the law as on 1 January 1995. Andrew Le Sueur was primarily responsible for Chapters 1-11; Javan Herberg for Chapters 12-18. We are greatly indebted to Susan Hall who wrote much of Chapter 9 (Ombudsmen) and read and commented on several other chapters, and to Lucan Herberg who wrote much of Chapter 15 (on bias). Other friends and colleagues, particularly Rodney Austin, Nicholas Bamforth and Nicola Shaldon, also took the trouble to look at parts of the book in draft. Naturally we remain responsible for the errors and failings of the book. Thanks also to Jo Reddy and Kate Nicol at Cavendish Publishing for their constant good humour and, above all, patience.

Javan Herberg
Andrew Le Sueur
March 1995

Outline Table of Contents

Detailed Table of Contents

Table of Cases

Table of Statutes and Treaties

Chapter 1

Introduction to the book

At some time during your constitutional and administrative law/public law course, you'll feel the need to reach for a book other than your main textbook. This may be after a lecture on a particularly difficult topic, or maybe when you're sitting down to write an essay. Or towards the end of the course when you want a clear overview of how things fit together. You may want some background knowledge on history and politics before you even begin to study the subject.

Up to now that 'other' book has most likely had to be one of the little crammer-style books which your teacher probably would rather you didn't buy. Many of those books are overly simplistic and deeply misleading. This book has been written as an alternative. Obviously, it cannot even begin to cover the same ground in the same detail as one of the big, classic textbooks such de Smith's *Constitutional and Administrative Law*. It tries to provide something different; this book is as much about how to study constitutional and administrative law as it is about the content of the subject itself. We've borrowed Glanville Williams' motto from his classic *Learning the Law* and have tried to produce a 'guide, philosopher and friend' for people studying public law.

- It's a *guide* in as much as it seeks to explain why writers and judges make the claims that they do; we highlight things to look out for on various topics and try to give some fresh, practical and critical ways of looking at topics.

- It's a *philosopher* because we believe that in order to be able to understand public law deeply, students need some awareness of history and an appreciation of trends in political thought and to understand how these have shaped 'legal' issues.

- It's designed to be *user-friendly* and the style is informal.

Some of the chapters in this book can usefully be read before or soon after you start studying constitutional and administrative law. These include:

- Chapter 2 on the main characteristics of the constitution;

- Chapter 3 on basic constitutional history;

- Chapter 6 on changes brought about by the Conservative governments since 1979.

1.1 A 'companion' for law students

1.2 When to read this book

We've called these 'gap-filling' chapters because they include important background knowledge which law teachers may assume or expect students to arrive with. Many students, however, have never studied history nor do they have a grounding in political theory; if this is you, you should find these chapters a good starting point.

Chapter 4 on a 19th century writer Dicey should be read after the first or second time your lecturer mentions his name (which will probably be quite early on in the course!).

Chapter 7 is written, in part, as a practical guide to research on constitutional and administrative law issues. It explains where to find sources of public law (statutes, statutory instruments, examples of the prerogative, conventions etc) in the library and summarises the constitutional problems associated with them. It ends by giving an overview, using a practical example, of how they all fit together.

1.3   Coverage

Many topics on the syllabus of your constitutional and administrative law course are not tackled head-on in separate chapters. (Parliamentary sovereignty, for example, is considered in Chapter 4 on Dicey and his critics and in Chapter 8 on European Community law.) Use the index to track things down.

Nor does this book give detailed accounts of particular institutions such as Parliament, local authorities or the organs of the European Community; many other textbooks do this. There are, however, several chapters with titles which are likely to match items on your syllabus. In these chapters we focus on the three topics which, experience shows, students have most difficulty in understanding *well*. These are:

- the inter-connection between European Community law and the English legal system in Chapter 8;

- the role and techniques of the so-called Ombudsmen in Chapter 9;

- above all, judicial review in Chapter 10 onwards.

1.4   A 'critical' approach to public law

One of the aims of this book is to encourage readers to adopt a 'critical' approach to studying constitutional and administrative law. Like all law degree subjects it can require students to learn quite a bit by rote and in this sense knowing facts is important. But to get a deep understanding of what modern public law is about, much more is needed. It is all very well to be able to describe the stages through which a Bill must pass through Parliament on its way to becoming an Act, or what needs to be done by a person who wants to apply to the High Court for an application for judicial review of an official decision. To get to the root of things, however, you need also to be *critical*.

Being critical is not the same as rubbishing everything; indeed it is possible to be 'critical' in a sympathetic way. A law student shouldn't say something like 'Parliament is just a talking shop which rubber stamps everything the government wants it to' and then stop. What's needed is an appreciation of how things came to be as they are, what different writers and theorists claim the problems to be, why they hold these views, whether you agree and what might be done to remedy problems. This approach can be applied to everything on your syllabus: from Parliamentary sovereignty, to the role of Ombudsmen, to the concept of legitimate expectation in judicial review. Being critical above all means *questioning* the academics and judges whose writing you'll be reading during your constitutional and administrative law course. If you work hard at developing this kind of informed, intelligent scepticism as your technique to studying public law, you'll find you get a deeper understanding. Dull, dry issues should then start to come alive.

Introduction to the Book

To get the most out of a course on constitutional and administrative law you should work toward a deep understanding of the subject. This is almost certainly what your examiners will be looking for. To achieve this, try adopting a 'critical' approach to your reading (and also writing).

The need for a 'critical' approach

Whenever you read a journal article, textbook or judgment it is worth asking some basic questions about it.

- Who wrote it? What do you know about the author?

- When was it written? A description of the constitution written in the 19th century, or even the 1970s, is unlikely to reflect what's happening today and so caution is needed.

- Why was it written? There is no such thing as neutral writing about the constitution; try to work out how writers' views on or analysis of a particular topic fit into a broader picture of his or her political views.

Chapter 2

Characteristics of the
United Kingdom Constitution

LECTURER'S HEALTH WARNING: An uncritical and complacent reading of this chapter can seriously damage a student's understanding of the modern British constitution.

2.1   Introduction

This chapter highlights some of the main features of the UK constitution. If you regularly read a quality British newspaper (as you should), much of this will be familiar territory. It's intended to be read sitting in a deck chair with a large glass of something cool during the summer before starting a course on public law. Or – more likely – sitting on a bus on the way to your first lecture on the subject. The 'health warning' is needed because all the descriptions and analysis of the institutions, principles and practices of the modern constitutions are presented in a very superficial way. But we need to start somewhere and taking a general overview of the topics dealt with in most courses seems a good place to begin.

2.1.1   An August day in London

Last summer I spent a very warm August day showing my friend Bill around some of the sights of central London. Bill is American and he lapped it all up. We emerged into the bright sunlight, blinking from the gloom of Westminster Abbey and walked across Parliament Square to look at the newly-cleaned Palace of Westminster. It was magnificent; even the gilt on the tower that houses Big Ben sparkled. I explained to Bill that this was, of course, where the two Houses of Parliament – the Lords and Commons – sit, but that it was the summer recess at the moment. 'So this is where it all happens, eh?' said Bill.

That set me thinking. Just how important is Parliament to the modern British constitution? We saw our bus coming and ran to the bus stop. Bill was disappointed that it wasn't one of the classic red Route Master double deckers. I explained that as part of the Conservative government's deregulation and privatisation policies, for a while now, several companies in addition to London Transport had been allowed to run bus services in central London.

We drove up Whitehall. I pointed out 10 Downing Street, official residence of the Prime Minister, with its impressive new gates designed to thwart terrorist attacks. (Perhaps this is where 'it all happens?' I wondered to myself.) We passed the great grey facades behind which are many of the government departments – the Treasury, the Foreign and Commonwealth Office, the Ministry of Defence, the Department of Health in its stylish new building. It was 5 o'clock and junior civil servants were streaming out of the doors. (Were *these* the places where real power lay? I thought). As we reached Trafalgar Square we just managed to snatch a glimpse down the Mall towards Buckingham Palace. (I was fairly sure that was no longer 'where it all happened'.)

The bus went past the National Gallery. We saw a taxi narrowly miss a cyclist and my blood ran cold thinking of the number of times that had happened to me. I complained to Bill that there were no proper cycle routes in London; some of the 32 boroughs had them, but many did not. I explained how the Greater London Council, the elected local authority for the whole of Greater London, had been abolished by Margaret Thatcher's Conservative government in 1986 and that there was no longer any elected strategic authority for the whole of London. Maybe, I suggested, things would be better for cyclists if we had a city-wide council again. Bill laughed embarrassingly loudly: 'No one,' he said, 'loves cyclists enough to spend money on them.'

Up the Strand. Round Aldwych with the BBC's Bush House and the Indian and Australian High Commissions. Then into Fleet Street. We jumped off just after the Victorian buildings of the Royal Courts of Justice. It was too late to go inside but I promised Bill we'd come back later on in the week. 'I like your Supreme Court, even if it is fake gothic,' Bill quipped.

'Oh, it's not the Supreme Court. I mean it is ... the building does house most of the bits of what's technically called that the "Supreme Court of the Judicature", but it's not a "supreme court" in the sense of being a constitutional court like yours in the US. We haven't got one of those,' I tried to explain. 'Gee! I don't think I'm ever going to get the hang of this British constitution of yours,' Bill sighed. 'Let's go and buy a copy of it in that legal bookshop over there and then grab a cup of tea,' he suggested. 'Ah ... that's a bit of a problem,' I said. 'You don't want "a cuppa"? I don't believe it!' Bill laughed. 'It's not the tea, Bill. It's the constitution. We don't have one. No, I mean, of course we have one ... it's just not written down ... of course bits are written down ... but not all in one place,' I stuttered. 'Come on, Andrew,' Bill said. 'You need some tea and sympathy.'

We sat down and the waiter brought us a pot of Earl Grey and a two sticky cakes. I was embarrassed. Here I was, a lecturer in constitutional law and I just wasn't doing a very good job of explaining the basics to Bill. I poured our tea and took a deep breath.

'Look Bill, there are only seven things you really need to know about the constitution,' I said, plucking a number from the air. I took out my pen and began thinking about the standard chapters in most student textbooks on constitutional law. I began writing a list on a paper napkin.

2.1.2   Tea and sympathy about the British constitution

Every English schoolgirl and schoolboy is told that we have an unwritten constitution. Their teachers are wrong. Many laws which can be described as 'constitutional' (because they deal with the relationship between different institutions of government or between the state and the individual's fundamental civil rights) is fundamental civil rights are, of course, in writing. There are statutes such as the frequently amended European Communities Act 1972 (making the United Kingdom part of the European Union), the Public Order Act 1986 (imposing restrictions on freedom of assembly), the Parliament Acts of 1911 and 1949 (dealing with the relative powers of the elected House of Commons and the unelected House of Lords) and the Act of Settlement 1701 (which among other things stipulates who becomes monarch on the death of the previous king or queen).

2.2   There is no single constitutional document

Even the constitutional rights, duties and powers created by judge-made common law are 'written'. They can be found in the law reports ... if a person knows how to use a law library. For instance, if you look up the reference [1948] 1 KB 233 you will find a report of a case called *Associated Provincial Picture Houses Ltd v Wednesbury Corporation* which contains a statement of a legal principle of great constitutional importance by Lord Green MR on p 230:

> 'It is true to say that if a decision on a competent matter is so unreasonable that no reasonable authority could ever have come to it, then the courts can interfere ...; but to prove a case of that kind would require something overwhelming.'

In that case the Court of Appeal upheld the validity of a condition imposed by the local authority that no child under 15 years could be admitted to see any film on Sundays. In England, general constitutional principles often spring from particular legal challenges to government. The cinema owners did not intend to establish a precedent that would be cited in every book on constitutional and administrative law. Yet today lawyers use the term '*Wednesbury* unreasonable' as shorthand for a complex bundle of principles which determine the lawful boundaries of how ministers, local authorities, tribunals and other public bodies may exercise their discretions.

The *Wednesbury* case also stands for a principle of judicial restraint: a judge judicially review a government decision may not quash it merely because he would have made a different one, eg that he would not have imposed the no-children-on-Sundays condition. Only if the decision is 'so outrageous in its defiance of logic or of accepted moral standards that no sensible person who had applied his mind to the question to be decided could have arrived at it' (in the words of Lord Diplock in *Council of Civil Service Unions v Minister for the Civil Service* (1984)) should a court intervene. (The grounds of judicial review are examined in more detail in later chapters.)

I reminded myself of the point I was trying to make to Bill: there is no single document in Britain which sets out in a principled, codified way the law on the constitution. A study of constitutional law cannot therefore really start with the examination of first principles. I searched for an analogy to explain what I meant to Bill; he cringed when I came up with this analogy ...

Some constitutions are like a piece of woven cloth designed by a committee who sat down (usually after some catastrophic event like war or revolution) and made planned decisions about the sort of thread to use, the colour and so on while bearing in mind their strategic goals – did they want the cloth to keep people warm? How big would it be? The British constitution is not like that: it is more like a patchwork quilt that has been made by many different people over many years. There is no master plan. When things need to be mended a new square is added or maybe one is replaced. Occasionally the various people doing the sewing get together to talk about how things are going. There is rarely much agreement about how to proceed, though there is a general feeling that progress is being made. There is, however, no founding committee with a grand plan to whom they can look. (I began to relax: Bill was smiling and nodding. Obviously I was making some sense ...)

Many academic writers and some politicians believe that many of the rules and practices of the British constitution should be codified into a single document. Part of that would be a Bill of Rights which would set out the fundamental civil and political rights of people living in Britain. But when people talk about Britain not having a written constitution, sometimes arguing that we should have one, the discussion is not just about making the rules of the constitution more accessible. The debate is about something altogether more important than that. Which brings us to thing-to-know-about-the-constitution-number-two.

Because Britain has no supreme constitutional document there are no legal constraints on what the government can do as long as it gives its decision legal-backing by having a statute passed through Parliament. (The barometer of Bill's frown suggested a concrete example was needed.)

Take abortion. It is a controversial matter over which people with deeply held views disagree. In Britain abortion of foetuses up to 28 weeks was legalised by the Abortion Act 1967. Pressure groups continued to campaign against abortion and in 1991 members of Parliament voted to amend the 1967 Act by reducing the time limit to 24 weeks. The English courts have from time to time had to hear cases dealing with abortion. For example in *Royal College of Nursing v Department of Health* (1981) the courts had to determine whether a circular issued by the department was legally correct in its statement that nurses could lawfully during an abortion perform certain functions. What the English courts did not have power to do was to decide whether the Abortion Act 1967 is itself 'lawful' or 'unconstitutional'. The judges must (subject to what's said below) accept statute law as given.

Contrast this with the role of judges in the abortion issue in the US. There the Supreme Court has been called upon to decide whether state legislation permitting abortion is or is not 'constitutional': see for example the famous case of *Roe v Wade* (1973). The provisions of the US constitution and the case law decided by the US Supreme Court are supreme law overriding all other ordinary legislation such as that passed by the legislatures in various states permitting abortion. In Britain there is no supreme law capable of overriding Acts of Parliament; generally the validity of a statute cannot be questioned in the English courts. There is no 'constitutional' or 'supreme' court in this sense. Many people claim that this is a key, perhaps unique, feature of the British constitution.

(Bill was nodding. He seemed to be following what I was saying. That frown suddenly reappeared when I started on point 3 ...)

2.3   Parliamentary sovereignty

Everything just said about Parliamentary sovereignty is subject to one very important exception to do with Britain's membership of the European Union. In fact, if we're being honest, the 'exception' is so big that it practically eats away the whole principle of Parliament's legislative sovereignty.

'Hey, I hesitate to interrupt your flow Andrew,' Bill said. 'But could you just fill me in about this European Union? We read about in the newspapers in New York almost every day but I've never been exactly sure what it's all about. I'm

2.4   Membership of the European Union

confused also about its name: we used to called it the European Community then all of a sudden everyone's saying European Union.'

The EU now consists of 15 Member States. It started life in 1950s as three free trade organisations with six members (not including the UK because President de Gaulle of France did not want us in the club) but has now grown into much more. Some people hope that the process of European integration will eventually result in something like a United States of Europe, with a common currency, a central bank and broadly similar laws in the Member States; others are appalled by this idea. The European Economic Community (later shortened to 'European Community') was the most important of the free trade organisations – others dealt with iron, steel and coal and atomic energy. It has grown and changed but is still concerned with the so-called 'four freedoms' of movement – of goods, services, capital and people. In 1993 a 'single market' was achieved in which all tariff barriers and physical boarder controls between Member States disappeared. For ordinary people in England this means that they can now take a van on the ferry to Calais to buy wine and beer (much cheaper in France) and cheese and cigarettes (much smellier) and bring it back to England without having to pay any customs duty. For business, too, the commercial advantages of the single market have opened up new opportunities.

In 1993 the Member States signed the Maastricht Treaty and formed the European Union. This has three parts. The well-established European Community remains one pillar. Second is a common foreign and defence policy. Third is that there will be cooperation over justice and home affairs (mainly crime and immigration).

Now, getting back to Parliamentary sovereignty and the UK's membership of the EC. The EC has its own law-making institutions (see Chapter 8) which now form a top tier of government in the 'British' constitution. The EC Treaty of (part of English law because s 2 of the European Communities Act 1972 says so) makes EC law supreme in all the Member States. This means that English judges now have power, which they have exercised several times, to strike down a statute passed by the UK Parliament on the ground that it is incompatible with EC law. This was a very profound change. Obviously this can only happen in relation to those types of activity that are governed by EC law – still mainly those to do with the four freedoms. In other areas of British life unaffected by the EC (for instance laws of inheritance) the principle of Parliamentary sovereignty remains.

I ordered some more tea. Bill looked as though he needed some. We watched the traffic trundle past us along Fleet Street. Then I continued.

Except possibly for a short period during the 17th century, Parliament has never *governed* the country. The executive functions government takes place in the name of the Crown. Obviously today this does not mean the Queen personally, but rather her ministers and their staff of civil servants. (The important story of how the change from personal rule of the sovereign to rule by ministers came about is told in the next Chapter 3.) The prime ministers and other ministers (often called Secretaries of State) are not, as such, directly elected. They are however mostly members of the House of Commons (a few are peers in the House of Lords) elected to represent one of the 651 geographical constituencies in the UK. John Major was elected as MP for Huntingdon by the electors in that area; he was not elected prime minister by the electorate as a whole.

Particular MPs become ministers and form the government because of their membership of a political party. John Major was leader of the Conservative Party which, after the last general election in 1992, had the largest number of its candidates elected as MPs. The Queen therefore sent for him and asked him to form the government. Political parties are accordingly an important part and parcel of the modern British constitution, though they do not have the same sort of status that they do in other countries. In Germany, for example, parties are formally recognised in the constitution. In the UK they do not receive funding for their campaigning and other activities from the state.

Hand in hand with the system of Parliamentary democracy goes the notion that the UK does not have any – or at least any strong – 'separation of powers', a principle which is regarded as important in many other countries. The notion is quite a complicated one but one version says that in a constitution legislative, executive and judicial functions should be exercised by different people in order to prevent abuse of power. In the US the president (who exercises executive functions) cannot be a member of congress (which legislates). The reverse is true in the UK: by convention all ministers including the prime minister have to be members of the legislature. The country's senior judges, the Lords of Appeal of Ordinary, are also members of the House of Lords and take part in its legislative work as well as sitting on the special Appellate Committee hearing appeals from lower courts. This is not to say that judges recognise that there are constitutional limits on their powers to intervene in 'executive decisions': for

2.5   Parliamentary democracy and the absence of separation of powers

example they exercise great caution before overturning government decisions involving the allocation of resources. But on the whole it is better to say that we have something more like a 'fusion' of powers.

Some people consider the domination of the House of Commons by the political party which also forms the executive government to be dangerous. Lord Hailsham, a former Lord Chancellor and Conservative politician has gone so far as to coin the phrase 'elective dictatorship' to describe the problem. So whenever the term 'Parliamentary sovereignty' is used you therefore have to remember what this frequently means in reality: the government will pressure the MPs in Parliament in its party to vote for its bill (a draft Act of Parliament). The government proposes and in practice secures the passing of whatever legislation it thinks fit.

2.6 Summary so far

Bill, who was planning to study law after college, tried to sum up: 'So what you're saying is that, apart from European Community law (which is part of English law because of an Act of Parliament in 1972), there is no constitutional law in England which has higher status than ordinary law. The role of judges is therefore normally limited to interpreting statutes, though they have created all this common law also. And providing the ruling political party can get a statute through Parliament, it can do anything it likes – though I guess it won't get re-elected if it does something that really gets up Joe Public's nose.'

I nodded.

'But I'm still not clear about one thing,' Bill said. 'I know I can't just walk into a book shop and buy a printed copy of the constitution – because there isn't one – but where do I find the laws on things like who gets chosen as prime minster and how many ministers sit in the Cabinet?'

Bill had put his finger on something important.

2.7 Constitutional conventions

Many of the 'rules' of the constitution cannot by any stretch of the imagination be described as 'laws' – they were not created by statutes or the judges, and the courts are powerless to enforce them. It is not *the law* that the prime minister answers oral questions from MPs in Parliament every Tuesday and Thursday just after 3 o'clock: this is just a rule of Parliamentary procedure over which the courts have absolutely no power to adjudicate. No law dictates how many ministers form the cabinet, though there is an established practice and expectation that ministers holding certain major portfolios will be members. In other words, quite apart from common law principles and statutory rules which can be called 'law', a range of other political principles, practices and constitutional conventions also constrain and facilitate government action. The constitution is often just 'what happens' (as Professor Griffith is fond of putting it). Some commentators have argued that conventions ought to be codified and given legal status but there are many problems with this suggestion. (Conventions are considered in more detail in Chapter 7, para 7.8, below.)

Bill seemed happy enough for the time being. He poured more tea and we looked out of the window again. Then he started to fidget.

'I hope this isn't a completely dumb question,' he said diffidently, 'but there is just one more thing I'm not clear on. On the 'plane on the way over I had to fill in a card including my country of final destination. What should I have put? Is it England? Britain? The United Kingdom? Or what?'

It was a good question.

The constitutional powers of the Crown have at various times in history extended over very different geographical areas. India and Pakistan, independent states since 1948, were for much of the 19th century administered from the India Office in Whitehall in London. As late as 1982 the British Parliament passed a statute having effect in Canada (the Canada Act, which 'repatriated' the Canadian constitution). But today the ambit of constitutional law is, for most purposes, confined to the state called 'the United Kingdom of Great Britain and Northern Ireland'. This is the entity which, on the international plain, enters into treaty obligations.	**2.8 The unitary state of the United Kingdom of Great Britain and Northern Ireland**

The UK is a unitary, rather than federal state, even though it comprises of four 'countries', to use a colloquial rather than a legal term: England, Wales, Scotland (which together may be referred to as Great Britain) and Northern Ireland. This book is mainly about England and Wales which share a common legal system (though some laws, for example about the use of the Welsh language, apply only in Wales). The legal system in Northern Ireland is different, and that of Scotland very different. But MPs from constituencies in each of them sit in Parliament at Westminster. There is no Welsh, Scottish or Northern Irish legislature or assembly, though many people in those countries think that there ought to be and from 1921 to 1972 there was one in Northern Ireland.

The UK is a highly centralised state. There is no tradition of regional government as there is in other European countries such as Germany and Spain. All there is below central government is a tier of quite small local authorities which have very limited powers. London, for example, is governed by 32 different borough councils. Local government consists of elected councils and a body of local government officers. (For more on the dramatic changes in the character of local government see Chapter 6.)

For many, many years there have been demands from some people living in Wales and Scotland for devolution of more power to Parliaments in those countries. Some demand complete independence from the UK. The problem is most pressing in Northern Ireland. Until 1920 the whole of the island of Ireland was part of the UK; then the larger part became an independent state, only six counties in the north remaining in the UK. Many people (but not a majority) living in Northern Ireland wish for it to be part of the Republic of Ireland rather than the UK. Men and women on both the Unionist and Republican sides have taken up arms and since 1969 the British army has patrolled the streets and country lanes in an attempt to keep the peace while politicians search for a longer term solution to the constitutional conflict.

2.9   Conclusion

Bill and I had had enough tea, cake and constitution. We walked through Temple down to the Thames. And then home on the District line. We had to wait ages. We carried on chatting about what I'd tried to explain in the tea rooms. One thing struck us both. The approach I'd taken was very much a 'top down' one. I'd started by wondering where power lay – in Parliament, with the Prime Minister, the Crown, civil servants or the judges. It hadn't occurred to me to think about the place of ordinary people in the British constitution. The idea of political power lying with the citizens, who in turn delegate some of it to the elected authorities, is at the bedrock of many constitutions (such as the French). But in Britain the starting point is still the Crown, meaning today the ministers of the Crown who sit in and dominate Parliament. Bill thought this was bizarre: 'It would be quaint', he said, 'if it weren't so dangerous.'

Characteristics of the United Kingdom Constitution

The characteristics of the constitution are:

- No single constitutional document as supreme law;

- Parliamentary sovereignty;

- Membership of the European Union;

- Parliamentary democracy;

- No strong principle of separation of powers;

- Constitutional conventions;

- Unitary state.

Chapter 3

Gap-filling: Constitutional History

In 1930, WC Sellar and RJ Yeatman, schoolmasters at an English public school, wrote a very funny, very inaccurate book called *1066 And All That*. It's now a classic and well worth reading. The subtitle is 'A memorable history of England comprising all the Good Parts you can remember including 103 Good Things, 5 Bad Kings and 2 Genuine Dates'. Any attempt to give an account of the constitutional history of the UK in 6,000 words (which this chapter does) runs the risk of being about as accurate but nowhere near as funny as *1066*; a little history is a dangerous thing. But many students find themselves beginning to study public law with no real knowledge of English history and feel disadvantaged compared to those others who know why James II threw the Great Seal into the River Thames and that 'The Levellers' were more than a cultish grunge band in the 1980s. If that is you, this chapter should be of help.

A historical perspective is needed because of one basic fact about the English constitution: it is not based on first principles or rational design. Professor Griffith says 'the constitution is simply what happens'. The constitution is also often what has happened in the past. Without some knowledge, however sketchy, of the events of the 17th century (when personal rule of kings was replaced by constitutional monarchy) and the 19th century (when many of the features of the modern state can first be detected), it is difficult to understand what is happening today.

If you are as new to history as you are to law, two warnings need to be given.

First, constitutional law and constitutional history are not at all the same sort of thing. Legal method is ahistorical: cases and legislation (such as Magna Carta 1215 and the Bill of Rights 1689) are often cited in court today without reference to their historical context. For an illustration of this approach have a look at Lord Donaldson MR's judgment in *R v Secretary of State ex p Muboyayi* (1991) where he states, in a case about a Zairian applying for political asylum in the UK, that the 'duty of the courts is to uphold [the] classic statement of the rule of law' in Magna Carta (1215), c 29:

3.1 Why an historical perspective is needed

3.2 The need for caution

3.2.1 History and law are different

'No freeman shall be taken or imprisoned, or be disseised of his freehold or liberties, or free customs, or be outlawed, or exiled, or any other wise destroyed; nor will we not pass upon him, nor condemn him, but by lawful judgment of his peers, or by the law of the land. We will sell to no man, we will not deny or defer to any man either justice or right.'

The notions of 'liberty' and who was a 'free man' were, of course, completely different in the 13th century from what they are today (they certainly did not include women); yet the principles which are supposedly enshrined in Magna Carta were applied to modern circumstances with the court seeing no apparent problems with this. An historian would consider this to be absurd!

3.2.2	Historians disagree	A second warning is that history is a controversial enterprise. Historians disagree not only about the facts but also about how to evaluate them. To take an example: many historians would say that the account of the constitutional events of the 17th century which follows focuses much too much on the squabbles among the ruling elite and pays insufficient attention to the role played by ordinary people – 'the mob' – around the time of the Glorious Revolution in 1688. There is also considerable debate about whether two rival theories of government were a cause or a consequence of the English Civil War. So caution is needed.
3.2.3	Scope of the chapter	The chapter sets out a basic chronology of events during two significant periods of constitutional development – the 1600s and then, roughly, 100 years from 1830 to 1930. Intellectual trends are also of great importance, particularly in the 19th century, but these are dealt with separately in Chapter 5.

3.3 English life in the 1600s

When James I succeeded Elizabeth to the throne in 1603, Shakespeare was in his prime: *Julius Caesar*, *Macbeth* and *King Lear* were all written around this time. The population was about 4 million, living mostly in rural areas. In the countryside the small gentry and yeoman freeholders – the rural 'middle class', to use an anachronism – had great influence. Some were appointed as local Justices of the Peace (JPs) who dispensed summary justice, administered the poor law relieving the destitute, regulated prices and wages, licensed alcohol and had some responsibilities for the upkeep of roads and bridges. They were 'maids of all work'. Statute conferred wide powers on them and their work was supervised by the Privy Council. Although they were Crown servants, they received no direct remuneration from the Crown. The Crown depended greatly on their loyalty – without them public administration would have collapsed.

Many JPs, and other men of property, aspired to be elected to the House of Commons. The two Houses of Parliament of the time were, of course, very different from today's. The Commons represented the landed gentry, merchants and lawyers as only a very small proportion of the population were enfranchised – by and large only males owning substantial land could vote. Also, Parliament met only sporadically, when called by the king, and was not in the almost continuous session it is today. Indeed, for very long periods during the 17th century, there were no sittings at all; Charles I ruled for 11 years without convening Parliament. However, the Stuart kings never abolished Parliament; they merely tried to manipulate it. They succeeded only in destroying the balance between crown and Parliament that had existed in Tudor England.

The 17th century was dominated by three key constitutional events:

3.3.1   Rebellion, restoration and revolution

- the run-up to the English Civil War and then rule by Oliver Cromwell;

- the restoration of the monarchy in 1660; and then

- the Glorious Revolution of 1688.

These were, of course, deeply complex events and historians are still arguing about their causes and their significance. There were significant disputes between adherents to three different branches of the Christian church – Roman Catholics, members of the Church of England (Anglicans) and dissenting protestants (non-Catholics who were not Anglicans). Religion was part and parcel of the constitution and the struggles for power in the 17th century. Also at the heart of the three key events lay notions about the proper relationship between the king and the House of Commons. James I and Charles I used their prerogative powers extensively to make law without the consent of Parliament. James I and his supporters believed in the 'divine right' of kings – in his own words:

> 'The state of the monarchy is the supremest thing on earth;
> for the kings are not only God's lieutenants on earth, but
> even by God himself they are called gods.'

But the disputes which shattered society were not in any straightforward way (as Professor Hill puts it in his book *The Century of Revolution*) 'about who should be boss' – the king and his favourites or the elected representatives of the men of property. Contemporaries simply did not think about sovereignty in these terms. The Parliamentarians had 'a stop in the mind': whereas Royalists had a long tradition of thinking on which to base their ideas, Parliamentarians, while they could deny sovereign power to the king, were not capable of asserting, on a theoretical basis, a claim that Parliament should be sovereign (one reason being that only the king could summon parliament). Only during the Commonwealth, the period of the civil war when the monarchy was abolished, was Parliament sovereign. Conrad Russell argues that

> '... the body of ideas about how the country should be governed were not really the central element in the cause for which [the Parliamentarians] fought: they were ... *ad hoc* ideas ... to serve the immediate purpose of clipping the wings of a king with whom they simply could not cope.'

(*The Causes of the English Civil War* (1990))

Looking back it can be seen that during the 17th century the decisive shift in sovereignty was from the Crown to the Crown-in-Parliament. By the end of the century, when William and Mary took over the throne, a constitutional monarchy, with the Crown clearly under the law and needing the consent of Parliament for most actions, was established. The narrative which follows is largely the story of how that came about.

3.3.2	The kings and queens of 17th century England

History is not the names and dates of kings and queens of England, but nevertheless it is useful to know the names and regnal dates of the monarchs (and others) at this time since their names will crop up frequently.

- James I 1603-1625

- Charles I 1625-1649

- Interregnum 1649-1653 (no monarch)

- Oliver Cromwell, Lord Protector 1653-1658

- Richard Cromwell, Lord Protector 1658-1659

- Interregnum 1659-1660 (no monarch)

- Charles II 1660-1685

- James II 1685-1688

- Interregnum 1688-1689 (no monarch)

- William III and Mary II 1689-1702

Professor Hill is blunt about the personal characters of the Stuart kings. James I was '... a shrewd, conceited, lazy intellectual ... a pedantic and undignified person with gross and unseemly personal habits'. His son Charles I (1625-1649) was '... much stupider than his father ... his high idea of his own station, his rigid inability to compromise in time, and his transparent dishonesty, made it impossible for him ever to have functioned as a constitutional monarch ...'. Charles II (1660-1685) 'was as intelligent, if as lazy, as his grandfather James I. But he had also learnt political prudence and a hard cynicism in his year of exile ...'. James II (1685-1688) '... had all the stupid obstinacy (or high devotion to principle) of his father [Charles I]: and the gentry thought the religion to which he was devoted [Catholicism] was the wrong one ...'.

Throughout the 17th century, the monarchy was in severe debt. Attempts were made to balance the budget, but James I and then his son Charles lived lives of luxury and extravagance, and increasing amounts of money were also needed for the defence of the realm. The clashes between the kings and the men of property (represented in the House of Commons) often surrounded attempts by the kings to raise revenue without the consent of Parliament, including, most famously, imposing import duty on currants (and other commodities), demanding 'ship money' and requiring the rich to make forced loans to the Crown. The judges were called upon to adjudicate on the legality of this and references to these cases still litter textbooks on constitutional law. The response of the judges to these disputes about royal power was not uniform; but this is not surprising since some judges were royalists and others Parliamentarian.

3.3.3   The king's prerogative and taxation

One of the early confrontations in the courts was over the attempt by James I to raise revenue from increased customs duties on imports. In 1605 Mr Bates, a merchant, refused to pay the new rate of duty on currants imposed by the king (over and above the 'poundage' tax stipulated by statute) and the matter went to court: *Bate's Case (The Case of Impositions)* (1606). The court found for the King on the ground that he did indeed have power to impose duties where his purpose was not primarily to raise revenue but to regulate foreign trade, as this was an aspect of the prerogative powers to control foreign affairs. (Bear in mind that the conduct of foreign affairs in the 20th century is still largely carried out under prerogative powers of the Crown, now exercised by the Prime Minister and cabinet: see Chapter 7, para 7.6).

The Commons was, perhaps understandably, unimpressed by the judgment, seeing it as a threat to subjects' property rights and also damaging to England's competitiveness in international trade. Under pressure from Parliament, James consented to a compromise: he would abandon some of the new duties, though some remained, and in the future the levying of 'impositions' would only be lawful if done with the

3.3.4   Mr Bates' currants

consent of Parliament. But he dissolved Parliament before this arrangement could be finalised.

3.3.5 Chief Justice Coke

Not all the judges approved of the way the king used his prerogative powers. This was a dangerous view to hold, or at least express, because judges held office only at the king's pleasure. They were his servants and could quite lawfully be removed from office if they handed down judgments which displeased him. Coke CJ (pronounced 'cook') (1552-1634) was the moving force behind a series of judicial decisions which sought to curb royal power. He was a Parliamentarian through and through. Before he was appointed to the bench he was an MP and after his dismissal he went back to the Commons. Coke was also a scholar and published a series of law reports and *Institutes* (legal commentaries), some volumes of which were banned from publication.

To mention just a couple of the 'anti-prerogative' decisions, in the *Case of Proclamations* (1611) it was held that the king no longer had the authority to create new offences by proclamation and could only exercise prerogative powers within the limits set by the common law. However, James I ignored this judgment and continued to make proclamations. And when, six years later in 1617, Coke refused to obey a command of the king not to try a case, he was dismissed by James and replaced by a royalist judge; in the years that followed many judgments finding the use of the prerogative lawful were handed down.

Another decision influenced by Coke was *Prohibitions del Roy* (1607) where the court (actually a conference of the judges) held that the king had no right to determine cases personally.

'... And the judges informed the King, that no king after the Conquest assumed to himself to give any judgment in any cause whatsoever, which concerned the administration of justice within this Realm, but these were solely determined in the Court of Justice ... The King said, he thought the law was founded on reason, and that he and others had reason, as well as the Judges; to which it was answered by me [ie Coke], that true it was, that God had endowed His Majesty with excellent science and great endowments of nature; but His Majesty was not learned in the law of the realm of England, and causes which concern the life, or inheritance, or goods, or fortunes of his subjects, are not to be decided by natural reason but by the artificial reason and judgment of law ... with which the King was greatly offended, and said, that then he should be under the law, which was treason to affirm, as he said: to which I said, that Bracton saith [the king should not be subject to any man, but to God and the law]'.

In 1625 Charles I came to the throne and another royal scheme to raise revenue – forcing subjects to grant him loans – brought questions of the Crown's authority before the courts again in 1627. In *Darnel's Case (The Five Knights' Case) (1627)* five knights refused to pay contributions to the loan and were imprisoned. They issued a writ of *habeas corpus* alleging their detention was unlawful. The gaoler told the court that the men were held 'by the special command of the King' and Hyde CJ accepted this amounted to lawful reason. As Professor Hill has said, 'The judgment was legally sound; but it placed impossibly wide powers in the hands of an unscrupulous government'.

<table>
<tr><td>3.3.6</td><td>Five knights: judgment for the king</td></tr>
</table>

3.3.6   Five knights: judgment for the king

In 1637 yet another of Charles' attempts to raise revenue without the consent of Parliament was challenged in the court. (Remember that Charles I managed to rule for 11 years without calling a Parliament). From feudal times, the monarch had been able to demand ships, or their equivalent in money (Ship Money), from coastal towns in England. Charles now sought to extend this tax to the whole of the country since money was needed to provide protection for English shipping. John Hampden, like Bates and Darnel in previous decades, refused to pay. Again, the court found for the King, though only by a majority (*R v Hampden (The Case of Ship Money)* (1637)). Professor Hill again comments that, 'Legally the judges had a case; but politics proved stronger than the law'. Many of the rich, upon whom Ship Money was levied, refused to pay and the Crown's financial difficulties deepened year after year.

3.3.7   Mr Hamden and the Ship Money: judgment for the king again

James I and his son Charles I's use of the prerogative was at least in one sense 'constitutional' – it was often held to be not against the law. Perhaps also in some instances the aim was not unreasonable: for example the levying of Ship Money across the country as a whole and not just the ports.

Tensions continued to rise between Charles I and the propertied classes represented in the House of Commons – especially over taxation. In 1640 the Commons passed the Triennial Act which provided for the automatic summoning of Parliament if the king failed to do so (remember Charles had ruled for 11 years without calling one). The judgment of the court in the *Ship Money Case* was declared unlawful. Across the water there was rebellion in Ireland in which thousands of Englishmen were killed. In England the king took armed men to the Commons with the intent to arrest the leaders of those who opposed him but they fled to the City. The king had lost control of London and the Civil War had begun, the first major

3.3.8   The outbreak of the civil war

bloodshed occurring at the battle of Edgehill in October 1642. By the end of 1645 the Parliamentarians controlled most of the country except for Oxford, the southwest of England and parts of Wales. Charles surrendered to the Scots in 1646 and was handed over to the English Parliament the following year. Attempts to agree upon a form of limited monarchy failed and Charles was executed in Whitehall as a traitor in 1649.

3.3.9   The Commonwealth
          under Cromwell

For almost 10 years England was without a monarch. During this period of 'the Commonwealth', the country was ruled by Oliver Cromwell, an MP and soldier, and other senior army officers. Cromwell was declared 'Protector' and, for a while, the House of Lords was abolished. The House of Commons offered the title of king to Cromwell but after some wavering he declined it. Although 'the Parliamentarians' (a loose coalition of factions) had won the civil war, arguably it had been no victory for democracy. During the war some of the Parliamentarians' side had flirted with forms of egalitarianism. By the Self-Denying Ordinance, peers had ceased to be officers in the army and appointments were made by merit rather than social rank, and throughout the period political ideas were debated as never before. One group, the Levellers, advocated giving the vote to all 'free Englishmen', the election of JPs and the abolition of the aristocracy. The sovereignty of Parliament (for there was now no king) could only be justified if that sovereignty derived from the people. Parliament should therefore represent all men (though not the 'unfree' – the destitute, women and servants). Another smaller and less important faction, the Diggers, went much further: all land, they said, should be held in common.

Cromwell was not for these radical reforms and over the years he suppressed the Levellers and Diggers and their propaganda. The limited reforms of the franchise actually led to fewer, rather than more, people being entitled to vote, though as a body Parliament had more power than before.

Under Cromwell's rule England was at war with the Dutch (1652-1654) and with the Spanish. He needed money and used familiar tactics: dismissing a judge whom he feared would declare the collection of a tax unlawful, manipulating MPs and preventing them from attending Parliament. Oliver Cromwell died in 1658 and was succeeded by his brother for a few months but the Commonwealth soon crumbled. Anarchy loomed and tax payers refused to pay (as they had 20 years before in protest against Charles I). The propertied classes were afraid. The Parliamentarians were irredeemably split into factions. The men of property, represented in the Commons, summoned Charles II to take the throne.

The country was to be ruled by Stuart kings again (Charles II and then his brother James II) for almost another 30 years. But there had been 'a change in the minds of men' which made absolutist monarchy an impossibility ever again. As Hill said:

> 'For nearly twenty years, Committees of Parliament had controlled Army, Navy, Church and foreign trade, more efficiently than the old government had ever done. No longer could these be treated as "mysteries of state", into which subjects must not pry'.

Religion – or rather which particular branch of Christianity was acceptable – became an increasingly important issue. The Test and Corporation Acts permitted only practising Anglicans to hold office in national and local government and removed the right to worship from Catholics and Unitarians. Those who opposed toleration did so more on political than doctrinal religious grounds: protestant dissenters (whose sects had often come to prominence during the Civil War) and especially Roman Catholics (who, it was seen, owed allegiance to a foreign power, the Pope) were regarded as threats to the constitution. After all, the King was supreme governor and 'Defender of the Faith' of the established Church of England. People were prosecuted for being absent from church services.

When James II, a convert to Roman Catholicism, succeeded his brother Charles II to the throne people asked: how can Protestant England have a Popish king? For James II, the persecution of Catholics was intolerable. In 1686 he granted a general pardon and later, by the Declarations of Indulgence, he prohibited prosecutions. For a while repression of Catholics and dissenters ceased. As Stuarts often had before, the king had used prerogative powers to suspend an Act of Parliament. James II's motivation for the policy of tolerance was complex: it was partly to win much-needed political allies among the non-conformist protestants, but he also cherished a hope that England could be converted to Catholicism by persuasion. In fact, there were few converts to Rome. On the contrary, London found itself in the grip of anti-Catholic hysteria and mob violence. Many people in the lower classes feared a Catholic coup (when in fact the precise opposite was about to happen!). Catholics were attacked and 'mass-houses' burned down. James' II position was untenable. Within four years of succeeding to the throne it was clear to him that his political allies – in particular the army and navy officers – had deserted him. The country once again was on the verge of anarchy.

3.3.10   The restoration of the monarchy

3.3.11   James II - a papist king for a protestant state?

3.4	**The Glorious Revolution**	In 1688, seven influential English men invited a Dutch Prince (William) and his wife (Mary, James II's daughter) to cross the channel, invade the country and become king and queen of England. William landed with 15,000 men at Torbay in November. The position in the capital continued to deteriorate and it became clear to James II that his position was untenable. In December he left London, and the country, famously throwing the Great Seal – the symbol of kingly authority – into the River Thames as William's army marched towards the capital. James II went into exile in France and never returned. Mobs broke into Catholic churches, looted them and burnt them to the ground. Crowds then turned their attention to the businesses and homes of the Papists; only the news that William was nearing London helped calm the crowds.

The day after Christmas 1688 an assembly of peers and MPs met and advised Prince William to call a convention of all peers and representatives of the counties and boroughs. The 'Convention Parliament' met in January 1689 and resolved that James, by 'breaking the original contract between king and people, and by the advice of Jesuits and other wicked persons having violated the fundamental laws and having withdrawn himself out of the kingdom, had abdicated the government, and that the throne has thereby become vacant'. The Parliament also passed a resolution 'that it hath been found, by experience, to be inconsistent with the safety and welfare of this Protestant Kingdom to be governed by a Popish Prince'. In fact there was considerable disagreement among the ruling class as to whether this was an abdication. It was more like a revolution. As Maitland (the 19th century legal historian) puts it: 'it was extremely difficult for any lawyer to make out that what had then been done was lawful'.

3.4.1	William and Mary take the throne in 1689	In February 1689 the two Houses of Parliament offered the crown to William and Mary – subject to clear understandings about the limited powers of the monarchy in the future. The Convention Parliament declared itself to be the Parliament of England and passed the Bill of Rights, firmly limiting the rights of the monarch. As has often been said, William was called upon 'to reign but not to rule'.
3.4.2	Trouble in Ireland	Almost immediately the new king had to cope with a new uprising in Ireland spurred on by James II's arrival there. ('King Billy' going into battle on horseback and the date '1690' remain ideological icons for Ulster protestants to this day). William went in person to fight the Battle of the Boyne, a battle as much with the French, whose forces had gone to aid their fellow Catholics, as with the Irish. His victory led in the years

that followed to Catholics being barred from the Irish Parliament and all public offices, attempts to eliminate Catholic landlords and the general subjugation of the Catholic population which made up the vast majority of the people of Ireland.

Historians are divided over the extent to which religious toleration of Catholics and non-conformist Anglicans improved in the wake of the Glorious Revolution. In 1689 the Toleration Act was passed 'for Exempting Their Majesties' Protestant Subjects, Dissenting from the Church of England, from the Penalties of Certain Laws.' This was very much more limited than the Declarations of Indulgence issued by James II a few years before, though it did place on a statutory footing the rights of certain protestant dissenters (those who believed in doctrine of the Trinity). Another of the achievements of 1689 was the settlement of succession to the throne: to this day it is the law of England that no Roman Catholic, or person married to one, can become king or queen of the UK.

3.4.3   Religion after the Glorious Revolution

It was during the reign of William and Mary that the foundations of the modern English constitution were laid (though not until the 19th century can the machinery of the modern state be seen to be emerging). A constitutional monarchy had been established. The judges now no longer held office 'during the King's pleasure', but on good behaviour: the Act of Settlement 1701 provided that they could only be removed with the consent of both Houses of Parliament. Parliament now asserted its clear power to control government finance and the Treasury began to draw up annual budgets for Parliamentary approval. The right to criticise royal appointments to government offices was also regularly used. A 'cabinet' of the Crown's ministers began to meet regularly, but again this was no real progress for democracy. As at the beginning of the 17th century, only a very small proportion of the population were represented in the Commons – the men who owned freehold property.

3.4.4   The legacies of the Glorious Revolution

For reasons of space, we have to gloss over the constitutional history of the 1700s. This does not mean that the period was unimportant. While the 1600s laid the foundations of today's relationship between the Crown/government and Parliament, the 18th century established of the geographical boundaries of the UK (though as we see later, these were again to change in the 1920s). Since 1603 there had been a 'personal union' of the Crown of England and Scotland when James VI of Scotland succeeded Elizabeth to become King James I of England. But each country continued to have its own Parliament and Privy

3.5   The 18th century

Council until 1706 when a Parliament of Great Britain was created comprising English (and Welsh) and Scottish MPs. In 1800 the Act of Union terminated the Parliament of Ireland, giving Irish MPs seats at Westminster.

In England, the constitutional settlement achieved in the Glorious Revolution of 1688 survived for over 100 years because it represented an acceptable compromise between the different groups of the population. But it could not last very far into the 19th century. Many of the elements of that earlier settlement were being seen as anachronisms by the early decades of the 1800s.

3.6 The 19th century

From the point of view of public law, two themes dominate the development of the constitution during the 1800s: first, the movement towards Parliamentary democracy and secondly, the creation of a government machine capable of coping with the new demands imposed on the state by the new industrial age. Both of these things were responses to the rapid and profound transformation in the character of English society from a rural economy dominated by landowners to an industrial society. The population grew phenomenally and polluted, squalid urban centres sprawled across the country. A few people grew wealthy – some of the old aristocracy from under whose land coal was mined, and also a new capitalist class – but the mass of the people lived lives of grinding misery in abject poverty. These were the challenges for law and government in the 19th century.

3.6.1 Steps towards Parliamentary democracy

As we have seen, the civil war and Glorious Revolution of the 17th century had little to do with the mass of the people. The struggles between king and Parliament were not about democracy, but the protection of private property against the arbitrary powers of the Crown. The House of Commons did not represent 'the people', only the small proportion of men-who-owned-freehold-property. At the beginning of the 19th century the position was as it had been for many years previously: the aristocratic landowners and the king continued to exercise considerable powers of patronage which influenced, often determined, the outcome of elections to the Commons, a task made easier by the fact that elections were not by secret ballot.

Society was changing rapidly in the 19th century. A new middle class was emerging and so was a large urban working class; but neither group had the right to vote. But there was no single reform movement for greater democracy. For some, the goal was confined to the extension of the franchise to the growing middle class. Radicals demanded more: universal manhood suffrage (literally, for few included women in their proposals). The ruling class and their representatives in Parliament were frightened and the events across the channel in 1789 – the French Revolution which swept away the old order – was still remembered. The year 1819 was a turbulent one in England. A crowd of 60,000 met in St Peter's Fields in Manchester to hear radical speakers. It ended with soldiers charging the crowd, killing 11 and wounding many hundreds – the 'Peterloo massacre' is ironic reference to Wellington's victory at Waterloo in 1815. The government's reaction was to pass the 'Six Acts' which, among other things, banned meetings of over 50 people for the discussion of public grievance, extended newspaper stamp duty to political pamphlets and prohibited the training of persons in the use of arms.

But reform, if not immediate radical reform, was inevitable. The first success was the Representation of the People Act 1832 (often called the Great Reform Act) which abolished the 'rotten boroughs' and extended the right to vote to men of property who did not own substantial freehold land. In 1867 (the Second Reform Act) many working men in towns were enfranchised and in 1884 so were agricultural labourers. Women had to wait until 1918 for the vote in general elections, though women in the propertied classes had been able to vote in local elections since 1869. It was not until 1928, however, that women could vote on the same basis as men, at 21.

The coming of Parliamentary democracy led to transformations. Mass political parties became part and parcel of the constitution and led to the evolution of conventions such as that of collective ministerial responsibility.

Anyone who studies English history at school will have examined the agrarian and industrial revolutions. Probably little, if any, attention will have been given to the 'revolution in government and administration' – yet its effects on society were as profound as the better turnip and the steam engine. During the 19th century ideas and practices of 'government' changed and new techniques and structures of public administration were created. In Chapter 5 some of the powerful intellectual ideas, such as 'Benthamism' and 'collectivism', which shaped this gradual but dramatic process, are examined; here it is enough for the time being just to trace some of the main landmarks in the process of reform.	3.6.2 The administrative revolution
In 1853 two senior civil servants with suitably Victorian-sounding names, Sir Stafford Northcote and Charles Trevelyan conducted a wide-ranging review of administration in	3.6.3 The Northcote-Trevelyan reforms of the civil service

Whitehall. Their short 20 page report was eventually to transform the British civil service. In future, they recommended, young men should be recruited on merit after sitting competitive examinations, rather than on the basis of favouritism and patronage. Uniform conditions of employment should apply in all government departments, the Northcote-Trevelyan report said, rather than the haphazard arrangements and sinecures which still existed. Many people in the establishment viewed these proposals with hostility when they were first published, some even seeing in them 'the seeds of republicanism' because examinations rather than the Crown were to determine who was appointed to the civil service. But public outrage over the lives lost in the Crimean war due to administrative inefficiencies helped prepare the ground for the adoption of the proposals.

In 1870, when Gladstone was prime minister, a new civil service order in council (legislation under the royal prerogative) was made implementing most of the proposals in the Northcote-Trevelyan report. England now had a modern, permanent, 'politically neutral' civil service. It was also a bureaucracy that was growing rapidly: it doubled in size between 1853 and 1890. But central government departments could not by themselves cope with the new demands on government.

| 3.6.4 | New forms of administration | Innovation in new bureaucratic structures did not start or end with the great departments of state in Whitehall (such as the Home Office). Throughout the 19th century, government increasingly intervened in commercial activity to ensure basic standards of health and safety by inspecting factories, passenger ships, railways, mines, etc. The state also assumed a greater role in 'dealing with' the poor by providing subsistence, basic health care and elementary education, gas, water, sewage disposal – and eventually the provision of affordable housing to the working class. This was the beginning of the modern regulatory, interventionist state; government no longer confined itself to being a 'nightwatchman'. |

A variety of new administrative techniques were used. Central government departments sometimes appointed their own inspectors or set up independent bodies of inspectors. Sometimes specially created 'commissions' or 'boards' were set up (such as the Poor Law Commission in 1834 which later became the Poor Law Board). Above all, local government was a vital part of the new emerging structures of public administration. The Justices of the Peace (described in para 3.3, above) were no longer appropriate 'maids of all work'. Their functions were taken over by elected rate-levying bodies responsible for police, the administration of the poor law, schooling, etc.

As with central government, local bodies underwent a process of reform during the century both in terms of democratic participation and their administrative effectiveness. During the 19th century the right to vote in local elections – as for the House of Commons – was progressively widened: first to the middle class (1832), then the working class in towns (1867) and agricultural labourers (1884). Eventually, the morass of different local bodies exercising different responsibilities were amalgamated into general purpose local authorities with paid clerks and treasurers with powers to make bye-laws (local regulations). They were subject to financial audit and began to receive financial grants from central government. The work of these authorities was directed by central government departments by means of delegated legislation, circulars and so on.

The political agenda immediately after the First World War was dominated by Ireland: there were ever more forceful demands for home rule or independence. Sinn Fein, a major political party in Ireland, set up an unofficial Parliament in Dublin in 1918 after the general election. As in India, where Gandhi campaigned against British rule, this amounted to civil disobedience on an extraordinary scale. The Irish Parliament behaved as if it were an official one; taxes were levied and courts established. At the same time, the IRA began a guerrilla war against the British in Ireland. Over 1,500 people died. Messy, confused negotiations led to the British Parliament agreeing in 1921 to Prime Minister Lloyd George's negotiated settlement which was to divide Ireland; four counties in the north – predominately protestant – were to remain part of the UK and the rest of the island – overwhelmingly catholic – would officially be recognised as the independent republic (which it had, in fact, been for several years already). A large part of the 'UK' had been excised.

3.6.5   A shrinking UK

It is appropriate to end the short history where it began, with the Crown. During the later years of Queen Victoria's reign the monarchy regained popular appeal. The monarch had a new significance. It was its symbolism – part of what Walter Bagehot called the dignified (as opposed to the efficient) constitution – that mattered now, rather than its direct political activity or use of prerogative powers.

3.6.6   The Crown

3.7   Pragmatism

If one theme emerges from this narrative it is that the British constitution changes pragmatically. Governments respond to pressures (eg to extend the franchise) cautiously and in a piecemeal fashion. Grand ideas carry little weight. Even the civil war – sometimes held up as a battle for Parliamentary government over absolute monarchy – is now subject to reinterpretation by historians. In *The Causes of the English Civil War* Conrad Russell argues that:

> '... the body of ideas about how the country should be governed were not really the central element in the cause for which they [the Parliamentarians] fought: they were, like their medieval predecessors, ad hoc ideas constructed out of any materials ready to hand, to serve the immediate purpose of clipping the wings of a king with whom they simply could not cope.'

This tradition of pragmatism needs to be borne in mind whenever you consider reform of the constitution today such as the abolition of the House of Lords or the enactment of a written constitution.

Gap-filling: Constitutional History

1603	James VI of Scotland succeeds Elizabeth to throne of England	**Chronology of the 17th century**
1606	Bates's case	
1611	Case of Proclamations	
1617	Chief Justice Coke dismissed	
1625	Charles I becomes king	
1627	Darnel's case (Five Knights Case)	
1637	Case of Ship Money	
1642	Battle of Edgehill: first major bloodshed of Civil War	
1645	Parliamentarians control most of England	
1649	Charles I executed as traitor at Whitehall, London	
1649-60	The Commonwealth: Oliver Cromwell, then his brother, rule from 1653 to 1659	
1660	Charles II returns to London and is crowned king	
1685	James II (a Catholic) succeeds his brother to the throne	
1688	The Glorious Revolution. William and Mary on the throne	
1700	Act of Settlement	
1706	Act of Union joins Parliaments of England & Wales with Scotland	
1819	'Peterloo' massacre led to the repressive Six Acts	**Chronology of the 19th century and beyond**
1832	Great Reform Act extends right to vote to middle classes	
	Poor Law Amendment Act establishes Poor Law Commission	
1835	Elected statutory municipal corporations replace old boroughs	
1837	Queen Victoria succeeds her uncle William IV to the throne	
1833	State intervenes to ensure health and safety by Factories Act	

1853	Northcote-Trevelyan Report on the civil service
1867	Second Reform Act: votes for the urban working class
1870	Gladstone implements Northcote-Trevely and recommendations
	Education Act: publicly-funded schools for children up to 13
1873-75	Judicature Acts: reforms of legal system
1884	Right to vote given to agricultural labourers
1906	Liberal party wins election: Lloyd George prime minister
1901	Queen Victoria dies; succeeded by her son Edward VII
1908	Old Age Pensions Act: means tested benefit for over 70s
1909	The People's Budget
1911	Parliament Act: House of Lords' veto and right to delay removed
	National Insurance Act: contributory unemployment and sick benefits
1918	Women over 30 enfranchised
1921	Independence for Irish republic
	Poplar Borough Council spearheads municipal socialism!
1928	Women over 21 given right to vote – on the same basis as men

Chapter 4

Who is Dicey?

Many undergraduates studying public law find one question nagging away at them during their course: just who was this man Dicey to whom their lecturers and the textbook writers keep referring? Obviously he is important. He seems to have defined everything from Parliamentary sovereignty to the rule of law to constitutional conventions. But can the views of a law professor really be so important that 100 years after the first publication of his book *Introduction to the Study of the Law of the Constitution* (1885) it is still on students' reading lists? Another thing puzzles many: presumably the constitution Dicey describes is the 19th century one. How can this be relevant to the constitution of the late 20th century?

Students will probably come across the views of Dicey in relation to at least three different topics: (a) Parliamentary sovereignty; (b) the rule of law; and (c) the nature of constitutional conventions. The aims of this chapter are:

- to provide a biographical sketch of Dicey;

- to consider how Dicey's work should be read in the 1990s;

- to sketch out the main arguments of the *Law of the Constitution*; and

- to outline the central criticisms of Dicey made by one later theorist (Ivor Jennings).

A broader consideration of the political beliefs which underpinned Dicey's work can be found in the next chapter. As Jennings said in *The Law and the Constitution*, Dicey 'honestly tried ... to analyse [the constitution], but, like most, he saw the constitution through his own spectacles, and his own vision was not exact'.

Albert Venn Dicey was born in 1835 into a middle-class, evangelical Christian family. He died, aged 87, in 1922. His life therefore spanned the period of great change in government and administration during the later part of the 19th century, described in the last chapter. He witnessed the establishment of Parliamentary democracy, the reform of the civil service, the 'administrative revolution' and the formation of an independent Irish republic. He was a well-known figure during his lifetime and twice refused a knighthood. (Had he lived in the 1990s he would undoubtedly have been a panelist on TV and radio programmes such as 'Question Time' and 'Any Questions'!)

4.1 A biographical sketch

Throughout his life he suffered from a muscular weakness which often made it difficult for him even to write. He failed exams more than once because the examiners couldn't read his handwriting. His prose style, though, was a model of clarity and succinctness. After graduating from Oxford he practised at the Bar for several years with no outstanding success. He continued to write articles, regularly had letters published in *The Times* and wrote a book. In 1882, at the age of 47, he was appointed to a chair at his old university and it was as an academic that he exerted a profound influence (though undoubtedly he would have preferred to have been an MP or judge). During his 27 years at Oxford he wrote two monumental books, both of which are still much used, discussed and criticised: *Introduction to the Study of the Law of the Constitution* (1885 1st ed) and *Law and Public Opinion in England* (1905).

Dicey's political views are often described as 'liberal', meaning he had a commitment to individualism and free trade. Above all he was against 'state collectivism', believing there was a contradiction between such 'socialism' and democracy. He was concerned by the increasing state regulation of economic activity and the growing provision of services by the state. Of all the particular political causes with which Dicey was involved, his strongest feelings were, however, about Home Rule and independence for Ireland. He was a passionate, obsessive Unionist and opposed all proposals that any part of Ireland should cease to be part of the UK. For Dicey, the maintenance of the UK was a fundamental principle and one of his answers to the growing problems of law and order in Ireland was to advocate suspending trial by jury. The Irish Republic became an independent state in 1920 shortly before Dicey's death.

4.2   How to read Dicey

Dicey's famous book *Introduction to the study of the Law of the Constitution* started out as a series of lectures given to students at Oxford University in the 1880s. The book was a runaway success with law students everywhere, not least because of its easy, clear style. They 'were attracted by Dicey's convenient format which encouraged certainty and precision in a subject which was vague and imprecise' (McEldowney in *Law, Legitimacy and the Constitution*). The book is arranged around three ideas:

* The sovereignty of Parliament;

* The rule of law;

* The conventions of the constitution.

It is important to understand not just each of these things in isolation, but also Dicey's attempt to explain their inter-relationships. The last edition of the book to be revised by Dicey himself was in 1908. But how should the book be read today? Professor ECS Wade has suggested three possible approaches (see his introduction to the 10th ed of Dicey's *Law of the Constitution*):

'(i) to accept Dicey's principles, and more particularly the sovereignty of Parliament and the rule of law, as portraying only the period of which he wrote;

(ii) to regard these principles critically and in the light of future events to admit that they were only partially true of the 19th century and certainly inapplicable today;

(iii) to accept these principles, supplemented if need be by later developments, and to show how they can be fitted into modern public law.'

Think carefully about the approaches set out above as you read the following summary of the main themes of Dicey's *Law of the Constitution*.

4.3 **Summary of *Law of the Constitution***

Dicey argues that 'the sovereignty of Parliament is (from a legal point of view) the dominant characteristic of our political institutions'. This means that the Queen in Parliament has 'under the English constitution, the right to make or unmake any law whatever; and, further, that no person or body is recognised by the law of England as having a right to override or set aside the legislation of Parliament'. It could be shown, as a matter of fact, that attempts to entrench legislation would be legally ineffective.

4.3.1 Chapter 1: the nature of Parliamentary sovereignty

Political sovereignty, however, lay with the electors. Their views were always represented by MPs. Sovereignty was as a matter of reality limited externally by the possibility that a large number of subjects will disobey or resist laws. There was also an internal check on sovereign power – 'the moral feelings of the time and society' which MPs, including those in government, shared. Dicey claimed that representative government produced a coincidence between the external and internal limits on sovereign power.

Here Dicey contrasts the powers of Parliament and non-sovereign law-making bodies (such as local authorities, railway companies empowered to make bye-laws and legislatures in federal systems). He details the characteristics of the UK Parliament.

4.3.2 Chapter 2 : Parliament and non-sovereign law-making bodies

- 'There is no law which Parliament cannot change ... or so-called constitutional laws can be changed by the same body and in the same manner as any laws, namely by Parliament acting in its ordinary legislative character.'

- There is no marked or clear distinction between laws which are not fundamental (or constitutional) and laws which are. There is no written constitutional statute or charter.

- No judicial body can pronounce void any enactment passed by Parliament on the ground of such enactment being contrary to the constitution or any other ground whatever (except of course its being repealed by Parliament). Earlier Dicey had demonstrated that the courts will not inquire into any alleged irregularities in Parliamentary procedure. Nor is the fact that an Act is contrary to international law or morality any basis for the courts declaring it invalid.

| 4.3.3 | Chapter 3: Parliamentary sovereignty and federalism | Dicey compares the system of Parliamentary sovereignty in Britain with systems of federal government, especially those of the US and Switzerland. He argues that a federal state derived its existence from the constitution just as a corporation (such as a railway company!) did from the charter by which it was created. This meant that the constitution of federal countries must necessarily be 'written' and 'rigid'. The distribution of powers was also an essential feature of federalism which led to weak government. Federalism also tended to produce conservatism and 'legalism' (the predominance of the judiciary in the constitution). |
| 4.3.4 | Chapter 4: The rule of law: its nature and general application | Moving on from discussion on Parliamentary sovereignty to examining the second of the main characteristics of the constitution – the rule of law – Dicey argues that it meant three things in the English constitution. |

- Government officials did not have 'wide, arbitrary or discretionary powers of constraint'. This meant that no man could be punished or be made 'to suffer in body or goods' except for a distinct breach of law established in the ordinary legal manner before the ordinary courts of the land. He warns sternly 'that wherever there is discretion there is room for arbitrariness ... [which] ... must mean insecurity for legal freedom on the part of its subjects'.

- A second meaning is that 'every man, whatever be his rank or condition, is subject to the ordinary law of the realm and amenable to the jurisdiction of the ordinary tribunals'. Dicey was not thinking about treating aristocrats and farm labourers equally; rather he meant that government officials, policemen, ministers, tax collectors etc could be sued in tort if they conducted their official duties unlawfully. There was no special body of law administered by tribunals which gave immunity to state officials. (Dicey chose to ignore the common law immunity from being sued which judges enjoyed – and still do. He also ignored the legal position of 'the Crown'; at the time there were considerable procedural hurdles facing anyone attempting to sue a government department.)

- Thirdly, the rule of law meant that 'the constitution is the result of the ordinary law of the land'. The general principles of the constitution to do with civil liberties, such as the right of personal liberty and freedom of assembly, were the *result* or consequence of judicial decisions in cases where individuals sued government officials. This was to be contrasted with countries which had a supreme written constitution where the rights of individuals resulted from the general principles embodied in that document.

In Chapters 5-10 Dicey examined certain areas of substantive rights, including the rights to personal freedom, freedom of discussion and of public meeting.

In this chapter Dicey addresses what might appear to be tensions – or even a contradiction – between 'the two principles which pervade the whole of the English constitution'. Parliamentary sovereignty means that the legislature can legally do whatever it wants to by enacting a statute; but the rule of law means, in part, that common law principles established by judges protect the civil liberties of subjects. In reality there was no conflict, Dicey argued, for two reasons.

4.3.5   Chapter 13: Relationship between Parliamentary sovereignty and the rule of law

First, 'The sovereignty of Parliament favours the supremacy of the law of the land'. The will of Parliament can only be expressed through an Act of Parliament which gives great authority to the judges who must interpret the words used in the statute. Also, except for a period during Cromwell's rule, the English Parliament has never 'governed' by exercising direct executive power or appointing ministers and civil servants (who are still 'servants of the Crown'). Parliament, though sovereign, cannot interfere with the administration of justice.

A second reason why there is no conflict between the two principles is that the 'supremacy of the law necessitates the exercise of Parliamentary sovereignty'. Dicey argued that the 'rigidity of the law' sometimes prevented government action, in which case the executive needed to obtain from Parliament 'the discretionary authority which is denied to the Crown by the ordinary law of the land'.

4.3.6   **Chapter 14: Nature of conventions of constitution**

In Part III of the book Dicey goes on to examine the last of the three main characteristics of the UK constitution – constitutional conventions. He draws a sharp distinction between constitutional 'law' (which are the rules enforced or recognised by the courts) and constitutional conventions which are 'customs, practices, maxims or precepts which are not enforced or recognised by the courts ...'. He quickly adds, however, that a lawyer cannot master 'the legal side of the English constitution' without understanding 'those constitutional understandings which necessarily engross the attention of historians or of statesmen'.

The common characteristic of most conventions was, Dicey argued, that they were rules for determining the mode in which the 'discretionary' (ie prerogative) powers of the Crown and ministers ought to be exercised. A few conventions also related to the privileges of Parliament.

Conventions had one ultimate object:

'Their end is to secure that Parliament, or the Cabinet which is indirectly appointed by Parliament, shall in the long run give effect to the will of that power which in modern England is the true political sovereign of the State – the majority of the electors ...'

In other words, conventions secured the political sovereignty of the people, he claimed.

4.3.7   **Chapter 15: The sanction by which conventions are enforced**

In the final chapter Dicey considers what sanctions exist to enforce conventions – he thought that this was 'by far the most perplexing' of questions in constitutional law. Remember that he has just said that conventions are not law (ie they will not be enforced by the courts). He rejects the idea that it is the force of public opinion which ensures ministers and others follow conventions: this was really just a restatement of the question.

The real reason for obedience was this: 'the fact that the breach of ... conventions will almost immediately bring the offender into conflict with the courts and the law of the land'. He gives illustrations of how this works. If, for example, a government breaks a convention by refusing to resign and call a general election when it no longer has the confidence of the majority of MPs, the government would be unable to get the annual Appropriation Act through

Parliament and this would leave government without any lawful means of expenditure. Therefore:

> 'the conventions of the constitution are not laws, but in so far as they really possess binding force, derive their sanction from the fact that whoever breaks them must finally breach the law and incur the penalties of a law-breaker.'

Just as you are likely to come across Dicey's work quite early on in your constitutional and administrative law course, so too are you likely to encounter the views of his many critics. As we have already noted (para 4.2, above), there are at least three different ways of reading *The Law of the Constitution*. You should bear this in mind when you consider what his critics say – they often criticise in different ways. Here we confine our attention to one early and highly influential riposte to Dicey: that of Professor Sir Ivor Jennings in *The Law and the Constitution* (1993). Jennings who was professor of law, first at the London School of Economics, then at Cambridge University. He was also a socialist.

On a broad level, Jennings criticised the scope of Dicey's book. He argued that Dicey failed to deal with the *powers* of government: Dicey 'seemed to think that the British constitution was concerned almost entirely with the *rights of individuals*'. In fact, even when Dicey was writing, central and local government had considerable discretionary legal powers to carry out all sorts of functions from the compulsory purchase of land to restricting overseas trade.

Jennings also makes more specific criticisms of Dicey's analysis of parliamentary sovereignty, the rule of law and the nature of conventions.

Having first regretted that Dicey used the word 'sovereignty' in this context, Jennings goes on to say that Dicey's comparison of sovereign and non-sovereign legislatures is 'entirely beside the point' and ridicules Dicey's suggestion that a local authority in England and the Parliament of Canada share characteristics because they are both non-sovereign. Jennings also attacked Dicey's assertion that a sovereign Parliament was incapable of entrenching legislation (ie making it more difficult for a subsequent Parliament to repeal or amend an enactment). The true rule was that 'the courts accept as law that which is made in the proper legal form'. 'Legal sovereignty' was just the name for the rule that the legislature has, for the time being, power to make laws of any kind in the manner required by the law. Parliament was therefore capable

4.4   Dicey's early critic: Jennings

4.4.1   Parliamentary sovereignty

of entrenching legislation because the power to change the law included the power to change the law affecting itself.

<table>
<tr><td>4.4.2</td><td>Rule of law</td></tr>
</table>

- **Dicey was wrong about arbitrary powers**

  In Appendix II of *The Law and The Constitution* Jennings considers Dicey's theory of the rule of law. In relation to Dicey's first meaning (the absence of arbitrary and discretionary powers) Jennings explains that what Dicey really meant was that 'wide administrative or executive powers are likely to be abused *and therefore ought not to be conferred*' (emphasis added). But the discretionary powers of ministers and local authorities were as much part of the 'regular' law of the land as any others. And while, of course, occasional abuse of power might occur, this was no reason for not conferring discretionary powers on officials. These powers, remember, were used to ensure things like minimum standards of health and safety in work places and to clear slum housing. This, Jennings said, was of no interest to Dicey:

  > 'Dicey ... was much more concerned with the constitutional relations between Great Britain and Ireland than with the relations between poverty and disease on the one hand, and the new industrial system on the other. In internal politics, therefore, he was concerned not with the clearing up of the nasty industrial sections of towns, but with the liberty of the subject. In terms of powers, he was concerned with police powers, and not with other administrative powers.'

- **'Equality' in tort law is only a small point**

  In relation to Dicey's second definition of the rule of law (equality before the law), Jennings flatly denied that there was any equality between the rights and duties of an official and that of an ordinary person. Dicey surely realised this, but had chosen to ignore the public law position of officials, eg the duty of local authorities to provide education to children and the powers of the tax inspectors to demand information. Dicey was only writing about the position in tort law, not public law. While it was true that, generally, officials could be sued personally by an aggrieved citizen for a tortious act or omission in the course of their duty, Jennings's withering retort was that 'this is a small point upon which to base a doctrine called by the magnificent name of 'rule of law', particularly when it is generally used in a very different sense'.

- **Dicey was wrong about the source of the constitution**

  Lastly, Jennings questioned Dicey's proposition that the rule of law meant that 'the constitution is the result of the ordinary law of the land'. Jennings could not understand this:

  > 'the powers of the Crown and of other administrative authorities are limited by the rights of individuals; or the rights of individuals are limited by the powers of the administration. Both statements are correct; and both powers and rights come from the law – from the rules.'.

Jennings rejects Dicey's definition of conventions. For Jennings, they are 'rules whose nature does *not* differ fundamentally from that of the positive law of England' (emphasis added). There were, he argued, problems with Dicey's sharp distinction between laws and conventions. First, Dicey generally over-emphasised the role of the courts; most public law issues never see a court. Public law powers and duties are created by statute and enforced by administrative authorities. Only in the rarest cases do the courts become involved, and even then an Act may restrict or exclude their jurisdiction. For Jennings, a wider definition of 'law' was appropriate which would include rules, such as that it is the Prime Minister and not the cabinet who advises the Queen to dissolve Parliament. As a matter of history, the courts recognised rules (such as Parliamentary sovereignty) which were established around the time of the Glorious Revolution, but conventions which developed later (eg to do with cabinet government) were as a matter of formality treated as not being part of the common law. But there was no distinction of substance or nature between law and convention.

4.4.3   Conventions

Jennings also sought to show that Dicey's argument that a breach of a convention would lead to a breach of law was not necessarily correct.

You should see by now that while Dicey's work continues to be regarded as highly important, it gives rise to a great many problems. Is *The Law of the Constitution* 'in some respects the only written constitution we have' (see the Preface to Jowell and Oliver's *The Changing Constitution (3rd ed, 1994)*)? Or should we regard it as containing now patently dated ideas of a man with a peculiar, blinkered vision of English government? The challenge for a law student is to come to an informed view as to how Dicey's analysis should be treated.

4.5   Dicey today

Who is Dicey?

As a way of understanding the views of Dicey, and those of his critic Jennings, why not complete the table below. Summarising their different definitions and analysis of Parlimentary sovereignty, the rule of Law and Constitutional conventions?

	DICEY	JENNINGS
Parliamentary Sovereignty		
Rule of Law		
Conventions		

Chapter 5

Political Thought for Public Law Students

The purpose of this chapter is:

- to explain why an understanding of political thought is important for public law students;

- to sketch out some of the main themes of general political thought which have been influential in Britain (a gap-filling exercise);

- to outline some of the recent writing specifically on the connection between political theory and public law.

Only a few years ago, distinguished commentators were complaining that British writing about public law was too untheoretical, that the textbook writers showed little interest in things like the idea of democracy or political thinking about the relationship between the state and individuals. One possible explanation may be the influence of Dicey, who in *The Law of the Constitution* wrote:

> 'With conventions or understandings [the law teacher] has no direct concern. They vary from generation to generation, almost from year to year ... If he is concerned [with conventions] at all, he is so only in so far as he may be called upon to show what is the connection (if there be any) between the conventions of the constitution and the law of the constitution. This the true constitutional law is his only real concern. His proper function is to show what are the legal rules (ie the rules recognised by the courts) which are to be found in the several parts of the constitution. Of such rules or laws he will easily discover more than enough ... The duty, in short, of an English professor of law is to state what are the laws which form part of the constitution, to arrange them in order, to explain their meaning, and to exhibit where possible their logical connection.'

Dicey had, to modern eyes, a very narrow view of what students of public law should be taught and what the task of the law teacher was: constitutional law courses should not dwell on things that strictly speaking were not 'law'; there was no need for public law teaching or writing to deal explicitly with things like the theory of the state or democracy.

5.1 The absence of political theory

5.2	**New theoretical writing**	In the last few years there has been a steady stream of writing on the relationship between public law and political thought in Britain. The writers have tended to have one (or both) of the following aims:

- To expose the political assumptions underlying other writers' analysis of constitutional and administrative law (eg how did Dicey's political views affect his analysis of the constitution?) and then devise schemes for classifying different trends or traditions of writing.

- To examine how different political theories have shaped and influenced the constitutional structures and the content of administrative law in the UK. (For example, a theory of participatory democracy would suggest that administrative law should give the citizen opportunities to make, at the least, representations to law-makers before rules are enacted.)

5.3	**How theory can help you**	You may find that questions about political theory and public law are not tackled head-on in your constitutional and administrative law course. This can be because some teachers consider the subject too difficult for first year law students – much of it is indeed very tricky and sophisticated stuff. A few teachers also still regard issues of political theory as a sort of optional extra to a public law course suitable only for the keenest students. The truth, however, is that it is inescapable. Some awareness of the rudiments of political thought can help students get to the sort of deep, critical understanding of constitutional and administrative law that is desirable. It can help in at least two practical ways.

5.3.1	Reform issues	Many questions in public law exams are about reform of the constitution, for example 'Although the House of Lords has some value it is an anomaly and should be abolished or radically reformed. Discuss.', or 'Examine the implications and desirability of enacting a Bill of Rights in the UK.' Reform does not happen in a vacuum! In order to be able to tackle questions like this really well you need to anchor your ideas – or the rival proposals you are evaluating – into some sort of framework. For instance, views on the future of the House of Lords depend on more general opinions about the value of different sorts of democracy, what gives institutions legitimacy and why constitutional reform should be carried out. Theory allows you to delve deeper and so write better essays!

5.3.2	Writers', judges' and teachers' viewpoints	A second reason why 'theory' is necessary is because it is a powerful antidote for students who begin to feel like literary

couch potatoes, staring glassy-eyed at the pages of textbooks and journal articles and taking it all in (or not, as the case may be) in an uncritical way. Unless you are alert to theoretical perspectives it is easy to slip into the habit of thinking that textbooks are value-free, technical descriptions of the 'facts' about the institutions and processes of the constitution. That is nonsense. Every textbook, article and judgment is written by someone with a standpoint, a set of political beliefs about public law. More often than not the writers and judges do not make this explicit by saying '... and now I am about to reveal my theoretical perspective ...'. But this makes it all the more important that students have some awareness of the different approaches that are adopted. This facilitates a more critical reading of texts.

The basic lessons to take away are (a) that there is no such thing as value-free or apolitical writing about the constitution and (b) that political ideas influence or determine real-life public law in a variety of ways.

Some people go to university to do degrees in political science, government and politics and public administration – but obviously you are not one of them. In one subject (constitutional and administrative law) on a *law* degree there is also quite obviously only very limited scope for learning about the methods and ideas of another academic discipline. Realistically, the most that a first year law student can probably be expected to do is develop an *awareness* (rather than a detailed knowledge) of a few aspects of political thought and to see how it affects public law and writing about public law. The task is therefore not as daunting as it might seem at first.

By the end of this chapter you should be aware of the main characteristics of three sets of political theories (liberalism, conservatism and socialism) which to a greater or lesser extent have had an impact on government in Britain. You will also be aware of some of the different ideas about what democracy is, in particular:

- representative democracy;

- pluralism; and

- participatory democracy.

By 'politics' and 'political' we are not suggesting that all academics and judges are card-carrying members of the Labour Party or flag-waving Conservatives. Political in this context does not mean party political. But any description or analysis of what has happened, is happening or should

5.4 What is political theory?

happen in the English constitution will be based on the writer's view of, among other things, the proper role of government and the legitimate scope of the state's coercive powers. Thus, when Dicey defined the rule of law and Parliamentary sovereignty he was not setting out any necessarily objective truth about how things are, but merely asserting one set of ideas based on the opinions he held about law and the state. Different commentators have different agendas.

5.5 Political ideas generally

Before you can understand the *particular* links between political theory and public law, you need to know something about the more *general* ways of thinking about the role of government, the nature of the relationship between individuals and the state, etc. Here, as with constitutional history (see Chapter 3), a little knowledge can be a dangerous thing: you must be careful when using labels like 'liberalism', 'conservatism' and 'socialism'. What follows tries to highlight a few of the main characteristics of these three traditions in political thinking (there are, of course, many others). Be aware that each of these terms are used to represent a wide range of ideas, even about some of their central characteristics. Also, bear in mind that these sets of beliefs cannot be identified in any straightforward way with the policies of the major political parties in the UK today. The modern Conservative Party is, for instance, as much influenced by 'classical liberalism' as they are by what we here call 'conservatism'.

5.6 Liberalism

The big problem with using the term 'liberalism' is that it has been used to mean very many and very different things over the years. However, one or two key features, about which most people who call themselves liberals broadly agree, can be identified. Central to liberalism is the importance attached to the individual and liberty. The term individualism can be used to express the idea that society is made up of an aggregate of individuals. (We will see shortly that many *conservative* thinkers view society as an 'organic' whole which is more than just the individuals who make it up.) Individualism can also mean that people (rather than government) are the best judges of what is good for them and so should be able to live their lives with the minimum of interference by the state.

Belief in the value of individuals has spawned two very different sets of liberal political beliefs. For convenience we can call them (1) *laissez-faire* (or 'classical' or 'libertarian') liberalism and (2) social (or new) liberalism. The difference between them is over *how* individual freedom is best achieved.

Laissez-faire liberals believe that freedom for the individual means the absence of coercion. They say that minimal government is the key: the state should intervene as little as possible in people's lives and businesses. In the 19th century they therefore supported free trade and the abolition of the Corn Laws, which limited the import of grain in order to maintain the price of domestically grown corn. They favoured freedom of contract and so thought it wrong that government intervened to restrict working hours or force employers to ensure minimum health and safety in factories and mines. For most *laissez-faire* liberals the principal means to ensuring individual freedom, and also social responsibility, was ownership of property, because property gave people autonomy and independence from the state. This was the central, traditional liberty which needed to be protected from the powers of government. (Remember that in the 17th century the Civil War had been about protecting the rights to property from the arbitrary prerogative powers of the Crown.) This belief in the ability of property to empower people, to make them autonomous, carries on today.

Laissez-faire liberals do not advocate anarchy: *some* laws, and the coercive mechanisms to enforce them, are necessary to protect property rights and uphold the sanctity of contract. But on the whole the role of government should be limited to ensuring that the market economy can operate effectively.

By the end of the 19th century many people who subscribed to liberalism faced a dilemma: if, as they believed, the individual's freedom was paramount, what about the mass of the population who continued to live uneducated in abject poverty and ill-health? The law might not prohibit the pauper from eating properly, but how plausible was it to say that such a person still had the freedom to do so? It was becoming clearer and clearer that in the modern world the quality of a person's life was determined by things quite outside his or her control. No amount of 'self-help' (the prescription of those who believed in *laissez-faire*) was likely to improve the conditions of a factory worker who had never been to school, worked 16 hours a day and lived in rat-infested terrace with insufficient money to feed his or her children adequately.

5.6.1   New liberalism

The solution was social legislation, designed to increase the opportunities of individuals to exercise their freedoms more effectively. This required a greater role for the state both in the provision of public goods (such as education, a sewage system, basic health care and even – later on – affordable housing for the working class) and also the redistribution of wealth through welfare benefits and taxation. Throughout the 19th century some important legislation had been passed which sought, for example, to protect the exploitation of children at work and ensure some health and safety standards in mines and factories. However, it was at the turn of the 19th century that social reform legislation took off. The new policies on education, housing, tax etc were not the same as 'socialism' (see below) because the aim was not merely to reduce inequality. Nor did new liberalism involve the public ownership or control of the means of production and exchange. Liberalism always stood for the continued right to own private property and for the market economy.

5.6.2   Liberalism and the welfare state

The 'new' liberalism was given practical effect by Liberal governments led by Lloyd George and Asquith around the turn of last century: death duties for the rich were increased; old age pensions for the poor were introduced by the Old Age Pensions Act 1908; a national insurance scheme to protect workers against the effects of illness and unemployment was created by the National Insurance Act 1911 (the old poor laws applied only to those absolutely destitute); progressive income tax arrived (and has never gone away) and investment income was taxed differently from earned income. Taxation became a tool for changing society and was no longer seen as merely a way of raising revenue to pay for things such as the defence of the realm and administration of justice. The role of the state was now to include responsibility for providing an income to people in their old age and during times of sickness and unemployment.

The era of *laissez-faire* therefore came to an end and 'social security' had arrived – but not without a constitutional struggle. The upper House of Parliament was unable to stomach this new-fangled and dangerous social democracy. The Lords used their legislative power to block the bill to implement the Liberal Party's 'people's budget' in 1909. There was a crisis. The government responded by calling a general election in January 1910. The Liberals won (because of the Irish, Welsh and Scottish voters; they did not win a majority of the English constituencies) and the Lords had little option but to pass the bill when it was reintroduced in the new Parliament. The government was determined to take away the Lords' powers to block money bills. Again the Lords refused to pass a bill to do this and in December 1910 a second general election was called. The outcome was another victory for the Liberals and a limited one for democracy; faced with a threat from King George V to create as many Liberal peers as necessary to get the bill through, the Lords reluctantly gave their approval to the Parliament Act 1911.

Arguably, much government policy in the 20th century up to 1979, whether Conservative or Labour, was shaped by ideas of social liberalism. Sometimes too much is made of the term 'consensus politics', used particularly to describe political debate in the UK during the 1950s and '60s, but there *was* widespread acceptance of the need for state intervention in the form of the welfare state, government control or ownership of major industries and a mixed economy. However, Margaret Thatcher's Conservative government was elected in 1979 and set a new agenda with a return to many ideas central to *laissez-faire* liberalism. (The significance of this period for public law is dealt with in Chapter 6).

A second important approach in political thinking is conservatism. As with liberalism, conservative perspectives on government and public law are not coextensive with the manifesto commitments of the modern Conservative Party. As has already been said, the Conservative Party today is as much associated with ideas of classical liberalism (described above) as anything else: it believes that the role of government should be kept to a minimum.

There is, however, another strand of conservative thought which is quite opposed to the notion of individualism. It does not see civil society as merely the aggregate of the individuals who make it up, nor the function of government as being primarily a means to the end of individual freedom. Conservative writers in this tradition often use the word 'organic' to explain their concept of civil society and make analogies with the family. Society is not, as some liberals and others suggest, based on the idea of a social contract between the people and the rulers. Instead it should be seen, like the family, as non-contractual and arising out of necessity rather than choice. Government is, however, only one part of civil society – institutions such as charities and other voluntary associations are also an important part of the fabric of society.

This form of conservatism is not necessarily in favour of limited government. The government may, for instance, interfere with private property rights where this is in the interests of society, eg by prohibiting house owners from altering the exterior appearance of their houses where this would have a detrimental impact on the character of a locality. Paternalism also prompts many conservatives to assert the right of the state to intervene in 'moral' issues. The fact that an activity (such as viewing pornography) is done by a consenting adult in a private place is not a good reason for saying that the law should not interfere with the individual's

5.7   Conservative and paternalistic traditions

5.7.1   Paternalistic intervention by government

freedom to do it; if government believes that the activity is damaging to society and its values, it ought to intervene and prohibit the activity.

Let us take an example. On a constitutional level, the clash between the paternalistic and liberal approaches can be seen in views about whether it should be legal for gay men to have sex. A liberal (whatever *her own* attitude about the fact that a significant proportion of the population is homosexual) would say the decision of two consenting individuals to make love to each other should be of no concern to the state; the individuals concerned, rather then the government, are the judges of whether their actions are right. The freedom to fall in love and have sexual relationships is, for almost everyone, a key part of what it means to be an individual. The paternalistic approach denies that there is a separation between 'private' and 'public' realms of life and says that if sexual acts between people of the same sex is damaging to society as a whole (eg because it may challenge the notion of the family), then it is proper for the law to prohibit it.

Obviously these different approaches to the question of how far, and why, government and law can legitimately intervene in people's lives is relevant to discussion about 'constitutional rights'. If the UK was to have a Bill of Rights what would go into it? Liberals and paternalistic conservatives could probably agree that the right to own and dispose of property should be constitutionally protected – though all but the most die-hard libertarians would want this to be qualified. But what about a constitutional right to privacy? Many conservatives would oppose this on paternalistic grounds.

5.7.2   The value of tradition

Another central conviction in conservative thinking is the stress on the value of continuity with the past. Reform of the constitution should take place only where there is a pragmatic need for it: there is no need to mend what does not need to be fixed. Change, when needed, should be incremental, building on the existing practices and institutions which have developed over the years and centuries. Many conservative thinkers even argue that the authority or legitimacy of government *derives* from the long-established constitution, not from some abstract, overarching principle like the need to promote individual freedom or from the principle of democracy.

From this perspective it is not self-evident that an institution such as the House of Lords – whose hereditary and appointed composition might be difficult to justify on a principled basis – ought to be reformed. As a second chamber it *in fact* works, so why reform it? The mere fact that it is not democratically elected is not, for conservatives, of itself a major problem. Conservatives in the end came to accept the need to extend the franchise for the House of Commons in the last century, but this was for pragmatic reasons – the need to accommodate the system of Parliamentary government to changing social conditions – rather than a dogmatic belief that democracy should be an overriding principle spurring on constitutional change.

Another strand in conservative thinking about law and government is to prefer the common law to statute law. Roger Scruton (a conservative philosopher and barrister) puts it in this way in *The Meaning of Conservatism*:

5.7.3   Preference for common law over legislation

> '... judicial reflection is governed by no ruling purpose other than the pursuit of justice within the framework of the given social order, while parliamentary reflection [ie in the legislative process], being purposeful, is inherently dangerous to the state ... [J]udges seek to align the decrees of Parliament [ie statutes] with an established legal system, and hence (indirectly) with institutions that find protection under the existing body of law. A politician who sought to destroy those institutions would therefore desire to remove law-making capacity from the judges and vest it entirely in Parliament, specifically, in the House of Commons, where the judiciary is neither directly represented, nor overtly influential ... Those who suspect the judiciary, under existing arrangements, of being a conservative force, are surely right.'

The point is not that judges overtly support the Conservative Party, but that the process of the common law, through concepts such as natural justice, protects traditional liberties (such as the right to property) against 'the formation of the egalitarian state' which has to be carried out by legislation.

The third major type of political thinking addressed in this chapter is socialism. As with the other political traditions, what constitutes 'socialism' is difficult to pin down, and, again, the bundle of beliefs which go to make up socialism cannot be associated directly with the policies advocated by a single political party. The Labour Party, at least as represented in Parliament, has never been made up exclusively of people who could accurately be described as socialists. Two key ideas are at the core of the socialist tradition in England: equality and criticism of capitalism.

5.8   Socialism

The first idea is a belief in equality – or (to say something rather different) a condemnation of inequality. Many theorists,

5.8.1   Equality

including *laissez-faire* liberals, make appeals to the principle of equality, saying that people should be treated equally unless there is a good reason for treating them otherwise. In the 19th century this was often patently not the case: not all adults were permitted to vote in Parliamentary elections and women did not have equal legal rights to men in many respects. Socialists tended to go further, however, than just demanding equality of opportunity. Equality needed to be not merely about how people were *treated* in formal terms, but had to go beyond this to redistribute resources in society. Just giving a factory worker living in abject poverty the right to vote, for instance, would do little to change the quality of that person's life; giving the worker a share in the ownership and profits of the factory would.

5.8.2   Rejection of the market

Secondly, socialists argue that capitalism is ethically wrong and economically inefficient. It is wasteful to permit mass unemployment and poor living conditions which result from the operation of market forces. The means of production and distribution should be owned and controlled collectively rather than by private owners. Clearly this goes much further than the state intervention to provide social security which was pursued by the new liberals in the early years of the century. Whereas new liberalism always saw a place for private ownership and enterprise, socialism did not. Socialists have expressed a wide variety of views as to what common ownership should be: some have advocated state ownership (nationalisation) while others argue for co-operatives and other smaller-scale collective forms of ownership.

5.8.3   Socialism and collectivism

Both new liberals and socialists do, however, share a common belief in the benefits of collective action directed by the state and for this reason both can be called 'collectivists'. (Dicey, for instance, used the terms collectivism and socialism interchangeably.) In the UK, during the 20th century, the greatest impact of socialist ideas has probably been at a local level when committed socialists have been elected to run local authorities. The policies of such councils have often brought conflict with central government and in the courts. For example, in 1921 the London Borough of Poplar decided to use its powers under s 62 of the Metropolis Management Act 1855 (to employ and pay such wages 'as the Council think fit') not to reduce wages even though the cost of living was falling, to set a minimum wage of £4 and also – horror of horrors – to pay men and women the same. The court quashed this decision on the basis that it was unlawful for the council to show such 'philanthropic enthusiasm' with ratepayers' money.

At a central government level, socialist principles can be seen in the program adopted by the Attlee Labour government which was elected in 1945. Many industries and services, including the coal mines, steel industry and railways, were nationalised, meaning they were compulsorily purchased from their owners. The high degree of state regulation and control of industry during the Second World War had accustomed people to the idea that the economy could and should be controlled – and owned – by government and managed in the national interest rather than for private profit.

In this last section of the chapter we look at a handful of recent books by public lawyers which make links between political thought and constitutional and administrative law. They are:

5.9   Overview of recent writing on political thought by public lawyers

- Carol Harlow and Richard Rawlings, *Law and Administration* (1984), Chapters 1 and 2;

- Martin Loughlin, *Public Law and Political Theory* (1992);

- PP Craig, *Public Law and Democracy in the UK and USA* (1990).

The fact that these three books were written in the last dozen or so years does not imply that the study of the links between political thought and law is something new. Although this chapter began by criticising Dicey's *Law of the Constitution* for a failure to make explicit or explain the strong political views which underpin it, Dicey did go on to do some pioneering research on the connections between political thought and law. When he had finished work on *The Law of the Constitution*, Dicey wrote another book called *Law and Public Opinion in England During the Nineteenth Century* (first published in 1905). In it he argued that there was a 'close and demonstrable connection during the 19th century between the development of English law and certain known currents of opinion'. He divided the 19th century into three periods: old Toryism (1760-1830), Individualism (1825-1870) and Collectivism (1865 onwards) and he diagnosed a trend away from individualism towards collectivism. (Remember that he was personally very much an anti-collectivist.) Many people have since criticised Dicey's analysis, but this does not detract from the importance and value of the enterprise; it is absolutely clear that teaching, practice and writing about constitutional and administrative law has not been immune from trends and different traditions in political thinking. But until the 1980s there had been no real attempt to examine this in detail; certainly Dicey himself had avoided doing this explicitly in *The Law of the Constitution*.

5.10   Harlow and Rawlings: red, green and amber

A good and fairly accessible place to start for first year students is the first couple of chapters in Harlow and Rawlings' book. They set out to show how public law writers fit into one of three broad traditions which for convenience they label 'red light', 'green light' and 'amber light'. Writers are classified according to their views about what the main role of public law should be; this, Harlow and Rawlings argue, is largely determined by each writer's broader conception of the proper role of the state.

5.10.1   Red-light theorists

Writers and judges in the red light camp tend to see the aim of administrative law as the protection of 'traditional' liberties (eg to do with the use of property) against the state. The label red-light is used to signify the view that state power ought to be stopped or at least slowed down. These writers' ideas are individualist, rights-orientated and court-centred. They believe that administrative law exists primarily to redress grievances, and that the administrative machinery of the state is controlled externally (principally by the courts) and retrospectively. Judicial review of administrative action is seen as central to this mission. Dicey falls within this category (though remember, of course, that he had little to say about 'administrative law' and judicial review).

5.10.2   Green-light theorists

In contrast, green-light theorists say the aim of administrative law should be to facilitate government action. In this model, lawyers tend to be apolitical technicians rather than upholders of the rule of law. The law is not seen as embodying any particular set of values but is a tool by which government can implement its policies. These writers approve of the interventionist state and consequently see regulation and legislation as more important than the case law produced by the courts. Government, rather than the law, is central to their interests. Administration should be controlled by internal and prospective methods such as participation and consultation.

The green-light theorists are especially associated with a group of writers at the London School of Economics during the 1930s. Jennings, whose criticisms of Dicey were outlined in Chapter 4, was one of them.

5.10.3   Amber-light theorists

Harlow and Rawlings are very careful to warn readers that if their selection of materials in the first two chapters suggests 'polarity, this is an over-simplification'. Most public lawyers today occupy the middle ground. For many years, they say, 'there has been a measure of consensus about the need for a sophisticated system of administrative law to monitor and discipline the powers of the state', but also an acceptance that the state needs powers – including the discretionary powers abhorred by Dicey – to carry out the governmental functions of the 20th century such as regulation and the provision of social security.

Like Harlow and Rawlings, Loughlin attempts to map out and suggest models for understanding the broad traditions of thinking and writing about public law in Britain. He constructs two main models – functionalism and normativism – which he defines in outline on page 60:

> 'The *normativist style* in public law is rooted in a belief in the ideal of the separation of powers and in the need to subordinate government to law. This style highlights law's adjudicative and control functions and therefore its rule orientation and conceptual nature. The *functionalist style* in public law, by contrast, views law as part of the apparatus of government. Its focus is upon law's regulatory and facilitative functions and therefore is orientated to aims and objectives and adopts an instrumentalist social policy approach. Functionalism reflects an ideal of progressive evolutionary change.'

You should be able to see how Loughlin's 'normativists' share similarities with Harlow and Rawlings' red-light camp: they highlight the role of public law in controlling government. Similarly, Loughlin's 'functionalists,' like green-light theorists, focus on how public law helps government achieve its tasks. A modern day 'functionalist', judge (through Loughlin does not classify him as such), is perhaps Lord Woolf, who in many of his judgments has emphasised the need for judges to be sensitive to the needs of government, and who advocates procedural protections for government bodies in judicial review to prevent disruption to public administration.

Overall, however, Loughlin argues that the dominant tradition in English public law is a 'conservative variant of normativism' – with Dicey as the towering giant among those who adopt this approach. Loughlin identifies HWR Wade 'as the pre-eminent contemporary writer' within this tradition and argues that 'Wade must essentially be seen as a contemporary disciple of Dicey' who implicitly advocates both a limited role for government and supports the role of the judges. They place great faith in the common law as a way of protecting citizens from the powers of the state.

The other subset of normativism, the 'liberal normativists', has also had some influence as can be seen in the campaigns of reform groups such as Charter 88. Liberal normativists see law as playing a central role in protecting individual rights against the state and advocate the entrenchment of a Bill of Rights. But as Loughlin points out, writers from many of the 'schools' support Charter 88. This concerns him and he argues that the group's campaign ends up fudging many fundamental issues.

5.11   Loughlin's *Public Law and Political Theory*

5.12 Craig's *Public Law and Democracy in the UK and USA*

A third recent book to explore the connections between public law and political thought is Paul Craig's very challenging *Public Law and Democracy in the UK and USA*. Its major theme is that 'the different conceptions of public law reveal themselves to be reflections of deeper controversies about different conceptions of the democratic society in which we live'. As the title suggests, the book looks at the experience both in the UK and the US. Craig's own view is that 'agnosticism is not possible': a choice must be made between the rival theories of democracy and his own preference is for 'some form of participatory democracy'. In relation to the UK, Craig examines several types of democratic theory including:

- unitary self-correcting (representative) democracy; and

- participatory democracy.

He is critical of all of them. He also considers theories of liberalism in detail, though he readily concedes that liberalism is not itself a theory of democracy. The book is difficult and, for a student just beginning to study constitutional and administrative law, not very accessible. It is impossible adequately to summarise his complex arguments here; instead we draw out just two themes. The first is Craig's criticisms of Dicey (on Dicey generally, see Chapter 4, above). The second is his argument about the need for participatory democracy.

5.12.1 Dicey's majoritarian self-correcting democracy

Craig argues that Dicey's approach to the British constitution was based on 'certain assumptions concerning representative democracy and the way it operated'. Dicey's vision of democracy was one 'in which the will of the electors was expressed through Parliament, and in which Parliament controlled the government'. As we have already noted, Dicey thought MPs reflected the views of the majority of electors; if they did not, this would be 'corrected' at the next general election. It is not at all clear, Craig suggests, how Dicey 'would prevent or forestall the danger of majority oppression' of minorities. If the majority in Parliament enacted legislation which detrimentally affected minority interests, the common law (which is a key feature of Dicey's conception of the rule of law) could not protect because the principle of Parliamentary sovereignty would prevail. In any event, Craig argues, Dicey's image of the British constitution was flawed even when he wrote, and is certainly no longer sustainable today. Dicey thought that power moved in one direction: from the electors, via Parliament, to the government. But the reality was always more complex; even in Dicey's time 'our constitutional system became one dominated by the top, by the executive and the party hierarchy'.

Craig goes on to examine the several ways in which Dicey's view of democracy affected his writing. For instance, Dicey's distrust of discretionary powers in the hands of the executive – the first limb of his rule of law – stemmed at least in part from his view that it was only through *Parliament*, which represented the views of the nation, that government should be allowed to infringe individual rights.

In the last chapters of his book Craig examines a concept of democracy very different from that which underpinned Dicey's work: participatory democracy. There are several forms. In Chapter 11 Craig looks at one of these – 'the radical view'. He examines the difficult work of several American writers. For one of them, Barber in *Strong Democracy: Participatory Democracy for a New Age* (1984), participatory democracy is 'strong' democracy, in contrast to the other theories which provide only 'thin' democracy. In practical terms, it would entail things like:

5.12.2   Participatory democracy

- setting up neighbourhood assemblies to discuss regional and national issues, grievances and the defence of local interests;

- local office holders would be drawn by lot; and

- information technology could be used to communicate and disseminate information about political and economic information.

Advocates of radical forms of participatory democracy have to address the question of possible majority oppression of minorities. Barber and others reject the US courts' role in striking down decisions as 'unconstitutional' and instead 'pin their hopes upon internal self-regulation and the transformation of conflict'. In other words, groups outside the legislature, or within it, will discuss and argue the matter through.

If you are asked to consider questions of constitutional reform, eg whether the UK should enact a Bill of Rights or the House of Lords be reformed, it is worth remembering that there are more radical alternatives to those often sketched out in many of the constitutional law textbooks.

This chapter has been able, at best, to raise your awareness of the different types of political thought that exist and how these may impact on questions of public law. The main message is that it is impossible for any description of the constitution – or suggestions for its reform – to be politically 'neutral'. Bear this in mind whenever you sit down to write an essay on the need for constitutional reform.

5.13   Overview

As an exercise, try to work out, roughly, into which of the traditions described by Harlow and Rawlings the following fit:

(a) the main textbook you are using on your course; and

(b) your lecturer/tutor.

The contents page of the textbook and the syllabus of your course should be useful clues. If they are dominated by explanations of judicial review then this may indicate a red-light/normativist approach: the focus is probably on how government action is *constrained* by law. If, on the other hand, emphasis is given to statute law, delegated legislation and internal complaints mechanisms, which show how government uses public law to *facilitate* action, then this is likely to suggest sympathy with the green-light/functionalist perspective.

Political Thought for Public Law Students

An understanding of political thought is important to understanding constitutional and administrative law. It:

- helps students evaluate proposals for constitutional reform; and

- emphasises that there is no such thing as 'value-free' writing about public law.

In Britain three broad schools of political thinking have been influential.

Three groups of political ideas

- *Liberalism* stresses the importance of individuals and their liberty. For laissez-faire liberals this means the absence of state coercion: the role of government should be limited and it should intervene in people's lives as little as possible. An alternative strand of liberal thinking focuses on the need for government to ensure that individuals have the opportunities to exercise their freedom.

- *Conservatism* attaches importance to tradition and accepts that government may intervene in peoples' lives on paternalistic grounds. The common law is seen as embodying many values: it protects traditional liberties such as the right to property and it can curb the powers of government (eg through the process of statutory interpretation and insistence on natural justice).

- *Socialism*, in its original forms, embodies two central ideas: a belief in the value of equality and a rejection of the free-market as a mechanism for producing and distributing goods and services.

Harlow and Rawlings sketch out a model in which writers (and to some extent also judges) are categorised according to their views of the dominant purpose of constitutional and administrative law. These views in turn are determined by different views about the proper role of the state.

The connection between political thought and public law

- *Red-light theorists* see administrative law as existing principally to redress the grievances of individuals against government and protect their rights. The courts, and judicial review in particular, are where this happens.

- *Green-light theorists* see administrative law as the rules and mechanisms through which government can carry out its task; they emphasise statute law rather than the common law.

- *Amber-light theorists* accept both need to facilitate government action and the need to protect individuals.

Chapter 6

Gap-filling: 1979 and All That

This chapter is an overview of some of the changes in government and the constitution since 1979. That, of course, was the general election in which the Conservatives under Margaret Thatcher defeated James Callaghan's Labour government. The Conservative Party won the subsequent general elections in 1983, 1987 and (under John Major) again in 1992. This chapter has to be highly selective and looks at:

* privatisation;

* central-local government relations; and

* the reform of the civil service.

It is hardly an exaggeration to say that a new constitution has emerged in the UK since 1979 – and it did so in a typically pragmatic British way. While many constitutional and administrative law courses continued to fill the 'reform' slot on their syllabuses with discussion of the desirability of a Bill of Rights, a written constitution, the need for proportional representation or the abolition of the House of Lords, in the real world new types of institutions, constitutional structures and problems were developing. For some commentators, such as Cosmo Graham and Tony Prosser (*Waiving the Rules: the Constitution under Thatcherism* (1988)):

> 'If one theme predominates it is that the approach of [the Conservative governments since 1979] has been instrumental and tactical rather than strategic and planned.'

For other writers there were also some ideological explanations for many of the developments. First, the Conservative government has been committed to 'rolling back the frontiers of the state'. In other words, they believed that the state ought to do less.

Second was a related desire to control and, wherever possible, cut public expenditure so as to reduce government borrowing and, it was claimed, levels of taxation. Nationalised industries and state-owned utilities (gas, water, electricity) were sold to private investors. This brought revenue to the government but the constitutional question of how the often monopolistic powers of these companies were to be scrutinised and made accountable was not always properly addressed.

6.1   What motivated the radical changes?

The ability of the 300 or so local authorities to levy and spend local tax was also very considerably curbed. During this period the relationship between central government and the councils was 'juridified' (see Martin Loughlin, *Local Government in the Modern State* (1986)): central government used legislation to control councils more than ever before and there was frequent resort to judicial review by both sides.

The need to curb public spending also prompted a sustained attempt to improve efficiency and effectiveness in the civil service (with Next Steps Agencies) and the National Health Service (with the creation of an 'internal market'). As with privatisation, these reforms all created problems of accountability which have yet to be resolved.

6.2 Nationalised industries

When, in the wake of the Second World War, the Labour Party under Clement Attlee won the general election in 1945, it compulsorily acquired many of the major industries and services. The various regional railway companies were amalgamated into British Rail. It ceased to be possible for a private business or individual to mine coal or make iron and steel – all companies were nationalised. Later, during the 1960s and 1970s other industries were also acquired by the state, including parts of the ailing motor manufacturing industry such as British Leyland.

If your library has older constitutional and administrative law books on its shelves, take a volume down and you will almost certainly find a chapter about these nationalised industries. They posed many constitutional problems. To what extent should a relevant minister be responsible to Parliament for the performance and policies of these public corporations? What degree of managerial independence should the head of each corporation be given? In what circumstances should it be proper for government to intervene in their running? Some of the nationalised industries were also chronically unprofitable (even taking into account that earning profit was sometimes seen as only one of their objectives).

6.3 The privatisation policy

Although a policy of privatisation did not form a central plank of the 1979 Conservative Party manifesto, after their second election win in 1983 it had become an important part of the government's programme. To the government it seemed a solution to several problems. One was that it would help stem government borrowing: when public corporations were turned into companies and the shares sold, this bought revenue into the Treasury; and loss-making enterprises ceased to be a drain on public funds. The privatisation policy also fitted into the government's view that 'less government is good government' and that individuals could be empowered by owning property (including shares).

By the 1990s many of the nationalised industries had been sold off, including: British Aerospace (1981), British Shipbuilders (1983), British Telecom (1984), British Airports Authority (1986), British Gas (1986), British Airways (1987), British Steel (1989), the regional water, electricity companies (1989) and British Coal (1994). Harold Macmillan, Conservative Prime Minister in the 1960s and critic of privatisation in the 1980s, likened this to 'selling off the family silver'. At the time of writing early 1995, British Rail was shortly due to be privatised.

Each of these industries form an important part of the British economy – the very reason they were nationalised after the War. What, if any, control should government continue to exercise over them now that they are privately owned? In theory the shareholders call the boards of directors to account for the efficiency and profitability of each company, but this form of accountability is clearly not always going to be sufficient. This is particularly so for companies in monopoly or near-monopoly situations such as the gas and water industries. Some form of government regulation was therefore inevitable in spite of Conservative slogans such as 'the business of government is not the government of business'.

6.3.1 The continued need for regulation

In many cases, a company is allowed to trade only after being issued with a licence by a minister, eg in the telecommunications industry. Also regulatory agencies, staffed by people appointed and paid for by government, have been set up to monitor the work of privatised companies. These agencies include OFWAT (for the water industry) and OFTEL (for the telecommunications companies). In some cases the director of the regulatory body has power to set maximum prices for services (eg telephone charges and gas). In early privatisations the government also retained a 'golden share' in the companies (a residual shareholding with special rights to intervene). In short, although industries have been privatised, a considerable degree of public control remains.

Exploration of how government does or should regulate private enterprises is more appropriate to advanced courses in public law; there is a great deal of theoretical writing on the subject. How, for example, should a regulatory agency decide to set prices? Should there be formal hearings with consumers and the business presenting evidence and a person adjudicating? Or are other procedures better? Also, what role should Parliament play in all of this – should it, for example, be allowed to debate ministers' decisions to grant licences to particular (eg telecommunication) companies? Graham and Prosser argue that these types of constitutional questions do 'not represent so major a change as appears at first sight' from those which applied to the old nationalised industries.

6.4 Local government in the 1980s and 1990s

Another area of constitutional change since 1979 – apart from the purported rolling back of the state by privatisation – occurred in local government. Since the latter part of the 19th century, local councils have been elected statutory bodies with responsibilities for providing a range of public services to their population. At one time this included hospitals, water and gas but by the 1950s each of these functions had been given to larger regional specialist authorities. However, councils continued to provide primary, secondary and further education, personal social services (meals on wheels, social workers etc), recreational facilities, maintenance of many roads, subsidised rented housing and other services.

During the 1970s local authorities, like the nationalised industries, were often criticised for their inefficiency and lack of accountability. During that decade the Labour government sought to limit the expenditure of councils, which at the time accounted for over a quarter of total public spending. When the Conservatives came to power in 1979 it was clear to them that changes were necessary. But as with privatisation, there was no overall strategic plan based on principle (eg the proper constitutional relationship between central and local government in a democracy), but rather a series of ad hoc policies aimed at solving particular problems. Sylvia Horton in S Savage and L Robins (eds), *Pubic Policy under Thatcher* (1990), gave this general assessment:

> 'The overall result amounted to a cumulative assault on almost every activity for which local government was responsible, but it lacked coherence and consistency. Some of the early policies failed to achieve their objectives and were either abandoned or changed. In others there were unforeseen effects and consequences to which the government reacted.'

6.4.1 Local government finance

The public services and facilities provided by local authorities are paid for mainly by grants from central government; most of the rest is financed through local taxation levied by the councils themselves. The story of the 1980s is of a cat and mouse battle between the Department of the Environment (the department responsible for local government) and local authorities about spending. There were frequent, confusing and highly complex changes to legislation and regular resort to judicial review by both sides. As part of the general economic goal of curbing total public spending, the Department of the Environment set spending targets for each authority and financial penalties were imposed on those that overspent. Some councils were 'rate capped' in 1985, meaning that legal limits were placed on the amount of local tax that each could impose.

In 1988 the system of local taxation (called rates) based on the notional rental value of every residential property in local authority areas was replaced with the highly controversial community charge (nicknamed the poll tax). With a few exceptions, every adult was to pay the same tax to their local authority. People on very low incomes were entitled to some rebate, but generally the new tax meant that a student nurse would pay the same community charge as a managing director earning £100,000. The government believed that this *per capita* tax would improve accountability of local authorities; that since a much larger proportion of people would be paying local government than had paid rates tax, they would vote in lower-spending Conservative councillors who keep expenditure, and therefore the poll tax, under control. The poll tax was not a success. There was a national campaign against it which culminated in a violent demonstration in London. John Major's Conservative government scrapped the community charge in 1993 and replaced it with a new system of council tax based again on property values but with discounts for people living alone.

6.4.2	Poll tax

There have been several reforms of the size and structure of local authorities during the 20th century. In 1972 a two-tier system was created across the country, with large county councils comprised of several district councils. The allocation of functions for planning and service provision between the two tiers often confused the public and in time many questioned the need for county councils, suggesting that a single layer of unitary authorities would be a better model. During the 1980s the county councils in the UK's seven major metropolitan areas (including London) were Labour-controlled. They wished to pursue policies such as subsidised public transport which found no favour with the Conservative government. In 1986, as promised in the 1983 Conservative Party manifesto, Mrs Thatcher's government abolished the GLC and the other six metropolitan county councils. The result in London was that the city is now governed by 32 quite small borough councils but there is no elected city-wide authority. After the abolition of the GLC some functions were passed down to borough councils. Other strategic planning

6.4.3	Structural changes

responsibilities, eg for fire, transport and waste, were given to new, joint boards (comprising representatives of the relevant borough councils). Many people questioned the lack of democratic control and accountability of these bodies.

6.4.4 Contracting out

As with the nationalised industries, the Conservative government saw the discipline of market forces and competition as tools which could be used to make local authorities more efficient in the way they provided services to their communities. The Local Government Act 1988 requires councils to advertise, inviting tenders from private businesses to carry out work such as catering in schools and old people's homes, maintenance of leisure facilities and refuse collection. The council's own work force may also submit a tender, but they will only be allowed to carry out the work if they can show that they can provide better value for money than an outside contractor. Contracts to carry out specified jobs for a period of time (usually a year or more) are then entered into by each council. Compulsory competitive tendering was later extended to professional services used by the councils themselves, eg legal advice and conveyancing.

The change has therefore been profound. One commentator has even suggested that 'it is quite possible to envisage the local authority of the future as a set of contracts, and a network of internal and external trading' (Kieron Walsh in J Steward and G Stoker (eds), *The Future of Local Government* (1989)). There has been a transformation from local government being a 'provider' to an 'enabler'.

6.4.5 Social housing and the right to buy

The provision of 'social housing' (subsidised rented flats and houses) has been a major function of local government since the 1930s. In 1977 the housing responsibilities of councils were enlarged when the Labour government enacted the Homeless Persons Act. This placed a legal obligation on every council to provide permanent housing for local people in priority need and who were homeless (including those living in inadequate private accommodation). For people who were not homeless there continued to be very lengthy queues for council flats and houses.

Throughout the 1970s doubts often surfaced about the ability of local authorities to manage their housing efficiently and sensitively. The Labour government, and after 1979 the Conservatives, gave more responsibilities to housing associations, charitable non-profit making bodies set up to provide low cost housing.

In 1980 the Conservative government gave council tenants the right to buy their council homes, at a discount according to how long they had been tenants and with the help of a mortgage provided by the local authority. Many tenants living in houses on more desirable estates did this, but councils were left with high-rise and other problem dwellings under their control. The Housing and Planning Act 1986 allowed councils to transfer whole estates to private landlords or housing associations. Councils were not, however, permitted to use the capital receipts from any of these sales to build new homes for rental. They were also required to stop subsidising the rents they charged to their remaining tenants.

The 1944 Education Act had created a partnership between local authorities and central government for the provision of education. Broad policy decisions (eg about the relative merits of selective and comprehensive education) were decided by the Department for Education, but local authorities had a considerable degree of autonomy. As in other fields, this arrangement largely broke down during the 1980s. 'Parental choice' became a slogan of the Conservative government. This was given practical effect in a number of ways:

6.4.6   Education

- Parents were given the right to 'express a preference' as to which local authority school their children would attend.

- The boards of governors of local authority schools were given responsibility for making decisions previously taken by authorities, eg staff appointments, sex education policy.

- Parents of local authority schools were given the right to vote to 'opt out' of local authority control and in future become 'grant maintained', receiving more favourable funding directly from central government.

- A national curriculum was introduced.

- The Department of Education introduced a controversial scheme for testing pupils.

- Local authorities ceased to have responsibility for polytechnics in 1988; they later became 'new' universities.

Many commentators argue that these policies amount to an unprecedented centralisation of power. Others, however, claim that although many of the policies have involved bypassing local authorities, real power has in fact been devolved to those in the best position to make decisions – parents, teachers and governors.

In countries with written constitutions, local government is sometimes given a protected status; principles such as local autonomy or decentralisation may be enshrined. There is of

6.4.7   Overview of local government

course nothing like that in the UK. Many of the battles and more or less constant tinkering with local government structures and finance stem from an absence of agreement about the proper role of local authorities in Britain. Some see them as primarily elected representative bodies which should have freedom to pursue policies in the best interests of their communities; importance is attached to there being *two* levels of elected government in the UK. For others, councils are seen mainly as agents of central governments, there to provide practical services to the public. There is little doubt that during the 1980s the relationship between central and local government has largely become one of principal and agent.

6.5   Civil service reform

As with the nationalised corporations and local government, the civil service is a part of the constitution to have undergone radical change since 1979. In contrast to the other two institutions where the transformations were (a) highly party politically contentious and (b) implemented by statute, reform of the civil service has been less fractious and more informal.

The motivation was to improve efficiency and effectiveness. Some critics (see Herberg, Jowell and Le Sueur (1995) 45 CLP Part 1 121, p 143) have suggested the end result has been like the curate's egg:

'While aspects of the new structures, procedures and working practices are to be welcomed, the headlong pursuit of efficiency has, in some contexts, left casualties in its wake. Efficiency may clash with other goals promoted by public law and result in less effective mechanisms of accountability and control of public power.

6.5.1   Next Steps agencies

The most constitutionally significant aspect of the efficiency strategy in central government is undoubtedly the Next Steps programme. It has transformed the British civil service in a way unprecedented since the Northcote-Trevelyan reforms in the 19th century (see Chapter 3, para 3.6.3). In 1988, Sir Robin Ibbs, Mrs Thatcher's efficiency advisor, put in motion the 'Next Steps' reforms (so-called because the question was what should be the next steps in the efficiency programme which had begun several years before). The key idea was to make a distinction between the two functions of the civil service; to separate (a) the delivery of services (eg issuing passports) from (b) the role of senior civil servants in policy-formulation and advising ministers. Responsibility for the former would be devolved to Executive Agencies headed by chief executives. Tasks such as the issuing of driving licences, payment of welfare benefits and the running of the Land Registry (to take just three examples) would no longer be carried out directly by central government departments.

By 1993, almost every executive function of central government was operating along these lines. Departments have become considerably smaller. The relationship between the agencies and their sponsor department is regulated by a framework agreement. The previously unified, monolithic civil service has become a 'more federal, varied structure' (Diana Goldsworthy, *Setting Up Next Steps* (1991)).

While Next Steps has been acclaimed by many as a success, for public lawyers the new executive agencies posed several potential problems. There was a need to fit the Next Step agencies into traditional constitutional conventions of ministerial responsibility (ie that a minister should be answerable in Parliament and before select committees for the actions of civil servants and, perhaps, resign in the last resort). But to continue to hold ministers accountable for the work of executive agencies would endanger the core concept of the reforms – that the minister 'delegates the managerial independence, within the pre-set budget, to decide how best to run the organisation and get the work done, with appropriate rewards for success and penalties for failure' (Goldsworthy).

6.5.2   Constitutional law problems with agencies

In July 1991, the Select Committee on Procedure made recommendations in relation to parliamentary questions. Until then, ministers, when asked a question on 'operational' matters, passed the question to the chief executive of the agency concerned. A practice developed of answers from agency heads being placed in the House of Commons library. Following the committee's recommendations, answers are now published in *Hansard*. The Treasury and Civil Service Select Committee supported this: 'The provision of information is vital if agencies are to be accepted by Parliament and the public.'

Several broad issues for public law emerge from the changes in government made by the Conservatives since 1979. First, the reforms and the way in which they were carried out illustrate the essentially pragmatic nature of constitutional change that has always been evident in Britain. As with the English Civil War, Glorious Revolution and 19th century reforms (discussed in Chapter 3), principled justifications for change often emerged only during or after the event.

6.6   General overview

Secondly, the reforms show the great importance now attached to the principle of efficiency – the idea that finite public resources should be used in as effective a way as possible. Perhaps 'value for money' is a constitutional principle as important as, say, the rule of law? Controversy will, of course, continue to surround how efficiency is to be achieved and future governments may not trust as much to market forces as the Conservatives have done. The work of the National Audit Office and local government auditors may be as deserving of the attention of public law students as other scrutiny mechanisms such as Parliamentary Select Committees and the ombudsmen.

Thirdly, the policies demonstrate vividly what Parliamentary sovereignty and the absence of a written constitution entail. Legislation was the key tool used by the government to implement its changes in local government:

> '... in contrast to previous governments, which utilised persuasion, negotiation, financial incentives and disseminated information on good practice to bring about change, the Thatcher government ... used law on an unprecedented scale' (Horton, above).

Gap-filling: 1979 and All That

Conservative governments since 1979 have brought about significant changes in the constitution and public law. There is a debate as to the extent to which the reforms have been essentially piecemeal and pragmatic or whether clear ideological explanations (such as the desire to 'roll back the frontiers of the state') can be given.

- Almost all that state-owned industries have been returned to the private sector. This does not, however, mean that they no longer pose constitutional problems. There is a continued need to regulate the activities of industries providing essential services such as electricity and water in monopoly or near-monopoly situations.

Privatisation

- Since the late 1970s the powers of local authorities to raise funds through local taxation have been limited by central government imposing 'caps' on their expenditure and introducing new forms of taxation (including the ill-fated Community Charge or 'poll tax'). This has resulted in lengthy conflict between councils and the Department of the Environment. In this battle central government has the whip hand because ultimately it can determine the rules by enacting legislation (including legislation to overturn judicial decisions in favour of local authorities). Other changes of constitutional importance in local government include restructuring (which many argue has lead to greater centralisation of power). There has been wide spread contracting out of the provisions of services which, according to some commentators, has lead to a transformation of the role of councils from being 'providers' to 'enablers'. The 'right to buy' council houses and radical changes to schooling have also led to a diminishing role for local authorities in these areas.

Local government

- Prompted by the search for ever-greater efficiency and effectiveness, much of the central government civil service had undergone radical reform. As part of the Next Steps programme, executive agencies were set up and they are now responsible for the delivery of most services to the public. Departments are now smaller and focus on policy advice to ministers rather than its day to day implementation. A number of constitutional problems

Civil Service reform

have arisen from this, particularly the question of accountability for acts and omissions by executive agencies. The traditional doctrine of ministerial responsibility has had to be adapted to these new circumstances

Chapter 7

Sources of Public Law

This chapter is about the sources of public law. It has three main aims.

- It contains *practical information* about where to find the sources of constitutional and administrative law. This will be of particular help to students writing essays and doing course work which require research in the law library.

- It also summarises the principal *constitutional problems* with the various types of public law powers and obligations. You may find the chapter a useful way to review or introduce many of the topics covered in your course.

- Finally, with the use of a practical illustration, the chapter shows how *different sources of public law inter-relate* with one another.

Many people new to studying law like to think of 'law' as a series of fairly precise rules which determine what people can and cannot lawfully do; and that people who breach a rule will be subject to some sort of sanction (either being punished by the state or being sued by another person). This is a very limited view of the nature of law generally. It can, however, provide a useful starting point for making sense of the subject. So far as constitutional and administrative law is concerned, the following are the main *sources* of obligations and powers of public bodies:

- Acts of Parliament;

- statutory instruments;

- quasi-legislation (ministerial circulars, codes of practice, etc);

- the prerogative;

- case law;

- constitutional conventions;

- European Community legislation (Treaties, regulations and directives).

Some of these sources of obligations, such as quasi-legislation and constitutional conventions cannot really be described as

7.1 Sources of public law obligations

7.1.1 Law and non-law

'law'. Some people studying constitutional and administrative law get concerned about this, believing that law students should, well ... just study law. This was once a very respectable approach and one that Dicey championed. He had a clear view of what a law teacher should do (*Law of the Constitution*, p 31):

> 'With conventions or understandings [the law teacher] has no direct concern. They vary from generation to generation, almost from year to year. ... If he is concerned [with conventions] at all, he is so only in so far as he may be called upon to show what is the connection (if there be any) between the conventions of the constitution and the law of the constitution. This the true constitutional law is his only real concern. His proper function is to show what are the legal rules (ie the rules recognised by the courts) which are to be found in the several parts of the constitution. Of such rules or laws he will easily discover more than enough ... The duty, in short, of an English professor of law is to state what are the laws which form part of the constitution, to arrange them in order, to explain their meaning, and to exhibit where possible their logical connection.'

For Dicey, non-legal sources of obligation such as constitutional conventions were of lesser importance than 'law'. Today, such a view of what needs to be studied is no longer plausible. Some modern writers even question whether 'law' can be distinguished from 'politics'. Martin Loughlin, professor of law at Manchester University, for example has written recently (*Public Law and Political Theory*, (1992) p 4) that:

> '... public law is simply a sophisticated form of political discourse; that controversies within the subject are simply extended political disputes.'

For people just starting to study public law, however, this type of debate is rather too sophisticated. We need to begin with some basics. Shortly, we will review the main sources of obligation (listed above) in the English constitutional and administrative system. Approaching the 'rule book' in this way is to focus on *who* makes the particular type of rules, *how*, and the rule's *formal status* (if any) in the legal system. In the next main section of this chapter (para 7.2 onwards) there is a statement of main characteristics of each type of rule, practical advice about where to find them in a law library and a summary of the main constitutional problems with each one.

7.1.2   Rules, discretions and rights

To begin thinking about public law obligations, however, it is necessary to go behind this type of formal description to consider what sorts of powers, obligations etc can be created.

- **Firm rules**

  One type of obligation which may be placed on an official, Minister or other public body is a firm and precise duty to do something. Thus, it is a firm rule (imposed by convention) that the monarch gives the Royal assent to all bills which have passed through both Houses of Parliament or in accordance with the Parliament Act 1911. The Queen has no discretion in particular instances to withhold her assent. Statutes and statutory instruments also often create firm rules. Thus, it is a firm and precise rule that men over the age of 65 years who satisfy clear criteria as to the national insurance contributions they have made over the years, are entitled to an old age pension. The Department of Social Security has no discretion to withhold payment of a pension because, for example, it considers that a person is not in financial need. The agency responsible for issuing driving licences similarly has to do so on the basis of pre-announced, specific criteria and cannot refuse to issue a licence because, say, it thinks that a person may be an inconsiderate motorist even though hs has passed his driving test.

  From the point of view of public bodies, applying firm rules can be a good way to make decisions. They can ensure that like cases are treated alike. Rules also help speed up the decision-making process: an official normally only has to compare the facts of an individual case with set criteria and does not have to make difficult value judgments.

- **Discretion**

  Not all public law obligations are imposed on public bodies in the form of firm and precise rules. Another method is to confer a discretion on the decision makers, giving them leeway to take account of individual circumstances in arriving at their decision. For example, a local authority may be given discretion to allocate licences to street traders by a statute using words such as:

  'A local authority may issue licences to such persons as it considers fit and proper'.

  The council is under no duty to grant a licence to everyone who applies for one and may decide to limit the number of licences. Nor are any firm and specific criteria laid down as to who should be given one. It is up to each council to decide what it means to say that a person is 'fit and proper'. This is not to say that the council has complete discretion. It could not, for instance, make an arbitrary decision that no man with red hair is a fit and proper person to run a market stall. This is because the courts, through the judicial review system, place constraints on the exercise of discretion to ensure that it is used for proper purposes.

- **Individual rights**

   In the UK, it is unusual for statutes or other sources of public law obligation expressly to confer rights on individuals; instead statutes tend to place obligations on public bodies. For instance, the homeless persons legislation does not say that 'A homeless person is entitled to be provided with accommodation by a local authority'. It is more likely to say that 'Where a local authority is satisfied that a person is homeless, they shall ensure that accommodation becomes available for his occupation.'

   Another illustration of this approach is that statutes tend to place a duty on public bodies to consult with people affected by their proposed decision, rather than confer on individuals an express right to make representations. In short, public law in Britain is mainly about the duties and discretions given to various officials and public bodies (and how these powers are to be controlled), rather than the rights of individuals and how they are to be protected.

   Having considered briefly the general nature of public law obligations, we can now turn to look at each source of law in more detail.

7.2 Absence of any special 'constitutional' law

We start with what does not exist! In the UK there is, of course, no single constitutional document setting out basic, supreme constitutional legal rules. There are, however, a number of draft constitutions in existence, so you can see what a written constitution for the UK might look like.

In 1991 the Institute of Public Policy Research (IPPR), a centre/left 'think tank', published a proposed constitution. Its principal features are as follows.

- Both Houses of Parliament would be elected by proportional representation.

- There would be assemblies with some legislative powers in Scotland, Wales, Northern Ireland and 12 regions in England.

- Many decisions currently taken under prerogative powers (on which, see para 7.6 below), such as those relating to defence, international relations and national security, would be put on a statutory basis.

- There would be a Bill of Rights.

This constitutional document would become the source of all government authority, replacing the prerogative, case law and conventions.

A more radical approach is taken by Tony Benn, the veteran Labour MP, in his Commonwealth of Britain Bill, the text of which is included in his book with Andrew Hood called *Common Sense* (1993). His proposed constitution would end the legal powers of the monarch: the Queen would cease to have any personal or political powers in the government of the country. A president would be elected by MPs from among their number for a period of three years. Benn sees the power of Ministers to vote in meetings of the Council of Minister of the European Community as dangerous, and would require that any Minister first obtain the assent of Parliament before voting in a particular way.

In deciding whether a written constitution and/or a bill of rights is needed in the UK there are at least three types of question which you may need to address.

7.2.1   Constitutional problems with adopting a written constitution and bill of rights

The first is to do with the *contents* of these constitutional documents. For instance, many advocates of a bill of rights suggest that this be achieved by incorporating the European Convention on Human Rights into English law by means of a statute. However, other people who would like a bill of rights see the ECHR, which was devised in the 1950s, as outdated. It fails to say anything much about protection of 'rights' such as the rights to effective health care provided by the state or education. Nor does the ECHR address environmental issues such as the 'right' of people to live in an unpolluted atmosphere. In short, there is little agreement about the types of rights which should be regarded as so fundamental that they need special constitutional protection.

A second type of question which is raised by the debate over a written constitution and a bill of rights is about the proper role of the courts. Some opponents of constitutional reform along these lines fear it would give too much power to courts and the law. Griffith, for example, argues that such reforms 'seem to indicate a way by which potential tyranny can be defeated by the intervention of the law and the invention of institutional devises. There is no such way. Only political control, politically exercised, can supply the remedy' ('The Political Constitution' (1979) 42 MLR 1, p 16).

Another type of question is a more technical one: is it possible in the British system for legislation to be protected from repeal or amendment by later Parliaments? This is an aspect of Parliamentary supremacy discussed below.

7.3   Acts of Parliament

Acts of Parliament ('statutes' or 'primary legislation') are the most important kind of legislation in the UK. In the absence of a supreme constitutional document much of the public law 'rule book' is contained in ordinary Acts of Parliament. These can be repealed and amended like any other: in formal terms, there is no difference between an Act of Parliament which regulates something as important as the relationship between the House of Commons and the unelected House of Lords (the Parliament Act 1911) and one which deals with relatively trivial subject matter.

Most public bodies, including local authorities, are statutory bodies and have only those powers and duties imposed on them by Act of Parliament or statutory instrument at any given time. If an official or public body cannot to point to specific legal authority for its actions and decisions, it is liable to be held to be unlawful by the courts on an application for judicial review (see Chapter 13 on 'Illegality' as a ground of judicial review).

7.3.1   How statutes are made

The purpose of most statutes is to give legal backing to *government* policy on various topics. The starting point will often be a period of consultation with the general public or interest groups. The government's initial proposals are often published in the form of a green paper. This class of document acquired its name because traditionally they were bound with green covers. After receiving responses, the relevant government department will often publish a white paper, setting out the government's firm policy on the subject.

Each year many departments will want to be given the opportunity to have 'their' bills put before Parliament. A committee of cabinet Ministers decides which bills are to be introduced during the next annual Parliamentary session. There is only limited time available. The bills chosen are announced in the Queen's Speech at the state opening of Parliament (usually held in October or November).

Once a department has been given the go ahead to introduce a bill, the next step will be for lawyers and civil servants in that department to instruct Parliamentary Counsel, the specialist legal draftsmen based at 36 Whitehall, to draft a bill. This is the text which the government hopes will eventually become an Act after its passage through Parliament. In most cases the government has a choice whether to introduce the bill into the House of Commons or the House of Lords, though if the bill involves taxation it must start in the Commons.

In whatever chamber it starts, a bill must go through a series of stages prescribed by Standing Orders of that particular chamber. These rules are published as *Erskine May's Parliamentary Procedure*. As we will see, in a long series of cases, the courts have held that they will not adjudicate on any procedural irregularities alleged to have occurred in Parliament during the passage of a bill: this is one aspect of the principle of Parliamentary sovereignty.

In outline the Parliamentary procedure for a bill is a follows.

- First reading

  This is a formality at which the title of the bill is read out and a date set for second reading.

- Second reading

  Here the general principles and policies embodied in the bill are discussed.

- Committee stage

  This is where there is line by line scrutiny of the text of the bill. In the Commons this may be done either by a 'standing committee' of up to about 40 MPs or as a committee of the whole House where all MPs are able to contribute to debate. Amendments to the text of the bill can be proposed by opposition MPs and also the government itself (eg to deal with matters overlooked during drafting or to respond to criticism). Amendments suggested by opposition MPs are normally voted down. Peter Riddell, writing in *The Times* (1993) 3 February puts the problem graphically:

  'The difficulty is the culture of Whitehall, which views the passage of legislation like a military operation. Both front benches regard the debates in standing committees as largely a charade; ministers claim a victory when they preserve a bill unamended, while the Opposition celebrates when it has clocked up enough hours.'

- Report stage

  This is when the bill, as amended in committee, returns to the floor of the chamber. This provides an opportunity for the government to try to change any unacceptable amendments that may have been made during the committee stage.

- Third reading

This is normally a short affair, with limited scope for MPs making further amendments.

Once it has passed through the House in which it was introduced, the bill is then considered by the other House.

For instance, if a bill was considered first by the Commons it then has to be considered by the Lords. If the text of the bill is amended by the Lords then the government may take the bill back to the Commons and attempt to overturn them, or the Lords may concede the points. If the two houses cannot agree then in the very last resort it is possible for a bill to move to its last formal stage, Royal Assent, without the Lords' agreeing to it. This may be done under the Parliament Act 1911 (as amended in 1949). These powers are very seldom used, the last time being the War Crimes Act 1991.

- Royal assent. This is a formality involving a quaint ceremony in the House of Lords every few weeks. The Queen herself is not present.

7.3.2 Private Members' bills

So far we have focused on *government* bills. Parliamentary procedure also permits backbench MPs to introduce bills in several different ways. Few of these bills manage to complete their passage through Parliament to reach the statute book. If, as is often the case, the government does not support a Private Member's bill it is able to use (some would say abuse) Parliamentary procedures to scupper the bill such as tabling a large number of amendments at the report stage or simply getting an MP to filibuster by talking at length on issues. A recent example of this was the failure of the Civil Rights (Disabled Persons) Bill in May 1994. On the positive side, Private Members bills, even if they do not become law, can be good ways of generating publicity about an issue and, perhaps, persuading the government to introduce its own bill on the subject.

7.3.3 Constitutional problems with statute law

From the point of view of the constitutional lawyer there are three main areas of concern to do with Acts of Parliament.

- **Parliamentary supremacy**

In short, the principle of Parliamentary supremacy (or 'sovereignty') states that judges have no power to declare Acts of Parliament to be 'unconstitutional' or 'unlawful' on any grounds. Since the UK joined the European Community in 1972 this principle has had to be modified: the British courts may now set aside any statute which conflicts with EC law. But in relation to primary legislation dealing with purely domestic issues, there are no legal constraints on either the procedure by which Parliament enacts legislation or as to the content of an Act. The courts will not adjudicate on any dispute as to whether or not the correct procedures were complied with (see leading cases such as *Pickin v British Railways Board* (1973)).

As to the content of Acts, because there is no bill of rights protecting fundamental liberties or the rights of minorities, there is no *legal* constraint on what may be enacted. An Act may nevertheless be described as 'unconstitutional' – at least in a broad sense of that word. Geoffrey Marshall writes that 'though it is rarely formulated as a conventional rule the most obvious and undisputed convention of the British constitutional system is that Parliament does not use its unlimited sovereign power of legislation in an oppressive or tyrannical way' ((1986) *Constitutional Conventions*, p 9). Many would dispute whether this is so. Examples of Acts which may contravene this convention arguably include some provisions of the Criminal Justice Act 1994 (outlawing 'raves') and s 28 of the Local Government Act 1988 (prohibiting public bodies from 'promoting homosexuality' or school teaching 'the acceptability of homosexuality as a pretended family relationship'). But, of course, neither of these Acts are in any sense 'unlawful'. You may wonder whether the word 'unconstitutional' has much value in this context – whether it is not just used as rather vague shorthand for a person's view that the statute offends against some moral principle which he or she considers important.

For many people, the principle of Parliamentary supremacy is a dangerous one as it provides no obvious way of protecting the rights of minorities in society. For some the answer is to incorporate and entrench a bill of rights into the English legal system which would prohibit, or at least make it more difficult, for Parliament by statute to treat any individuals or groups unfairly. Most proposals for a bill of rights envisage that the courts would have the task of ensuring that statutes did not infringe fundamental rights; the judges would be able to review the constitutionality of any statute. It would, however, also be possible to design a system in which Parliament itself, rather than the courts, had primary responsibility for ensuring that the basic liberties enshrined in a bill of rights were not affected by proposed legislation. A committee of MPs could vet every bill to ensure that it was compatible with the bill or rights before it was introduced into Parliament.

Another problem with the concept of Parliamentary supremacy is that since 1973 the UK Parliament has been limited in its ability to legislate in relation to some policy areas. In the areas of policy which fall within the competence of the European Community, eg agriculture, fisheries, transport, competition, sex discrimination, free movement, since 1973 European Community law takes precedence over anything enacted by Parliament and an Act of Parliament which conflicts with it will be declared ineffective by the UK courts: see *Equal Opportunities Commission v Secretary of State for Employment* (1994). Some critics from both the political left and right regard it as wrong that the British Parliament has lost much of its power to control or influence important areas of government policy. The UK Parliament plays no formal role in the making of European Community legislation (regulations and directives). Committees of MPs and Lords have been established to investigate and scrutinise draft legislation emanating from Brussels, but their influence is necessarily limited. Some MPs argue that Parliament has become too much of a conveyor belt, simply turning EC legislation into English law without much debate.

- **Inadequate Parliamentary scrutiny**

A second general constitutional problem with primary legislation is that MPs not in the government are given inadequate opportunities to scrutinise and, if necessary, defeat it.

One cause of this is role of the government whips (a small group of MPs appointed by the Prime Minister to maintain party discipline and ensure that MPs vote for government bills and motions). Writing in the 1970s, Lord Hailsham, a former Conservative MP and Lord Chancellor, complained that there existed an 'elective dictatorship' in the UK in which the House of Commons was dominated by government. It is often said that backbench MPs of the government party have little freedom to vote against government bills. In Britain there is no strong doctrine of the separation of powers and so members of the government (Ministers) are also part of the legislature (the Commons and the Lords). This helps the government to control MPs from its own party. In most instances, backbenchers of the government party are happy to support bills and need little persuasion to do so. Would-be 'rebels' are persuaded by government whips to vote for the bill. The government's power of patronage can act as a powerful incentive: backbenchers know that if they rebel too often they are unlikely ever to be appointed as a Junior Minister by the Prime Minister, a goal to which many aspire. Backbench pressure can however, on occasion, force the government to re-think its legislative plans. In 1986 many Conservative backbenchers defied a three-line whip (the strongest indication the whips can give to MPs in their party to vote in a particular way) and voted down the Sunday Trading Bill at the second reading stage. And in November 1994 the government decided not to introduce a bill to privatise the Post Office because it was believed that insufficient backbench Conservative MPs would vote for it.

The use of whips and executive domination of the Commons is not the only reason for inadequate scrutiny. Another cause is the sheer volume of legislation: there are too many bills. In order to get its legislative programme through Parliament, the government has to resort to procedures which allow it to curtail debate. 'Guillotine' motions are used by the government to set limits on the amount of time spent debating amendments to each clause of the bill during the committee stage. In December 1993 the government twice used guillotine motions to force bills (on national insurance contributions and statutory sick pay) through the Commons each in a single day. In protest, the Official Opposition withdrew cooperation from the government over the management of business in the Commons. This meant that 'pairings' were abandoned (these are arrangements between a Labour MP and Conservative MP that if one does not vote in the less important divisions then nor will the other one, leaving both free to do other things rather than queue up to vote) and Labour MPs forced debates on uncontroversial statutory instruments.

- **Style of drafting**

A final general problem with statute law as a source of obligation concerns the style of drafting used in Acts of Parliament. This is often overlooked by constitutional and administrative law textbooks, yet it is probably the most pressing practical difficulty. The main criticisms made of drafting style are:

(i)   Acts of Parliament rarely contain any clear statement of principle.

(ii)   Acts are overlong and over-detailed because draftsmen attempt to anticipate every contingency and aim to avoid being misunderstood rather than striving to be understood.

Clear drafting helps not only the ultimate end-user of the Act but can make scrutiny of the bill more effective. It can be difficult for backbench MPs (who cannot call on the advice of civil servants and government lawyers) and others to understand the implications of highly technical bills or propose effective amendments.

In 1993 the Hansard Society for Parliamentary government (a non-party political organisation set up to promote Parliamentary democracy) issued a report on legislation and the legislative process: see Report of the Hansard Commission on the Legislative Process, *Making the Law*. It was critical of the ways in which statutes are prepared, drafted, passed and published. Its proposals included the following:

(a) The legislative programme announced in the Queen's speech should run for a period of two years, not just a single Parliamentary session as at present.

(b) There should be pre-legislative enquiries into the policy of bills by committees of MPs with powers to take evidence. This consultation could help avoid the types of policy problems which occurred in legislation such as the Acts establishing the poll tax, setting up the Child Support Agency and the scheme for dealing with dangerous dogs.

(c) The minimum time periods between the various stages of bills should be increased.

(d) Acts should include notes explaining in straightforward language the purpose and intended effect of each section.

7.3.4	Where to find statute law

The most useful publications of Acts of Parliament are those which have annotations and commentaries. *Halsbury's Statutes* is made up of over 40 volumes containing statutes arranged according to subject matter ('Agriculture', 'Housing', etc). There are also cumulative supplements containing recent statutes not included in the specific subject volumes. The commentary on each Act and the individual sections is rather bland and, for a law student, of limited use. A much better bet, if your library has them, is to look in the multi-volume *Current Law Statutes*. Here the statutes are arranged according to date rather than subject matter, but they normally contain excellent commentary on the background of each Act, explaining why it was enacted and often referring to the relevant Parliamentary debates, green papers etc. The drawbacks are that *Current Law Statutes* only goes back as far as 1947 and, unlike *Halsbury's Statutes*, the volumes are never updated or reissued and so both text and commentary become superseded by later amendments and events.

Another place to look for commentaries on Acts is in the academic journals. *The Modern Law Review*, published six times a year, often includes a section called 'Legislation' in which recent Acts are discussed and analysed. The journal *Public Law* also contains short summaries of some recent Acts in its 'Current Survey' section.

Until 1993 it was a rule of the common law that the courts, when interpreting an Act of Parliament, would not examine what had been said about the intention or meaning of any provisions during the passage of the bill through Parliament. But since the House of Lords' decision in *Pepper v Hart* (1993) lawyers have been able to refer to reports of Parliamentary proceedings when a question of interpretation of an Act arises. The ruling in *Pepper v Hart* only allows limited reference to *Hansard* in court:

7.3.5   Background to Acts

- the section under consideration must be ambiguous, obscure or lead to an absurdity;

- only statements made by the Minister or promoter of the Bill, together with such other Parliamentary material as is necessary to understand them, can be considered; and

- those statements must be clear.

Verbatim reports of what Ministers and backbench MPs say during the passage of a bill through Parliament are contained in *Hansard*. To find out the date on which a bill was considered in the Commons or Lords it is best to look at the commentary to the Act in *Current Law Statutes Annotated*. There are two series of *Hansard*, one for the House of Commons (bound in green) and another for the Lords (red). Reports of the standing committee stage of bills in the Commons are published separately. The citation to a passage in Hansard is normally given in the following form: HC Deb Vol 233, col 815 (29 November 1993). If the debate is in the House of Lords, the citation is 'HL Deb.'.

It is often important to check that a section of an Act is in force. There are two main things to look out for. First, you should check that it has not been repealed by a later Act. Secondly, be aware that many Acts do not automatically come into force upon receiving Royal assent. Many are effective only when the relevant Minister has made a 'commencement order', ie a statutory instrument ordering an Act, or parts of it, to be in force. Many sections remain on the statute book for years without ever being brought into operation: see, eg *R v Secretary of State for the Home Department ex p Fire Brigades Union* (1994) discussed below.

7.3.6   Is it in force?

Repeals and commencement orders can be checked in a publication called *Is it in Force?* which will probably be near

Halsbury's Statutes in your law library. The *New Law Journal*, published weekly, also includes information about the passage of bills and commencement orders.

7.4 Statutory instruments

The other main type of domestic legislation, apart from Acts of Parliament, are statutory instruments (also known as delegated legislation, subordinate legislation, orders and regulations). Over 2,000 SIs are made every year. The main rationale for SIs is to prevent burdening Parliament with bills which deal with matters of detail or make minor or routine changes to the law. This type of legislation differs from a statute in several important ways:

- First, a SI is made by a Minster (or other public body) rather than the Queen-in-Parliament. In doing so, the Minister is exercising powers delegated to him or her under a section in an Act. This is known as the 'enabling provision'.

- Secondly, SIs receive only rudimentary Parliamentary scrutiny (see below).

- Thirdly, SIs may be quashed by a court on judicial review if it is shown that the Minister exceeded the powers of the enabling provision in the parent Act. An SI may also be quashed on the grounds of a procedural irregularity (eg the Minister failed to consult relevant parties before making the SI). Although this involves the courts in adjudicating on the lawfulness of legislation approved by Parliament, it does not contradict the concept of Parliamentary sovereignty: in theory the courts are upholding Parliamentary sovereignty by ensuring that *delegated* legislation is in conformity with the highest form of domestic law, an Act of Parliament.

7.4.1 How SIs are made

SIs are normally drafted by lawyers in the government department responsible for the policy area (transport, social security, etc) rather than by the specialist Parliamentary Counsel who draft bills. An important task for the lawyer is to ensure that the enabling provision in the Act gives the Minister sufficiently wide powers to make the rules he or she wants to.

Occasionally the Act may impose a legal requirement for the Minister to consult with people likely to be affected by the proposed SI. Failure to consult properly in these circumstances may lead to the SI being quashed on an application for judicial review, eg *Agricultural, Horticultural and Forestry Industry Training Board v Aylesbury Mushrooms Ltd* (1972). Even if there is no such legal requirement to consult, as a matter of practice departments usually do.

The next stage is for the SI to be laid before Parliament. As we have noted, Parliamentary scrutiny of SIs is very much less rigorous than for bills. Most SIs are not debated at all. There are two main types of procedures which can be used (which used in each case is determined by the Act which gives the Minister power to make the SI). Under the negative resolution procedure a SI becomes law 40 days after being notified to Parliament unless an MP challenges it. In the affirmative resolution procedure, used for the small number of SIs regarded as making significant changes to the law, there has to be a short debate and positive vote in Parliament before the SI becomes law. Whether the affirmative or negative resolution procedure is used, MPs are limited by the fact that they are not permitted to table amendments to an SI: whenever there is a debate the only options are either to approve it or reject it as a whole. And, of course, MPs from the governing party will be whipped to support the SI.

In addition to this, *all* SIs are vetted by a committee of MPs and peers called the Joint Committee on Statutory Instruments; their role is to draw Parliament's attention to any SIs which they believe contain 'technical' problems such as:

- the SI purports to have retrospective effect where the parent statute confers no express authority for this;

- the drafting appears to be defective; or

- there is doubt whether the SI in within the powers conferred on the Minister or it appears to make some unusual and unexpected used of powers conferred by the Act; or

- the SI is made under an Act containing specific provisions excluding the SI from challenge by judicial review.

7.4.2   Where to find SIs

There are four main places to look for the text of a SI. *Halsbury's Statutory Instruments* has the most important SIs arranged according to subject matter (eg 'Animals' etc), with annotations and subsequent amendments. A second source is the pale blue bound volumes published by HMSO annually. Here SIs are arranged chronologically and there are no annotations. Thirdly, if you are looking for a recent SI, your library may have the individual SI as published by HMSO. Finally, the text of SIs currently in force are available on LEXIS and CD-ROM.

Every SI is given a reference number as well as a title. For example, the Dangerous Dogs Compensation and Exemption Schemes Order 1991 is SI 1991 No 1744. If you don't know either the title or the number of an SI but you do know the section of the enabling Act under which it was made, look at the annotations to that section of the Act in *Halsbury's Statutes* where relevant SIs made should be listed. If this fails, try a key-word search on LEXIS or CD-ROM.

7.4.3   Constitutional problems with SIs

Concerns have been expressed about the use of SIs for many years. Back in 1932 the Donoughmore Committee on Ministers' Powers considered the problems associated with delegated legislation but concluded that its use was inevitable. Today, concerns continue to be expressed. One common complaint is that SIs receive inadequate Parliamentary scrutiny. It is not, however, immediately obvious how this could be improved. Remember that the main rationale for having SIs is to prevent the Parliamentary legislative timetable becoming completely overburdened with bills dealing with routine or minor matters. It is therefore no answer simply to suggest that more SIs are debated for longer. Perhaps the aspect of Parliamentary procedure which could effectively be improved is the 'technical' scrutiny by the Joint Committee on Statutory Instruments. Even the members of the committee complain that they are overwhelmed with piles of draft SIs and most members of the committee also lack the legal expertise to spot the often subtle and sophisticated legal problems with SIs which may only emerge later in the occasional judicial review proceedings which may be brought. Perhaps what is needed is a real committee of experts rather than politicians?

A second constitutional problem with SIs is that they are sometimes used by Ministers to wield extremely wide powers – not just to deal with routine and minor matters. Sometimes Acts of Parliament include so-called 'Henry VIII clauses'. These permit a Minister to make an SI *to amend or repeal an Act of Parliament*. There has been growing concern about the use of such powers and the Deregulation and Contracting Out Act 1994 was described during its passage through Parliament by Lord Rippon as 'one big Henry VIII clause'. In response to these concerns a committee of the House of Lords now scrutinises bills and draws attention to any such clauses giving Ministers wide powers to change primary legislation by SI.

Even if the Minister does not have power to amend or repeal primary legislation, SIs may nevertheless confer very wide powers. Many Acts are now merely 'skeletons' or 'frameworks', with many major issues of policy left to Ministers to flesh out with SIs.

Another use of SIs which goes beyond making minor amendments and routine matters is their use to transpose European Community directives into English law. When a directive is made by the Council of Ministers every Member State must amend its domestic law within a set time (often 18 months) to bring it into line with the policy collectively decided upon and set down by the directive. Section 2(2) of the European Communities Act 1972 gives Ministers power to incorporate directives into English law by using an SI. This means that even far reaching legal change can be brought about without full discussion in Parliament. For example, the EC directive on unfair terms in consumer contracts is to be given effect by means of a SI; what was really needed was for that directive to be integrated with existing English law, as set out in the Unfair Contract Terms Act 1977, but presumably the government did not have either the political will or space in the legislative timetable to introduce a bill to amend the 1977 Act.

In addition to formal UK legislation (Acts of Parliament and statutory instruments), rules may be laid down in ministerial circulars, codes of practice, official guidelines etc. These can be issued by government departments, local authorities and other public bodies.

7.5   Quasi-legislation

- Some are well-known even to the ordinary people in the street, eg the Highway Code.

- Some quasi-legislation is of great importance, affecting individual liberty and other fundamental rights, eg the Immigration Rules and the Codes of Practice made under the Police and Criminal Evidence Act 1984.

- In some contexts, such as town and country planning, education, prisons and the National Health Service, ministerial circulars set out rules and guidance to be followed by local authorities and health authorities. These circulars are written so that they can be read by non-lawyers and elaborate current government policy within the legislative framework of Acts and statutory instruments.

Quasi-legislation generally does not create binding legal obligations or impose legal duties. It can, however, have indirect legal consequences. For instance, if the police do not conduct an identity parade in accordance with the Codes of Practice made under the Police and Criminal Evidence Act 1984 they run the risk of that evidence being held inadmissible by a trial judge. If a government departments issues a circular stating that it will act in a certain way, this may give rise to a legitimate expectation that they will which may be enforced by a court on an application for judicial review (see eg *R v Secretary of State for the Home Department ex p Khan* (1986) and Chapter 16).

The advantages of using quasi-legislation, instead of say a statutory instrument, is that codes and circulars can be drafted and redrafted very quickly to meet changing circumstances, that they can use plain language and that 'informality, exhortation and persuasion' are sometimes better than relying on formal legal rules backed by sanctions.

One problem is that it is often difficult to find items of quasi-legislation because there are no uniform arrangements for their publication. Parliamentary scrutiny is also haphazard. Some quasi-legislation, eg the Immigration Rules, are subject to debate and scrutiny in the House of Commons, but most is not.

7.6 **Prerogative powers**	Ministers, and to a limited extent the Monarch herself, have some governmental powers, recognised by the courts, which do not derive from statute law. They derive instead from the powers once exercised by the monarch personally without Parliament. In time, most of these powers passed to Ministers who exercised them in the name of the king or queen. (For a more detailed explanation of this historical development, see Chapter 3). Dicey therefore defined prerogative powers as:

'... the residue of discretionary power left at any moment in the hands of the Crown ... every act which executive government can lawfully do without the authority of an Act of Parliament is done in virtue of this prerogative.'

The result is that in some circumstances a Minister may make legally binding rules and decisions without there having been any prior debate or authorisation by Parliament. This is seen by some as undemocratic and potentially dangerous. There is no comprehensive list of prerogative powers, and so it is difficult to go into the law library and find examples of the prerogative. You will need to look in one of the main textbooks on constitutional law for a general description of the main ones. The following are some of the more important areas in which prerogative powers are important.

• Powers to send British troops into war.

• Powers to enter into international treaties and conduct foreign relations.

• Powers to control appointments, terms and conditions of civil servants.

• The power of the Home Secretary to grant Royal pardons.

• Powers to issue passports to British citizens.

As Dicey noted, the prerogative powers are *residual*: they can be, and frequently are, removed and replaced by statutory powers. For instance, the security services (MI5 and MI6) once existed under prerogative powers, but were put on a statutory footing by the Security Services Act 1989 and the Intelligence Services Act 1994. There is no reason why other prerogative powers could not also be put onto a statutory basis: most of the proposed written constitutions for the UK (see para 7.2 above) would do this.

It is well-established that a Minister cannot use a prerogative power which is inconsistent with a subsequent statutory power enacted by Parliament. Thus in *Attorney General v de Keyser's Royal Hotel* (1920) the Crown argued that it need not pay compensation to the owner of a building requisitioned during World War I since it had occupied the hotel under prerogative powers. The House of Lords rejected this and held that the Crown had in fact occupied the hotel under powers conferred by the Defence Act 1842 which imposed a duty to pay compensation. Lord Dunedin stated:

7.6.1 Relationship between statute and prerogative

'Where ... Parliament has intervened and has provided by statute for powers, previously within the prerogative, being exercised in a particular manner and subject to the limitations and provisions contained in the statute, they can only be so exercised. Otherwise, what use would there be in imposing limitations, if the Crown could at its pleasure disregard them and fall back on prerogative?'

In the recent case of *R v Secretary of State for the Home Department ex p Fire Brigades Union* (1994) the Court of Appeal was faced with a slightly different situation. In 1964 the government of the day set up the Criminal Injuries Compensation Scheme (CICS) under prerogative powers to make payments out of public funds to victims of violent crime. They were awarded sums on the same basis as if they had sued the perpetrator in tort. In 1988 the government took the opportunity to place the CICS on a statutory footing: see s 17 of the Criminal Justice Act 1988. The Act stated that compensation would be on the basis of common law damages principles.

As is commonly the case, s 17 was to be brought into operation 'on such day as the Secretary of State may by order' made by statutory instrument appoint (see para 7.3.7 above on when statutes are in force). In 1992 s 17 had still not been brought into force and the CICS was still operating under the prerogative. In a statement the Home Secretary announced that the basis of compensation under the scheme was to be changed: awards would no longer be calculated as if the victim was receiving damages for tort but according to a tariff system. This would reduce awards. The Home Secretary said that the CICS scheme would continue be run under prerogative powers and he had no intention of bringing s 17 of the 1988 Act into force.

By a majority, the Court of Appeal declared that it was unlawful for the Home Secretary to introduce a new and radically different scheme based on tariffs using prerogative powers. Although s 17 had never been brought into force, it did show that Parliament had approved the principle that compensation be based on what would have been recoverable as common law damages. The only options open to the Home Secretary to make changes were therefore either: (a) to repeal s 17 and then use prerogative powers to set up the new scheme; or (b) to repeal s 17 and introduce a bill for a tariff-based statutory scheme.

In the two cases just discussed, *de Keyser's Royal Hotel* and the *Fire Brigade Union*, the problem was over a contradiction between prerogative powers sought to be used by government and an Act of Parliament. A rather different situation may arise where a statute deals with the same subject matter as one of the prerogative powers but without being in conflict. This was considered by the Court of Appeal in *R v Secretary of State for the Home Department ex p Northumbria Police* (1988) where it was held that the Home Secretary was still entitled to supply CS gas to a police force under prerogative powers even though the Police Act 1964 had given statutory power to do this to local police authorities. Looking at the wording of the statute, the court concluded that the Act did not give the local police authority monopoly powers to decide whether a police force should have this riot control gas and therefore the Home Secretary could continue to do so under the prerogative.

| 7.6.2 | Prerogative powers and judicial review |

Until the mid-1980s, the courts had a quite timid attitude to reviewing Minister's decisions made under the authority of prerogative powers. The courts would normally go no further than to ask the question whether or not the prerogative power claimed by the Crown in fact existed (see eg *De Keyser's Royal Hotel*). Then in the landmark *GCHQ* case, *Council of Civil Service Unions v Minister for the Civil Service* (1984), the House of Lords held that the mere fact that source of power exercised by a Minister was the prerogative did not in itself prevent the courts reviewing that decision on ordinary judicial review principles.

In subsequent cases the courts have reviewed decisions taken under the prerogative such as the refusal of a passport

(*R v Secretary of State for Foreign and Commonwealth Affairs ex p Everett* (1989)) and the refusal to grant posthumously a royal pardon (*R v Secretary of State for the Home Department ex p Bentley* (1993)). Some prerogative powers, such as decisions to send British troops to war, probably remain unreviewable but this is not because the legal authority for the decision is under the prerogative but rather because it is a decision which, of its nature, is not justiciable.

Another important source of obligations in the English constitutional and administrative system is the common law. Indeed, for Dicey, the fact that constitutional principles emerged from individual judgments in particular cases, rather than being set out in a single document, was part of the definition of the Rule of Law (see Chapter 4, above).

7.7   Case law

One important debate today surrounds two broad views of the role of the judges. (To say there are two views is, of course, an over-simplification and what follows is necessarily a caricature of the complex views expressed by different writers and judges). There are some who argue that judicial decisions developed over the centuries by the courts on a case by case basis provide effective protection for basic rights and also provide civil servants and Ministers with a clear guide to what they can and cannot lawfully do. On the other hand, some critics suggest that the case law shows little more than that judges make policy decisions which reflect their preferences for established authority and the status quo.

The types of argument put forward by the first set of writers and judges are well expressed by two current judges, both writing articles in academic journals. In 'The Infiltration of a Bill of Rights' [1992] PL 397, pp 404-405, Lord Browne-Wilkinson argues that:

7.7.1   Case law as fundamental principles

> 'It has become so fashionable to urge constitutional reform by means of a Bill of Rights or by incorporating the European Convention on Human Rights in our domestic law that attention has been diverted from the principles of our indigenous domestic law ... Whenever the provisions of the ECHR has been raised before the [English] courts, the judges have asserted that the Convention confers no greater rights than those protected by the common law.'

Sir John Laws, a High Court judge, echoes this:

> '... the contents of the ECHR, *as a series of propositions*, largely represent legal norms and values which are either already inherent in our law, or, so far as they are not, may be integrated into it by the judges.'

(See 'Is the High Court the Guardian of Fundamental Constitutional Rights' [1993] PL 59 p 61). Views such as these are becoming increasingly influential: see eg the decision of Sedley J in *R v Secretary of State for the Home Department ex p McQuillan* (1994).

A slightly different, but still broadly similar stance, is taken by Professor Jeffrey Jowell in a recent article 'Is Equality a Constitutional Value?' (1994) CLP 1 where he argues that the principle of 'equality' can be seen in many judicial decisions.

So far as civil servants and Ministers are concerned, it has also been argued that judicial review cases can be viewed as providing a positive framework of good administrative practice: see for example Professor David Feldman, 'Judicial Review: A Way of Controlling Government?' (1988) *Public Administration* 21. Certainly, many textbooks assume that judicial review is capable of having a beneficial effect on the quality of decision-making by public bodies. Whether this is so is considered further in Chapter 17 below.

7.7.2	Case law as policy and politics

Rather different conclusions about the nature of case law in the public law field are reached by a different group of writers. They deny that any strong 'principles' can be detected from judicial decisions. Instead they try to expose what they see as the *policies* underlying the case law. Professor John Griffith, formerly professor of public law at the London School of Economics, is particularly associated with this type of analysis. His controversial and much-criticised book *Politics of the Judiciary* is well worth reading. But a good starting point is his article 'Decision-making in Public Law' [1985] PL 564. Griffith argues that in some kinds of case the function of the court goes beyond adjudicating between two parties; in some judicial review cases

'by their nature and the nature of the law that governs them, courts are required to make decisions that transcend the parties and deeply involve political issues and the public interest' (p 565).

In cases such as *GCHQ* (1985) and the *Fare's Fair* case (*Bromley London Borough Council v Greater London Council* (1983)), in which it was held that the Greater London Council could not lawfully subsidise public transport as it wished to, the courts were not, according to Griffith, applying neutral legal principles. Rather, the judges were actually making 'policy' judgments, eg that it was undesirable for public funds to be used to subsidise fares on London buses and the tube. Griffith sets out to show that the courts and litigation are by their nature ill-suited to making such decisions. His somewhat surprising conclusion is that there ought to be a 'public officer whose responsibility it would be to act as advocate general, to present such evidence as he considered necessary in the public interest, and generally to draw the attention of the court to those matters affecting the public interest which he considered the court should take into account' (p 582). In this way if the courts have to make 'policy' decisions, at least they would be better informed about the issues; in the *Fare's Fair* case, for instance, they could have heard evidence from economists as to the pros and cons of subsidising public transport to the level proposed by the GLC.

You should already be familiar with the main series of law reports (*Law Reports*, *Weekly Law Reports* and *All England Reports*) which contain many of reported decisions in the public law field. In addition there are several specialist reports. The *Administrative Law Reports* (abbreviated to Admin LR) can be a useful source if your library has them, but they are not, at present, widely used. Other series of law reports deal with particular substantive areas of public law such as the *Housing Law Reports* (HLR), the *Property and Compensation Reports* (P & CR) which include cases on town and country planning and the *Immigration Law Reports* (Imm LR).

7.7.3 Finding case law in the library

Another useful source is the *Crown Office Digest* (COD). Published six times a year, this contains summaries of judicial review cases, many of which are not reported elsewhere.

Even more difficult to pin down than the prerogative are constitutional conventions. 'By convention is meant a binding rule, a rule of behaviour accepted as obligatory by those concerned in the working of the constitution' (Sir Kenneth Wheare, *Modern Constitutions*, p 179). As well as creating obligations conventions may also confer rights. It would be impossible to draw up an exhaustive list of conventions, but some obvious ones include the following.

7.8 Conventions

- Government Ministers have to be a member of one of the Houses of Parliament.

- The Queen must assent to bills which have been passed through both Houses of Parliament or in accordance with the Parliament Act 1911.

- Regular meetings of the Cabinet will be called by the Prime Minister; indeed, the very existence of the Cabinet is based on convention.

None of these are 'legal' rules in the sense that they are not set down in any Act of Parliament, statutory instrument or case

7.8.1 Finding conventions

law. If the UK were to adopt a written constitution many conventions would undoubtedly be reduced into writing in that document, but even in states with written constitutions many conventional rules regulate government, the courts and the legislature.

There are many good descriptions of constitutional conventions in academic books, including Geoffrey Marshall's *Constitutional Conventions* (1986) and chapters in Rodney Brazier's *Constitutional Practice* (1988). In his classic book The *Law and the Constitution* (1959) Sir Ivor Jennings suggests three questions have to be asked to work out whether or not a particular convention exists:

(i) Are there any precedents?

(ii) Did the actors in the precedents believe that they were bound by a rule?

(iii)Is there a reason for the rule?

In some instances this is straightforward. Take the convention that the sovereign never refuses to grant royal assent to a bill which has passed through Parliament. There are many precedents – not since Queen Anne tried to refuse consent in the 18th century has any one doubted it. Monarchs have believed themselves bound by a rule. And there are good democratic reasons for it.

Other cases are less clear. For example: it emerges that a government Minister has had an extra-marital affair. Does a constitutional convention dictate that he or she should resign from office? Finding precedents may involve searching through back issues of newspapers, biographies, autobiographies and history books. Some Ministers have resigned in these circumstances (eg Cecil Parkinson); other have not. Even if most did resign one would need to ask *why* they did so? They may have done so in order to save the government from embarrassment rather than because they felt obliged to do so because of a convention. It is also not entirely clear whether there are any good reasons for a resigning rule in these circumstances: it can be argued that these are essentially matters private morality which do not impinge on a person's fitness for public office.

7.9 European Community law

The sources of Community law, and how they may be used in British courts and tribunals, are considered in the next chapter, as are the main constitutional problems. Here we need only examine the practical problems of finding Community law in the law library.

- The Treaties

  By far the easiest place to find a provision in the constituent treaties of the European Community/European Union is in one of the books which consolidate them. Try Peter Duffy and Jean Yves de Cara's *A Lawyer's Guide to the European Union* (1992) or AG Toth, *Oxford Encyclopedia of European Community Law*.

- Regulations and directives

  There are several different places to find the texts of regulations and directives. The *Official Journal of the European Communities* is published almost daily and is mammoth in its size. For this reason, your library will probably have all but the most recent issues of the *Official Journal* on microfiche rather than in paper format. To be frank, this is best avoided. There are two series. The L series contains legislation and it is this you will need to find. (The other, the C series, has information and notices about EC matters.) To find a directive or regulation it's best to have as much information as possible: there should be a name (not that important), a statement of which Community institution made the legislation, its reference number and then (importantly) its citation in the *Official Journal*.

  A better place to look for directives and regulations, if your library has it, is in the multi-volume loose-leaf encyclopedia published by Sweet & Maxwell called the *Encyclopedia of European Community Law*.

A final resource you will need to use is the vast academic literature in the field of constitutional and administrative law. When doing research for an essay, it is sensible to draw up some sort of research and writing strategy rather than just let things drift along.

7.10   Academic literature etc

A useful starting point is to do a search for relevant literature. Your reading list will normally contain references. To find other books on the particular subject type in key-words into the LIBERTAS catalogue in your library. It is also a good idea just to browse along the relevant bookshelves.

7.10.1   Books

Tracing relevant journal articles needs to be done systematically. One way of doing this is to look in the index to the annual bound volumes of the major legal journals such as the *Modern Law Review, Public Law, Law Quarterly Review* and *Cambridge Law Journal*. Also, at the end of each issue of Public Law you can also find a list of some recent articles in

7.10.2   Journals

government and politics journals such as *Parliamentary Affairs* and *Public Administration*.

A short cut, however, to searching for articles about UK law is the *Legal Journals Index*. Your library should have this publication either in the form of bound volumes and or a CD-ROM. There are several indexes:

- you can look up names of authors;

- subject areas (eg 'Judicial Review') for all articles on the subject;

- there is also an index of case names through which you can trace any case notes that have been published.

You may also try the *Index to Legal Journals* which contains primarily US journals, though it does also contain references to some of the more important British ones.

A few journals (eg *New Law Journal*) are available through LEXIS.

| 7.10.3 | The Internet |

One final source, which is still of rather limited value, is the 'information superhighway' or Internet. This is a vast and rapidly growing system of public computers throughout the world. Texts in all sorts of subject areas, including law, can be accessed from a PC and downloaded (ie saved). If you want to find out more about this good starting points are Ed Kroll's book *The Whole Internet User's Guide and Catalog* (1994) 2nd ed and Bennett Falk's *The Internet Road Map* (1994). On the internet there is a great deal of material available on US constitutional and administrative law, including decisions of the US Supreme Court and documents issued by the White House. This, however, is likely to be only of marginal use to most students studying English public law. There is much less UK and European Community related legal material, though it can be fun to search for it.

7.11   Fitting it all together

So far this chapter has presented an overview of the main sources of constitutional and administrative obligations. Now we can turn to look briefly at how these 'fit together'. Let's start with a hypothetical problem.

Expert scientific advisers to the Department of Transport have done research which shows that people riding red bicycles are much less likely to be involved in serious accidents than those riding bikes of other colours. Senior civil servants and the Secretary of State for Transport decide that action is needed. They conclude that as from the middle of next year all bicycles sold in England and Wales should be red.

For government lawyers, the task will be to turn this policy into law. Using the prerogative to do this can be ruled out immediately because health and safety of road users is simply not an area in which there are any residual prerogative powers. The main options for formal law-making are therefore either enacting primary legislation (introducing a bill into Parliament) or making delegated legislation (laying a statutory instrument before Parliament). What are the relative advantages and disadvantages of these two different routes?

First, consider making a statutory instrument. This is dependent on there already being an Act of Parliament in existence which confers on a Minister relevant powers, in this case to make rules regulating safety features of bicycles. It is not always clear whether such an enabling statute really does confer the power actually needed in a given situation: there may be ambiguity or other types of uncertainty. For instance the words of the statute may be: that 'The Secretary of State may make regulations prescribing safety features of bicycles.' It might be argued that the colour of a bike is not really a safety 'feature' in the same sort of way as the strength of the frame or the type of brakes.

The main advantage of making a statutory instrument, in comparison to introducing a bill, is speed and convenience. Its passage through the Parliamentary procedures will be considerably shorter than for a bill, and there will be less opportunity for opponents to criticise it. Using an SI will also enable the legislation to be drafted inside the department rather than having to instruct Parliamentary Counsel (as in the case of a bill).

One disadvantage of delegated legislation, however, is that, unlike an Act, it can be judicially reviewed on the usual grounds of review (illegality, procedural impropriety and possibly irrationality). Government lawyers, and lawyers acting for people wanting to challenge the validiry of the SI, will need a good knowledge of the judicial review case law. The Minister's policy could therefore be held up if someone attempts to challenge its validity in the courts. But lawyers in the department will also bear in mind that today *Acts of Parliament* can be subject to judicial review challenge on the ground that they are incompatible with European Community law. In the present case it might be possible for (say) a French bicycle manufacturer to argue that a law prohibiting the sale of non-red bikes is contrary to provisions of the EC Treaty ensuring freedom to import and export goods between member states. Lawyers in the department will therefore need to consider carefully what, if any, constraints are imposed by EC legislation and the case law of the European Court of Justice. If a policy falls into an area over which the EC has competence (such as the safety of vehicles), then the UK may well not be able to 'go it alone' in imposing new or more stringent requirements.

In addition to the legal constraints on a department, many matters are regulated by well-established conventions or by political practices. Almost certainly in this case there will be consultation between the department and organisations representing bicycle manufacturers and retailers. This is unlikely to be a legal requirement but by convention it is likely to happen here.

As an alternative to formal law-making by Act of Parliament or SI, the department may well consider more informal methods of achieving its policy goal. It might, for instance, be possible to negotiate some sort of voluntary code of practice with bicycle manufacturers and retailers under which most bikes sold would be red. As with formal methods, arrangements such as this raise broad constitutional problems to do with accountability and scrutiny, though these fall outside the scope of most introductory courses on public law.

Sources of Public Law

The main formal sources of public law obligation are:

- Acts of Parliament;
- statutory instruments;
- quasi-legislation (ministerial circulars, codes of practice, etc);
- the prerogative;
- case law;
- constitutional conventions;
- European Community legislation (Treaties, regulations and directives) and the case law of the European Court of Justice.

A general characteristic of the English constitutional and administrative system is that duties and discretions are conferred on public bodies rather than rights being given to individual citizens. The focus of much public law is therefore on the creation and control of public law powers.

The absence of a written constitution and Bill of Rights as a supreme source of public law is regarded by many as a major weakness in the British system. Several questions arise. First, as to the content of those documents. Second, as to the role of the courts in interpreting them. Third, whether given the doctrine of Parliamentary sovereignty it is possible to entrench a written constitution and bill of rights.

Absence of a written constitution and Bill of Rights

Many criticisms can be levelled at the ways in which statutes and statutory instruments are drafted and made. In particular, Parliamentary scrutiny is inadequate. This results both from the executive's domination of the Commons and the sheer volume of legislation.

Statutes and statutory instruments

Prerogative powers are residual and may be replaced by statute. Since 1983 the fact that the legal basis of a Minister's power is the prerogative rather than an Act of Parliament is no longer, of itself, a bar to the Minister's decision being judicially reviewed.

Prerogative powers

Conventions

Constitutional conventions regulate a great many aspects of the constitutional and administrative system in the UK. Jennings suggests three questions have to be asked to work out whether or not a particular convention exists:

- Are there any precedents?

- Did the actors in the precedents believe that they were bound by a rule?

- Is there a reason for the rule?

Case law

Judicial decisions are an important source of constitutional and administrative law. Some commentators praise the common law for upholding fundamental rights through the development of principles. Judicial review cases can also be seen as providing a 'Code of Good Practice' for ministers and officials. Others are, however, more sceptical: they critise the courts for making policy decisions which ought to be left to ministers or elected local authorities. Judicial 'policy' (it is argued) is often conservative or Conservative.

Chapter 8

The Impact of the European Community

This chapter looks at those aspects of European Community law which students studying English constitutional and administrative law often have most difficulty with.

- The distinction between EC law and the European Convention on Human Rights.

- Understanding what the EC *actually does*; many public law text books don't say anything much about the areas of policy over which the EC has competence.

- Getting to grips with how practitioners in England use EC law in their day to day work. This is often presented in a quite abstract way using the jargon of 'direct effect' etc; by using a practical illustration and a table we show what this means in practice.

- Finally, the chapter gives an overview of the different ways in which membership of the EC has impacted on English constitutional and administrative law. It is easy for students to get the impression that this is confined to the issue of Parliamentary sovereignty, but in reality there is much more to it than this.

Many people – including some law students – get very confused about what 'Europe' means. They are not helped by the often vague ways in which European legal issues are covered in the news media. Even the quality press is often guilty of inaccurate reporting: you read about a person 'appealing to the European Court' without there being any explanation as to whether this means the European Court of Justice in Luxembourg (for the European Community) or to the quite distinct European Commission and Court of Human Rights at Strasbourg (which deals with the European Convention). In any event the word 'appeal' is misleading in both cases.

8.1 The community and the convention

The UK belongs to two separate (but, as we will see, related) international treaty organisations which bind it to other states on continental Europe:

- The European Community (EC); and

- The Council of Europe, an important aspect of whose work relates to the European Convention on Human Rights.

The treaties of the EC, and secondary legislation made under them, are part of the legal system in the UK because

8.1.1 The position in a nutshell

EC law was incorporated as a source of law by the European Communities Act 1972. In contrast, the European Convention on Human Rights has not yet been incorporated into English law and so cannot be used directly in argument in court.

8.1.2 **The Human Rights Convention**

The international treaty organisation known as the Council of Europe, much of whose work is concerned with the European Convention for the Protection of Human Rights and Fundamental Freedoms, comprises 32 states. It was founded in the aftermath of the Second World War with the aim of furthering the ideals of political democracy, the rule of law and the protection of fundamental human rights. Some of the most important provisions include the following:

- Article 3

  'No one shall be subject to torture or to inhuman or degrading treatment or punishment'.

- Article 8

  'Everyone has the right to respect for his private and family life, his home and correspondence.'

- Article 10

  'Everyone has the right to freedom of expression. This right shall include freedom to hold opinions and receive and impart information and ideas without interference by public authority and regardless of frontiers ...'.

- Article 11

  'Everyone has the right to freedom of peaceful assembly and to freedom of association with others, including the right to form and join trade unions for the protection of his interests.'

Many of the rights enshrined in the human rights convention are qualified by statements that they may be restricted in the interests of national security, public safety, for the protection of health and morals and for the protection of the rights and freedoms of others.

8.1.3 **Human Rights Convention is *not* part of English law**

The English legal system is 'dualist', meaning that international treaty obligations entered into by the government are not part of English law unless and until they are specifically incorporated by an Act of Parliament. The Human Rights Convention has not been incorporated into English law, though many argue that it *should* be in order to give the UK a justiciable Bill of Rights (on which see Chapter 7).

It is therefore impossible to argue in a British court that an Act of Parliament, statutory instrument or administrative act is unlawful because it is contrary to one of the provisions of the Human Rights Convention (see *R v Secretary of State for the Home Department ex p Brind* (1991) and *R v Secretary of State for the*

Environment ex p NALGO (1991)). To an increasing extent, however, judges are recognising that it is 'unreal or potentially unjust' to continue to develop English public law without reference to the human rights convention: see Sedley J in *R v Secretary of State for the Home Department ex p McQuillan* (1994). This is because many of the principles and standards already set by the common law are similar to those of the convention (see above, para 7.7.1) and also because the law of the European *Community* – which is supreme law in the UK – is informed by the principles of the human rights convention (see below, para 8.1.5). Nevertheless, the basic point remains: a lawyer appearing in an English court cannot rely *directly* on the human rights convention as a basis for arguing governmental action is invalid. The human rights convention may, though, be persuasive as to how the English common law should develop or how an Act of Parliament should be interpreted if there is an ambiguity.

Having exhausted all remedies in the English legal system it is possible for an individual to apply to the Human Rights Commission and then the European Court of Human Rights for a ruling that legislation or government action conflicts with the convention, but this is in no way an 'appeal'. The issues will be different from those which concerned the English courts. For instance, when in 1984 the government banned civil servants working at GCHQ from belonging to a trade union, the issue in the domestic courts was whether there ought to have been prior consultation (see *Minister for the Civil Service v Council for Civil Service Unions* (1984)). When the unions then took their case to the Human Rights Commission the main issue was whether the UK government had breached Article 11 of the convention; the Commission ruled that the government had not.

As from 1995, 15 states belong to the European Community. They are committed to the establishment of a single market based on 'the four freedoms' – the free movement of goods, persons, services and capital. It is Europe in this sense which is the focus of this chapter.	**8.1.4** EC law *is* part of the English legal system

In the English legal system, the status of Community law is quite different from that of the human rights convention. It can be used in the English courts because it has been incorporated into the domestic legal system by statute: the European Communities Act 1972 (as amended). Not only is Community law part of the legal order in the UK but it is supreme law because s 2(4) of the 1972 Act says so (though not in very clear terms). This means that when an English court is faced with a conflict between domestic law and EC law, the latter prevails. As well as the treaties establishing the Community, and other types of legislation made by the Community institutions, EC law includes the developing case law of the Community court (the European Court of Justice or 'ECJ'). The use of Community law in English courts is explained in more detail below.

8.1.5   Relationship between the convention and community

Although it is best to think of the EC and the human rights convention as entirely separate, the reality is that disputes arising from similar facts can fall within the jurisdiction of both sets of European institutions. For example, both the Community court (ECJ) and the European Court of Human Rights had to consider the legality of the Irish Republic's constitutional ban on the dissemination of information about abortion services in the UK. (Abortion is unlawful under the Irish Constitution and Irish women often travel to Great Britain for one.) The ECJ considered the matter from the perspective of whether such a prohibition prevented a free market in services between Member States and held that the Irish restrictions were justifiable. The European Court of Human Rights looked at whether there was a breach of Article 10(1) of the human rights convention which guarantees the right to receive and impart information and held that the ban was contrary to the convention.

The *Community* has attached a great deal of importance to the human rights convention in several declarations. In the preamble to the Single European Act (a treaty amending the Treaty of Rome discussed below), the Member States of the Community pledged themselves to 'work together to promote democracy on the basis of the fundamental rights recognised in the Convention'. Also, in a number of cases, the Community court has directly applied the Convention, eg *National Panasonic (UK) Ltd v Commission* (1979). For a much more detailed explanation of the links between EC law and the human rights convention see Nicholas Grief, 'The Domestic Impact of the ECHR as mediated through Community Law' [1991] PL 555.

8.2   Origins and scope of the EC

Having clarified the differences, and interconnections, between the EC and the human rights convention, we can now move onto a second area of difficulty for students. Many constitutional and administrative law textbooks say little about what the EC actually does. What follows is a brief 'gap-filling' exercise intended to outline some of its main features.

8.2.1   Origins

The UK became a member of the European Community (then colloquially referred to as the 'Common Market') over 20 years ago in 1973. Since then the organisation has grown in size: from 1995 there will be 15 Member States.

The origins of the Community lie in the devastation of Europe at the end of the Second World War in 1945. Jean Monnet, a Frenchman and international statesman, brought about what a few years previously would have been unthinkable: an agreement for economic co-operation between France and West Germany. Italy and the small Benelux countries (Belgium, the Netherlands and Luxembourg) also joined in the scheme and in 1952 the European Coal and Steel

Community (ECSC) came into operation with the countries agreeing to pool decision-making in those industries under a single multi-national authority. Britain, under Atlee's Labour government and then Churchill's post-war Conservative administration, refused to join this new organisation. The ECSC was seen as a great success by its Member States and they formed two other similar organisations: the European Atomic Energy Community (EURATOM) and the much broader European Economic Community. The three communities, ECSC, EURATOM and the EEC, were for most practical purposes amalgamated in 1967.

The UK began negotiations to join the Communities in 1961, but these were at first unsuccessful because the French government vetoed the proposal for British membership. Finally in 1973 the UK, along with Ireland and Denmark, became members and the Six became the Nine. Greece joined in 1981; Portugal and Spain in 1986; and Sweden, Finland and Austria in January 1995.

A good way to understand the development of the EC from the 1950s to now is by looking at the main treaties which, in effect, provide it with a written constitution. The treaties set out the institutional arrangements: how, when and by whom decisions are taken. Unlike a national government, the institutions have no general competence or inherent powers but only those powers specifically conferred under the treaty, as it is interpreted by the European Court of Justice.

8.2.2   Towards 'an ever closer Union'

- **The EC Treaty**

  The first is the Treaty Establishing the European Community (often referred to as the Treaty of Rome). It is here that you will find the important provisions to do with the 'four freedoms', the basic principles for policy areas such as the Common Agricultural Policy and statements as to the role of each of the institutions through which decisions are made. The EC Treaty was incorporated into UK law by the European Communities Act 1972.

- **Single European Act**

  The Single European Act of 1985, despite its name, was not a British statute but an international treaty amending the Treaty of Rome. It was incorporated into UK law by an Act amending the European Communities Act 1972. Changes were made to some of the EC institutions in order to encourage further progress towards the creation of the single market. It set a target date of the end of 1992 for the removal of the remaining trade barriers between Member States. It also made it more difficult for any one Member State to veto some types of decision and it increased the powers of the European Parliament.

- **Treaty of European Union**

    The Treaty of European Union (also known as the Maastricht Treaty after the Dutch city where it was agreed in 1991) further amended the Treaty of Rome. It marked a very significant step forward in the process of 'ever closer union' (an expression used in all the treaties). It increased the powers of the European Parliament still further and set a target date of 1999 for one of the last major elements of the common market: a single currency and central bank to control monetary policy throughout all Member States. It also created union citizenship. In addition to this it added two new facets to the relationships between the 15 Member States. The new European Union thus has three pillars:

(i) The first is the European Community which has been developing since 1958.

(ii) The second pillar creates a framework for inter-governmental co-operation on foreign and security policy.

(iii) The third is inter-governmental co-operation in the fields of justice and home affairs.

There are important differences in the ways in which decisions are taken in these so-called pillars. In the Community almost all decisions are now taken on the basis of majority voting so that no one Member State has a veto. The style of decision-making in the second and third pillars is quite different, much more along the lines of classic international diplomacy with sovereign states meeting as equals. Unanimity is required and institutions such as the Court of Justice, the Commission and European Parliament play much smaller roles (or none) than they do in relation to 'Community' matters.

There will be another inter-governmental conference in 1996 where further decisions about the further of European integration will be taken.

8.2.3   The single market

At the heart of the idea of the Community lies the notion of a common (or single) market. This was finally achieved at the end of 1992 when physical, technical and fiscal barriers between the Member States were removed. In practical terms this means that a company manufacturing bolts in Sheffield can now load them onto a lorry and they can be driven for sale in Naples without the driver needing to fill in dozens of forms as he crosses each national boarder. The bolts will now have to conform to a common standard (so the Italian purchasers will know exactly what they're getting); and the British company can have confidence that its trademarks and other intellectual property rights in the design of the bolts will be protected in all 15 Member States. Value Added Tax and excise-duties are now charged at approximately the same rates throughout the Community and so there is less distortion to the market than before. Another aspect of the single market is that there is free movement of people, so the British company can know employ a skilled German engineer in its Sheffield factory without the need for any work permit from the British government or there being any problems with immigration controls.

The Maastricht Treaty set a target date (1999) for one of the last major requirements of the single market-economic and monetary union. Given the continuing political controversy on the matter, it is far from clear that a common currency will be in place by then. In the mean time, the Italian firm buying the bolts still has to buy pounds sterling with its lira in order to pay the Sheffield company.

Most of the community's legislation, and much of the work of the European Court of Justice, arise out of one area of policy: agriculture, fisheries and food. One of the community's biggest successes, but also the source of massive problems, is the Common Agricultural Policy (CAP). The CAP established free movement of farm goods between all Member States and a common tariff barrier against imports from the rest of the world. Since the Second World War, there have been extraordinary increases in productivity and the EC is now self-sufficient in most types of food. This has, however, been achieved at a phenomenal cost in subsidies paid to farmers to encourage production. In some products there is massive over production and governments have to intervene to maintain stable markets by buying produce and keeping it in store for years on end (including the infamous wine lakes and butter mountains). Subsidies to farmers, to which they are entitled because Member States guarantee them minimum prices for their produce, swallow up a massive proportion of the EC's budget. Reform of the CAP is a high priority for the Community.

In 1983 the Member States finally managed to agree on a common fishing policy (CFP). Member states limit fishing within 12 miles of their shores to boats from their own country. The rest of seas around the Community are open to the fisherman from any EC country. In order to preserve stocks of fish, an annual limit is set for the catches of different species of fish. Each Member State is allocated a quota of this, but the system has not worked as the British government thought it would. It was concerned that Spanish trawlers were registering as 'British' vessels and having their catches counted

8.2.4   Agriculture and fisheries

against the UK fish quotas. The Merchant Shipping Act 1988 was enacted to prevent this, but it was subsequently held to be inconsistent with other principles of EC law (to do with freedom of establishment) and for the first time a British court held that an Act of Parliament could not be applied by the British government: see *R v Secretary of State for Transport ex p Factortame Ltd (No 2)* (1993)

| 8.2.5 | Competition policy | From the very outset of the EC it was recognised that the common market would need to be protected from enterprises with monopolies abusing their dominant position, mergers between companies, agreements between firms to fix prices and other restrictive practices. The governments of the Member States also needed to be prevented from giving subsidies to businesses in their own countries if this would distort competition. The EC Treaty therefore includes rules regulating competition. |

8.2.6   Social policy and workers' rights

As well as being a free market in goods, services and capital, the EC has responsibilities for protecting and improving the living and working conditions of employees. Apart from ensuring equal pay for men and women doing comparable work and some improvements in health and safety standards, success has been quite limited. There are high levels of unemployment in many Member States, little has been achieved by way of harmonising entitlement to social security benefits, and the hope of promoting greater participation of workers in the management of firms has not been realised. The British Conservative government (but not it alone) has been hostile to most attempts to set common standards on working conditions across the Community, arguing that to do so would unacceptably increase the costs of business.

The Maastricht Treaty includes provisions on workers' rights called the Social Chapter. These were unacceptable to the UK Conservative government and an 'opt out' was negotiated in 1991. The other 11 Member States agreed to proceed collectively without Britain. The strange position now reached is that British ministers are now not entitled to sit in the Council of Ministers' meetings whenever social policy governed by the Social Chapter is discussed and take no part in the decision making. Nor is the UK bound by any directives on the subject that may be adopted by the other members. It remains to be seen whether this arrangement is sustainable either legally or in policy terms. Many commentators were highly critical of it, arguing that this à la carte approach threatens the basic character of the Community.

The area of Community social policy which above all others has had an impact on British law is women's rights. Article 119 of the EC Treaty provides that 'each Member State shall ... ensure and subsequently maintain the application of the principle that men and women should receive equal pay for equal work'. A number of directives on equal pay and other aspects of equal treatment set out the policy on equality in more detail. They also provide a potent illustration of the practical impact of the supremacy of Community law over UK law (including primary legislation). The British government had to amend the Sex Discrimination Act 1975 by the Equal Pay Act 1986 to bring UK law into line with the Treaty and directives. And in the early 1990s, the Equal Opportunities Commission (a statutory body responsible for promoting equality of opportunity) began judicial review proceedings in the British court arguing that certain sections of the Employment Protection (Consolidation) Act 1978 were incompatible with EC law. These gave less favourable rights to part-time workers than to full-timers in relation to rights to redundancy pay and unfair dismissal. The EOC argued that as most part-timers were women and most full-time employees were men, these provisions were indirectly discriminatory. The House of Lords accepted the argument and declared parts of the Act of Parliament to be in conflict with Community law (see *R v Secretary of State for Employment ex p Equal Opportunities Commission* (1994)).

So far in this chapter we have looked at two problem areas for many public law students: (a) the distinction between the EC and the human rights convention; and (b) the background to the origins and work of the Community. We now move on to look at a third: understanding how EC law is used in practical ways by practitioners and courts in England. Most practising lawyers are not very interested in abstract concepts such as Parliamentary supremacy; many of them have little or no knowledge of the legislative process in the Community institutions. Let us look at things from their perspective–in a very practical way.

Solicitors today should know that Community law issues can crop up in all sorts of disputes. Take just one example: a few years ago it probably would not have occurred to a solicitor advising a market trader whose licence had been suspended by a local authority that there was a Community law dimension to the case. Yet in 1991 a Mr Watts, who had his licence to trade in Petticoat Lane Market revoked on the ground that he had failed to run it personally, went as far as the Court of Appeal with an argument that Southwark council's action was contrary to Articles 30, 34 and 52 of the EC Treaty (discussed below) (see *R v Southwark Crown Court ex p Watts* (1992)). He was not successful, but his case illustrates just how pervasive Community law issues can be.

8.3   Handling Community law in a practical way

What, then, does a solicitor have to look at to find out what rights or obligations a client has under Community law? There are four main sources:

- treaties establishing the Community;

- regulations;

- directives; and

- case law of the European Court of Justice.

8.3.1   Treaty provisions

We have already outlined the three general treaties, each amending their precursors, which now make up the written constitution of the Community (see para 8.2 above). From the busy solicitor's very practical perspective, the real importance of the treaties is not their prescription for the institutional framework of the EC but the fact that some articles confer rights and impose obligations on individuals, businesses and the governments of the Member States. These provisions are described as 'directly effective', meaning that they can be relied on by a person in any British court or tribunal in a similar way as if the rights were contained in an Act of Parliament. Not all the treaty provisions are directly effective, but in numerous cases the European Court of Justice has held that those which establish clear, precise and complete obligations and rights are. These include the following:

- Article 30 which prohibits quantitative restrictions on imports and discriminatory measures having equivalent effect.

- Article 48 which prohibits discrimination between workers on the grounds of nationality where this restricts the free movement of persons.

- Article 52 conferring the right of freedom of establishment.

- Articles 85 and 86 which prohibit anti-competitive practices and abuses of dominant position.

- Article 119 conferring the right of equal pay for equal work for men and women.

These rights can be relied on by a person in a British court both 'vertically' against the government and 'horizontally' against another private citizen or business. The rights and obligations under the treaties take precedence over any existing English law which is inconsistent with them (see s 2(4) of the European Communities Act 1972 discussed further below). Thus, the argument put to the Court of Appeal on behalf of Mr Watts, the street trader, was that Article 52 gave any person in the Community:

'the right to take up and pursue activities as self-employed persons and to set up and manage undertakings, [including] companies and firms ... under the conditions laid down for its own nationals by the law of the country where such establishment is effected.'

It was submitted that the UK legislation which required street traders to supervise their stalls personally was inconsistent with Article 52 because it would, say, prevent a French person from simultaneously operating a stall in Paris. The Court of Appeal held that this argument was misconceived as the English rules on stall holders applied to everyone – to an English person and a French person alike – and so were not discriminatory. Article 52 was also central in the *Factortame* litigation.

The treaties, however, make up only a small part of Community law and so a practitioner is likely to have to look at other sources. The treaties confer upon the Community institutions power to make secondary legislation. The main forms of this are directives and regulations.

Regulations are a type of secondary legislation made by the Council of Ministers or the Commission. (Confusingly, the term 'regulation' is also used to describe some types of UK *domestic* legislation, statutory instruments made by a minister under authority of an Act of Parliament: see Chapter 7.) As with the treaty provisions, EC regulations are 'directly applicable' in the UK. Article 189 of the EC Treaty states: 'A regulation shall have general application. It shall be binding in its entirety, and directly applicable in all Member States.' This means that they are a source of law in the English legal system without the British government or Parliament needing to incorporate every one of them into English law. (Section 2 of the European Communities Act 1972 incorporates regulations, as a general class, into English law). Many regulations set out detailed rules to do with the workings of the Common Agricultural Policy and competition policy.

8.3.2   Regulations

Again, as with the treaty provisions, not all regulations create rights and obligations enforceable in the English courts. A provision in a regulation has to meet the following criteria (first set out in *Van Gend en Loos* (1962)) before it can do so: it must be clear and precise, unconditional and leave no room for the exercise of discretion in its implementation.

Another type of secondary EC legislation is directives.

8.3.3   Directives

Article 189 provides that 'a directive shall be binding, as to the result to be achieved, upon each Member State to which it is addressed, but shall leave to the national authorities the choice of form and methods'. This means that they have a different status in the English legal system from either articles in the EC treaty or EC regulations. Normally they create rights and confer obligations enforceable in the English courts only after they have been specifically incorporated into English law.

Once a Directive is adopted by the Community each Member State has to implement it into its own domestic law within a set time period (usually between 18 and 24 months). In the UK this can be done by Act of Parliament, eg the Consumer Protection Act 1987 brought Directive 85/374/EEC into English law.

8.3.4   Transposing a directive into English law

More commonly, the government may choose to transpose a directive into English law by making a statutory instrument (SI), eg the directive on unfair terms in consumer contracts 93/13/EEC will be translated into UK domestic law by an SI. Section 2(2) of the European Communities Act 1972 gives ministers a general power to use SIs to implement directives (though the government may not use SIs to impose taxation, retrospective legislation, sub-delegated legislation or the creation of new criminal offences: see Schedule 2 to the Act). Other statutes also confer more specific powers on ministers to use SIs to transpose directives, eg s 17 of the Food Safety Act 1990 and s 156 of the Environmental Protection Act 1990.

Using statutory instruments has obvious advantages for the government; given the already overcrowded legislative timetable for bills in Parliament, it would be impossible to use primary legislation to transpose all directives. The down-side is that statutory instruments receive little Parliamentary scrutiny in comparison to bills. In particular, there is little opportunity to debate a draft SI and MPs have no opportunity to make amendments, only to approve or reject it as it stands.

One problem for government ministers and their legal advisers is the style of drafting to use. There is no obligation for the Act of Parliament or SI to use precisely the same wording as the directive, which tends towards broad statements of policy. In the past there was a tendency for British legislative drafters to use traditional English styles which meant spelling out the policy in great detail and trying to anticipate as many contingencies as possible. The danger with this is that discrepancies may arise between the Act or SI and the original directive on which it was based. An alternative, which is being used more and more, is known as the 'copy out' technique; here the text of the directive is just set out almost word for word. A potential problem with this approach is that directives normally only set out broad principles and there is a fear that this will give English judges too much discretion to fill in detail when they are called on to interpret the legislation.

You may be thinking that if directives are implemented into English law by Act of Parliament or statutory instrument, then there will be no need for our busy practitioner to look at the actual wording of a directive. Unfortunately this is not true. A variety of practical situations may occur where it is still necessary to look at the directive itself.

- The government may have failed to implement the directive into English law by the set date. Generally, the UK has a very good record of managing to do this on time unlike some other Member States (such as Italy) where many directives remain to be incorporated several years after the due date.

- The English Act of Parliament or SI may not properly reflect the provisions of the relevant directive. This could happen due to a mistake in drafting, eg a right conferred by a directive is erroneously omitted from the domestic legislation.

- Another reason for inconsistency may be that the British government deliberately took a narrow view of the policy contained in the directive when it was drafting the Act or SI designed to implement it, and the ECJ subsequently gives a wider interpretation (or visa versa).

If a solicitor spots an inconsistency – or a directive has just not been transposed into English law at all – how can this help his or her client? The answer is a little complicated.

First, many directives are simply incapable of having direct effect in English courts because they do not create any relevant obligations or confer rights which are unconditional and sufficiently precise.

Secondly, directives (unlike the treaty provisions considered above) can never have 'horizontal effect'. In other words an individual cannot directly rely on the provisions of a directive against another individual or private business, only against an institution of the state (see *Marshall v Southampton and South West Area Health Authority (Teaching)* (1986)). This is because of the wording used in Article 189 to define directives (see para 8.3.3 above) which stresses that directives are binding 'upon each *Member State* to which it is addressed'. Directives are not, as such, binding upon individuals and private businesses.

Recent developments have, however, rather undermined the idea that directives can only have direct effect vertically, ie against public bodies. This is because in *Marleasing SA v La Comercial Internacional de Alimentatacion SA* (1992) the ECJ held that national courts had, so far as possible, to interpret national legislation so that it conforms with directives: see para 8.3.6 below. The practical effect of this is that rights or obligations contained in a directive may, by this sidewind, be enforced by a British court even against a private person or business.

To make things clearer, consider this practical (but fictitious) example. Suppose that a shop treats its women employees less favourably than its men by making them retire at 60 instead of 65 and that this is not prohibited by the Sex Discrimination Act 1975. If the solicitor for one of the women considers that a directive on equal treatment requires English law to say that this sort of discrimination is unlawful, the solicitor cannot just argue that the directive should be applied by the court or tribunal and that a female employee (whom we will call Margaret) should be reinstated in her job. Margaret's complaint will have to be made against the British government and its failure to implement the directive, rather than against her ex-employer (who, after all, had just followed English law). The directive is supreme law and 'trumps' anything inconsistent with it in, say, the Sex Discrimination Act; but the directive will not bind a private business or another individual until it is actually transposed properly into English law.

The correct course of action for Margaret in these circumstances may be to make an application for judicial review against the relevant government minister to establish whether or not the existing English law was incompatible with the directive. The normal time limits for judicial review (applications must be made promptly and in any event within three months) do not apply in this situation and so a challenge may be made even to statutes enacted, or statutory instruments made, several years previously (see *Equal Opportunities Commission v Secretary of State for Employment* (1993)). If Margaret succeeds in showing that existing British legislation is inconsistent with the directive, then that legislation will be declared ineffective and the government will need to introduce new legislation to bring English law into line with the directive. In these circumstances the government *may* be liable to pay Margaret compensation for the loss she suffered as a result of its failure properly to implement the directive in question (see below).

An important footnote is needed to this explanation. If instead of working in a shop Margaret had been a civil servant or employed by the National Health Service or other 'organ or emanation' of the state, then her position would have been different. This is because directives can be directly effective in the 'vertical' relationship between the citizen and the Member State. If it can be shown that the obligations imposed *on the*

Member State by the directive are sufficiently clear, precise and unconditional, and that the time limit for implementation has passed, then Margaret could rely on the directive directly (see the *Marshall* case and *Foster v British Gas plc* (1990).

The reason why public authorities (including very recently privatised national industries such as British Gas) are treated differently from individuals and private firms is that Member States should not be allowed to rely on their own failure to implement a directive into domestic law. From a different perspective, however, this leads to arbitrary treatment of individuals merely on the basis of who their employer is; this is rather hard to justify in policy terms.

Even if a directive does *not* have direct effect, it is still possible for a practitioner to refer to it in court by arguing that ambiguous domestic legislation should be construed in such a way as to make the Act or SI reflect the policy of the directive. In the illustration about Margaret we assumed that English law contained no provisions prohibiting differential retirement ages for men and women. Assume now, however, that there was some provision in English law, but that it was unclear whether this legislation really covered retirement ages. In such a situation the English courts and tribunals should construe domestic legislation so as to accord with any relevant directive whether the domestic legislation came before or after the directive (see *Marleasing SA v La Comercial Internacional de Alimentatacion SA* (1992)). The House of Lords have added a gloss to this approach laid down by the ECJ: the court or tribunal must carry out its task of interpretation 'without distorting the meaning of the domestic legislation' and words of the Act or SI must actually be capable of supporting an interpretation consistent with the directive (see *Webb v EMO Air Cargo UK Ltd* (1993)). In other words the English courts apply the *Marleasing* principle to choose an interpretation of legislation consistent with a directive where this is one of several plausible interpretations.

In our example Margaret may have lost a considerable amount of money by way of lost wages from the time she was compulsorily retired. Following an important judgment by the European Court of Justice in *Republic of Italy v Francovich* (1992), citizens of a Member State may now claim damages against their government for failure to implement a directive into domestic law – whether or not it had direct effect. In *Francovich* the Italian government should have implemented a directive into its domestic law to set up some sort of scheme (it was up to each Member State to decide precisely what kind) to ensure that employees received any outstanding wages etc if

8.3.6   Interpreting domestic law to conform with directives

8.3.7   Compensation for failure to transpose a directive

their employer became insolvent. Italy failed to do this by the due date. Francovich's employer went bust and he was not paid. The directive was not directly effective against the Italian government because the provisions lacked sufficient 'unconditionality' – the government needed to carry out several things before the scheme could be operational. But Francovich sued the Italian government for their failure to establish a scheme. The ECJ held that there was a right to damages for non-transposition of a directive if three conditions were satisfied in a case. These were:

(i)   the directive created individual rights;

(ii) the content of those rights must be ascertainable from the directive itself;

(iii) there was a causal link between the government's failure to transpose the directive and the individual's loss.

Like *Marleasing*, the *Francovich* case shows that even if a directive has no direct effect it nevertheless may be used by an aggrieved citizen. It is not yet clear whether Member States may be liable to pay compensation for their misinterpretation of a directives as opposed to just not having implemented one by the due date.

8.3.8	Summary

This section of the chapter has examined in outline how, in practical ways, EC law can be used by practitioners in England. The picture is quite complex. The tear out page at the end of this chapter summarises the main points in tabular form.

8.4   Impact on the British constitution and administrative law

In the final part of this chapter we can turn to look at the ways in which membership of the Community has impacted on the UK. Some textbooks give the impression that the only important impact of Community membership has been on the principle of Parliamentary sovereignty, but this is a rather narrow view. We can look at the impact in three contexts:

• the impact on administration;

• the impact on Parliament; and

• the impact on the British courts.

8.4.1	Impact on administration

In many ways membership of the Community has had little impact on the structure of central government departments and local authorities. There is no 'minister for Community affairs' or 'department for the EC'. Some departments, such as the Ministry of Agriculture, Fisheries and Food (MAFF), have set up specialist units of civil servants to deal with particular policy areas. Generally, however, Community law is seen as being 'all in a day's work' for the average department and its lawyers. Community law is not seen as presenting any unique problems different from those thrown up by domestic law. But if there has been relatively little change in the *structure* of public administration, the same cannot be said about the substance of work in some departments and local authorities. The work of three departments have been particularly affected: MAFF, the Department of Trade and Industry and Customs and Excise.

For central government one problem has been the need to create a system to ensure that there is an appropriate collective response from the government to Community law and policy. Two bodies have responsibility for ensuring that there is a unified and consistent line.

- The European Secretariat of the Cabinet Office

  The Cabinet Office provides general administrative support to the work of the Cabinet and co-ordinates policy briefing for Cabinet and Cabinet committees on all issues. A handful of civil servants form the European Secretariat with in it and advise departments of issues as they emerge from the European Commission and Council of Ministers.

- Foreign and Commonwealth Office and UK Rep

  The FCO has a general responsibility for British relations with the Community and the 14 other Member States. The UK Representatives to the European Community (UK Rep for short) is a small body of officials from the FCO who meet with the opposite numbers from the other Member States in a body called COREPER (the Committee of Permanent Representatives). These officials prepare for meetings of the Council of Ministers and hold negotiations before and afterwards.

Community law and policy has had a massive impact on some aspects of the work of local authorities in the UK. Many areas are now governed more by Community law than domestically initiated legislation, eg the work of trading standards officers and public procurement of goods and services. Some councils have appointed 'European officers' to keep an overview of Community matters and ensure that the council applies for any relevant funds available from the EC, eg for development of industry in areas of high unemployment. Many local authorities feel that they are at a disadvantage compared with the much larger units of regional government in other Member States which are able to negotiate and lobby more effectively in the Community.

8.4.2   Impact on Parliament

We have already seen how Parliament is involved in implementing directives into domestic law by passing Acts or approving statutory instruments. In many ways this is quite a mechanical process: the UK has no choice but to follow the policy included in the directive. Criticisms are made over the extensive use of statutory instruments to implement directives since this gives MPs no opportunity to suggest amendments and very little chance to debate matters. (For further discussion of statutory instruments, see Chapter 7, para 7.4).

Concern is also often expressed about Parliament's extremely limited role *before* a directive or regulation is made. The British Parliament has no *formal* role under the EC Treaty in scrutinising draft directives before they are adopted by the Council of Ministers. This is a problem. It means that British ministers are able to cast their votes for or against proposed legislation at meetings of the Council of Ministers without there having been any prior discussion or vote by MPs at Westminster. This, it is often argued, gives much too much power to the executive. One solution, suggested by Tony Benn, is that ministers should be mandated on how to vote in the Council of Ministers by a prior vote and resolution in the House of Commons. (See further Tony Benn and Andrew Hood, *Common Sense*).

Although the British Parliament has no formal role under the EC Treaty in scrutinising Community legislation, committees have been established in both the House of Commons and the House of Lords to consider both the policy and drafting of proposed directives. These select committees pass their reports to the relevant government departments in the UK and also to the EC Commission. To this limited extent, Parliament is less on the margins of policy and law making in relation to Community matters than it once was.

Others have argued that rather than increasing the powers and role of legislatures in the Member States, it would be preferable to enhance the role of the European Parliament. To some extent this has happened with the powers given to the EP under the Maastricht treaty.

8.4.3   The impact on the courts

Membership of the Community has had important, though often subtle, impacts on the judges in Britain. Most obviously, they are now empowered to consider the validity of Acts of Parliament: statutes can be declared legally ineffective insofar as they are incompatible with the provisions of the EC Treaty or any directive. This is seen most clearly in the recent case of *Equal Opportunities Commission v Secretary of State for Employment* (1994) when the House of Lords held that sections of the Employment Protection (Consolidation) Act 1978 were inconsistent with Article 119 of the EC treaty and directives on equal treatment. Prior to accession in 1973, the principle of

Parliamentary supremacy meant that the English courts had no power to strike down primary legislation (though they could quash statutory instruments which were *ultra vires*). The European Communities Act 1972 s 2(4) does its best not to draw attention to this important shift in constitutional power by using highly technical language. There was no bold statement of principle that 'henceforth the Judges of the United Kingdom may quash any statute which is incompatible with EC law'. But this is precisely the effect of s 2(4).

Another feature of membership of the EC which has constitutional importance is that English courts and tribunals, from a lowly industrial tribunal to the House of Lords, is now bound by the jurisprudence of another court – the ECJ. The role of the ECJ is to ensure 'that in the interpretation and application of the Treaty the law is observed'. The judges are assisted by six Advocates-General who, acting with complete impartiality and independence, make reasoned submissions in open court. A Court of First Instance may decide certain classes of action, subject to an appeal on point of law to the ECJ. Several different types of proceedings come before the ECJ. Of great importance for the domestic courts in the UK is the power of the ECJ under Article 177 to give 'preliminary rulings' concerning:

- the interpretation of the Treaty; and

- the validity and interpretation of the acts of the institutions of the Community.

Any court or tribunal in the UK may make an Article 177 reference to request a preliminary ruling. In *R v International Stock Exchange ex p Else* (1993) the Court of Appeal stated that British courts and tribunals should not take upon themselves the burden of difficult questions of the construction and application of Community law unless they feel in any case they can with 'complete confidence' resolve the question. Courts and tribunals are therefore encouraged to make references to the ECJ. Recent examples of the many Article 177 references made by English courts include the following:

- In the *Factortame* litigation, the question whether the English courts had power to grant interim injunctions against a minister of the Crown.

- In *R v Secretary of State for the National Heritage, ex p Continental Television BVio* (1993) the question whether the statutory instrument banning a satellite TV channel 'Red Hot Dutch', which broadcast pornographic films from Denmark to the UK, was contrary to an EC Directive on broadcasting.

Because of backlogs, there is often a wait of over two years before the ECJ gives its decision. In the meantime, a person may seek an interim injunction in the English courts to preserve the status quo until the case is finally determined: this is what happened in *Factortame.*

Once the ECJ gives its decision, the UK court then applies this to the facts of the particular case before it. The ECJ is not therefore an 'appeal' court.

Less dramatic, but equally important, is the impact of Community law on the day to day work of courts and tribunals through the principles of direct effect and the *Marleasing* approach to interpreting domestic legislation discussed above.

The impact of Community membership is felt in still more subtle ways. The principle of proportionality in judicial review cases is discussed in Chapter 18 below. As we will see in the case of *Brind*, the House of Lords is usually understood to have decided that proportionality was not a separate head of judicial review in English law. Yet proportionality is clearly a separate principle of review under Community law, and when determining whether domestic legislation is in conformity with EC law, English courts have to apply the principle. An example of an English judge applying the principle of proportionality can be seen in Hoffmann J's judgment in *Stoke-on-Trent City Council v B & Q plc* (1991). That was a case where it was argued that s 47 of the Shops Act 1950, which restricts Sunday trading, was incompatible with the provisions of the EC Treaty which outlaw measures that have the effect of restricting imports from other Member States. It is quite difficult to see why it is acceptable for a judge to use proportionality as a ground of review in one context (cases which happen to raise Community law points) but not in others.

The fact that Community law now empowers British judges to review the legality of Acts of Parliament may also remove one objection to having a bill of rights in the UK. If the courts can already set statutes aside on grounds of incompatibility with Community law, it is not such a large step to do the same in respect of non-conformity with the human rights convention.

The Impact of the European Community

Type of EC law	Does it create legal rights and obligations enforceable by people in English courts?	The type of argument in court.
EC Treaty provisions	Some articles do: those which are (i) clear and precise, (ii) unconditional and (iii) leave no room for the exercise of discretion in their implementation. Ultimately, it is for the ECJ to decide if these criteria are satisfied.	The Treaty article can straightforwardly be used in argument – against public or private bodies – like any other legislation in the English legal system. If there is a conflict with UK law, the article takes precedence.
	Some articles don't: if they do not satisfy the criteria set out above.	
Directives	Some provisions in directives do, but only if: (a) the time for implementation of the directive into English law has expired; *and* (b) the article is (i) clear and precise; (ii) unconditional and (iii) leaves no room for exercise of discretion in its implementation; *and* (c) the legal dispute is with a government body or other 'emanation of the state'.	• The directive can straightforwardly be used in argument like any other legislation in the English legal system. If there is a conflict with UK law, the directive takes precedence *(Marshall)*. • If the plaintiff has lost money as a result of a failure properly to implement a directive, then they can claim compensation *(Francovich)*.
	If the directive doesn't create legal rights because (a) to (c) in the box above aren't satisfied ...	... you can still use the directive in court. • The court must, so far as possible, interpret UK legislation so that it accords with the directive *(Marleasing)* • If the plaintiff has lost money as a result of a failure properly to implement directive then may be possible to claim compensation *(Francovich)* * It's possible to apply for judicial review of UK legislation in conflict with the directive to have it 'disapplied' (eg *EOC* case).
Regulations	EC Treaty Article 189 says that provisions in regulations create rights and obligations enforceable in the UK courts – but to do so they must be (i) clear and precise; (ii) unconditional and (iii) leave no room for discretion in its implementation.	As with a Treaty article, a regulation can straightforwardly be used in argument – against public or private bodies – like any other legislation in the English legal system. If there is a conflict with UK law, the regulation takes precedence.

Chapter 9

Commissioners for Maladministration ('Ombudsmen')

> 'A characteristic all ombudsmen schemes have in common is their potential to adjudicate between disputing parties without the trappings of going to court.' (Lord Mackay, the Lord Chancellor, Hamlyn Lectures 1994).

On one level, 'the ombudsmen' can seem like one of the more straightforward topics on the public law syllabus. It is, however, difficult to tackle well. This chapter tries to help. As with the rest of the book, this chapter should be treated as an overview of the subject. There is some excellent recent writing on the topic of the ombudsmen, including:

- JUSTICE, All Souls Review of Administrative Law (1988) Chapter 5.

- Lewis and Birkinshaw, *When Citizens Complain: reforming justice and administration* (1993).

- Drewry and Harlow, 'A "Cutting Edge"? The Parliamentary Commissioner and MPs' (1990) 53 MLR 745.

If possible you should also try to read at least some of the actual reports of the ombudsmen mentioned in this chapter.

The instinctive reaction of most lawyers when they meet a person with a grievance against a public body is to consider whether there are any grounds for making a legal challenge, either by making an application for judicial review, a claim for damages in tort or taking the matter to a tribunal (if there is an appropriate one). The various ombudsmen provide an alternative to these methods of grievance redressing. Complaining to an ombudsman is different from taking court or tribunal proceedings in several ways.

- The techniques used by the ombudsmen are inquisitorial and investigative rather than adjudicatory.

- Many people complain to the ombudsmen without having to consult a lawyer; in this respect it may be a cheaper alternative to court proceedings.

- Any findings or recommendations made by an ombudsman at the end of the investigative process are not legally binding on the public body complained against.

The ombudsmen have no sanctions but rely instead on cooperation.

In order to get to grips with the ombudsmen, you will need to be able to evaluate the efficacy of the ombudsmen as *a method of redressing grievances*, and be able to draw comparisons with the efficacy of redress in the courts, by MPs and by more informal methods of redress such as that provided under the Citizen's Charter (on which see para 9.7.2 below). You'll need to be aware of the political and legal context of the British ombudsmen system. You should also consider the usefulness of the ombudsman system *as a method for maintaining and improving the quality of public administration*. Again, how well the ombudsmen achieve this can be compared with the courts, the Citizen's Charter and scrutiny of public services by MPs and local councillors.

9.1 Who are the ombudsmen?

There are four main public sector 'ombudsmen' in England and Wales.

- **The Parliamentary Commissioner for Administration (PCA)**

  The PCA was set up in 1967 to investigate cases of injustice caused by maladministration in central government departments and some other institutions. The current office holder is WK Reid, a former civil servant. (His immediate predecessor was Mr Andrew Barrowclough, a lawyer.) The PCA office is based in London and is staffed by civil servants on secondment from government departments; this is sometimes said to be a weakness since the ombudsman's office should be seen to be neutral and independent. The Commissioner enjoys similar status and tenure of office to that of a High Court judge.

- **The Health Service Commissioner (HSC)**

  The HSC was established in 1973 to look at allegations of maladministration in the National Health Service. Mr Reid also holds this post.

- **The Local Commission for Administration (LCA)**

  The LCA was set up in 1974 to deal with complaints of maladministration against local authorities in England and Wales. England is split into three areas, with a commissioner for each.

- **The Prisons Ombudsman**

  The Prisons Ombudsman (formally known as the Independent Complaints Adjudicator) was set up on the recommendation of the Woolf report into the serious riots at Strangeways Prison. This was part of a package of reforms introduced in 1992 in which Prison Boards of Visitors ceased to hear disciplinary charges against prisoners; prison governors are now entirely responsible for this. If a prisoner believes that a disciplinary finding is wrong or that proper procedures were not followed, he can now appeal to the prison ombudsman. Unlike the other public sector ombudsmen described above, the Independent Complaints Adjudicator has not been set up by Act of Parliament and therefore has no statutory powers. For further discussion see Rod Morgan, 'Prisons Accountability Revisited' [1993] PL 314. This ombudsman began work in October 1994.

In addition, be aware that a plethora of private sector ombudsmen have been created to investigate complaints in service industries such as banking, insurance and estate agents. Most of these ombudsmen have been established and financed by the industries themselves and have no special statutory powers. Others, however, have been set up by statute, e.g. the Building Societies' ombudsmen. Another example is the Legal Services Ombudsman, which was established by s 21 and Schedule 3 of the Courts and Legal Services Act 1990. This ombudsman oversees how the professional bodies deal with complaints against solicitors, barristers and licensed conveyancers. He is, however, precluded from investigating allegations relating to matters for which there is immunity from actions in tort, such as advocacy in court. In 1993 1,235 complaints were received, of which about half were investigated. The number of complaints is increasing.

9.1.1   Private sector ombudsmen

The fact that some private sector ombudsmen are set up by statute, and others are just voluntary, creates an untidy picture – especially when it comes to the way in which complaints *against* the ombudsmen may be made. If an ombudsman has statutory powers then a person dissatisfied with a decision not to investigate a case of maladministration (for example) can apply for judicial review of that ombudsman (see, eg *R v Parliamentary Commissioner for Administration ex p Dyer* (1992)). But if the ombudsman is merely 'voluntary', and has no statutory powers, then judicial review is probably not possible (see eg *R v Insurance Ombudsman Bureau ex p Aegon* (1994)).

Ombudsmen for both the public and private sectors have begun to work closely together, and meet regularly under the auspices of the UK and Ireland Ombudsmen Association formed in 1993, the aims of which includes improvement of public awareness of the functions performed by ombudsmen.

It follows from all of this that when you are thinking and writing about 'the ombudsmen' you need to be cautious: while sometimes it will be possible to talk in general terms about the ombudsmen, at other times you will need to distinguish between them as they have somewhat different powers and functions. This chapter focuses mainly on the work of the Parliamentary and Health Commissioners and the local ombudsmen.

1993	Complaints	Percentage investigated in full (approx)
Parliamentary Commissioner	1,244	25%
Health Service Commissioner	1,384	15%
Local Commission for Administration	13,307	3%
Judicial Review	2,878 applications for leave	30% cases have a full hearing

9.2   The statistics

The table below summarises some useful statistics about the ombudsmen and also, for comparison, judicial review.

Two things should jump out of the page at you. First, the relatively small number of complaints received by the offices of the Parliamentary and Health Service Commissioners. Bear in mind the vast number of decisions taken by public servants on behalf of a population of almost 60 million, and then the tiny number of complaints can be put in perspective. Later, we shall consider the causes of this and whether it is a problem.

Secondly, notice how few complaints receive a full investigation. As we shall see this is in part because many complaints made fall outside the scope of the ombudsmen's jurisdiction and so are filtered out at a preliminary stage. Also, the ombudsmen often manage to resolve complaints by informal contact with the public body without any need for a full formal investigation.

9.3   'Injustice as a consequence of maladministration'

The function of the ombudsmen is to investigate cases where an aggrieved person claims to have sustained 'injustice' as a result of 'maladministration' by the relevant public body. None of the statutes establishing the various ombudsmen actually define what is meant by 'maladministration'. A useful, but not comprehensive guide was provided by Richard Crossman, a minister at the time the PCA was first established. It's now known as the 'Crossman Catalogue':

> '... bias, neglect, inattention, delay, incompetence, ineptitude, perversity, turpitude, arbitrariness, and so on.'

'And so on' may prove useful to the Commissioners, giving some discretion and flexibility regarding that which can be investigated.

The 1993 PCA report lists additions to the Crossman Catalogue which includes unwillingness to treat a complainant as a person with rights, neglecting to inform, failure to monitor faulty procedures, and the failure to mitigate the effects of rigid adherence to the letter of the law where this produces manifest inequity.

The best way to understand what maladministration means is to look at some reports of some ombudsmen investigations. Drewry and Harlow are less than impressed by the Parliamentary Commissioner's reports, calling them 'dreary'. This did not prevent the JUSTICE/All Souls Review suggesting in 1988 that reports into maladministration should be more widely publicised and circulated among public servants. The 'case law' built up by the Parliamentary Commissioner since 1967 could be selected and published as a reference source to aid good public administration by avoiding pitfalls suffered in the past. The current Parliamentary Commissioner strongly supports this idea in the 1993 Annual report.

Some recent Parliamentary Commissioner investigations are as follows:

9.3.1   Some recent Parliamentary Commissioner investigations

- The Commissioner upheld a woman's complaint regarding a lack of concern by the Home Office when an escaped prisoner accosted her and stole her car. She received an ex gratia payment from the department.

- Delays in handling Disability Allowance claims, where 'glaring shortcomings' on the part of the Department of Social Security resulted in the loss of allowance to thousands of disabled people were investigated by the Parliamentary Commissioner and a special report was produced. Procedures were improved and compensation paid.

- A complainant suffered loss of Invalidity Benefit due to incorrect advice given by the Department of Social Security. The department agreed to make her a payment of £11,000.

- There were also many complaints against the Legal Aid Board, where, according to the Commissioner, there is 'woeful confusion and delay'. Among the complainants was a barrister, who for the second year running had not been paid by the Board.

In addition, the Parliamentary Commissioner received very many complaints about the highly controversial Child Support Agency set up by the government in 1993 to trace absent parents (usually fathers) and make them contribute towards their children's upkeep. As yet no report has been published, but the first investigations should be finished in 1995.

The majority of complaints to the Parliamentary Commissioner are against the Department of Social Security and the Inland Revenue. The latter has now appointed a high-profile Adjudicator which may lead to a reduction of complaints reaching the Commissioner.

9.3.2   Some recent Health Service Commissioner investigations

Some recent Health Service Commissioner investigations are as follows:

- A consultant decided not to investigate or treat a man for suspected cancer, because he thought the man was too old. He did not inform either the man, his family or the medical and nursing team. The old man died suddenly, shocking his close relatives, and members of staff. The Walsall NHS Trust apologised, and agreed to improve communication.

- Delayed diagnosis, treatment and inadequate nutrition of a patient led to his premature death. The hospital was unable to name the doctors on duty because there were so many locums and juniors. Three out of four of the radiologists were on leave. Nobody ensured that the patient received the fat-free diet that was needed. The nurses' notes were inadequate, the care plans poor and signatures illegible. This occurred at the Basildon and Thurruck General Hospital NHS Trust.

- An elderly man was taken into Southend Health Care NHS Trust for respite care. There he developed thrush which prevented him eating. He was not treated until the family complained several times. He was also dropped by nurses. During a visit, his family noticed that he had cuts to his face and they were told that he had been attacked by another patient. Three days later, a nurse telephoned the man's wife to say that he did not want any visitors because he wished to sleep. Four hours later, he died alone. In fact, the doctor had thought that he would die at any time, but had not told the family, denying them the chance to be at his bedside when he died. There had been no discussion with other staff, and the man's notes were incomplete and fragmented.

Many complaints to the local ombudsmen (CLA) are about housing (5,037 in 1993) and planning (3,250). As can be seen from the cases below, non-compliance with the recommendations of the local ombudsmen is a problem; we will return to this point later.

- The CLA criticised Barnet Council for the manner in which it dealt with planning permission for the largest house to be built in London since the Second World War. The lack of liaison between departments resulted in the complainant having to live next door to this huge building, which was both bigger than it should have been, and in the wrong position. The district valuer assessed the loss of value to the complainant's house at £50,000. The council apologised, but has refused to pay compensation.

- The London Borough of Tower Hamlets failed to investigate allegations of harassment and refused a reasonable request to address some members of the council. Though the council did accept the CLA's finding of failure regarding this complaint, they refused to pay the £500 compensation and instead paid a 'derisory' £5. The CLA found this 'insulting both to the complainant and to me'.

- Boothferry District Council was found guilty of maladministration in delaying rehousing an 80 year old tenant, who needed accommodation suitable for a wheelchair. Her needs had not been properly assessed. The council refused either to apologise or to pay compensation, choosing instead to publish a statement. In the opinion of the CLA 'this only added insult to injury'.

Not every incident of 'maladministration' by a public body can be taken to the ombudsmen for investigation: all the ombudsmen are subject to statutory restrictions on the scope of their powers. The ombudsmen are able to investigate only those public bodies specifically referred to in the ombudsmen's respective statutes. Some of these limitations are relatively uncontroversial; others less so. The following are all excluded: from the Parliamentary Commissioner's jurisdiction.

- Complaints relating to matters affecting the UK's relationship with other countries or international organisations.

- Criminal investigations and national security.

- The commencement or conduct of civil or criminal proceedings.

9.3.3   Recent investigations by the Local Commission

9.4   **Scope of the ombudsmen's investigations**

- Any exercise of the prerogative of mercy by the Home Secretary.

- Matters relating to contractual or commercial transactions of government departments.

- Grievances concerning the pay, discipline, pensions, appointments and other personnel matters in the armed forces and civil service.

- The grant of honours, awards and privileges within the gift of the Crown.

- The Health Service Commissioner cannot investigate complaints which involve clinical judgment.

In addition, complaints are subject to a time limit; they have to be made within 12 months from the day the aggrieved person first had notice of the problem.

The Parliamentary Commissioner himself believes that his jurisdiction needs to be enlarged. He has expressed regret that he is not able to investigate personnel matters in the public service.

An area of real concern has been the exclusion from the jurisdiction of both the Parliamentary Commissioner the health service ombudsmen and the local ombudsmen of matters relating to commercial or contractual transactions. Since the 1980s many public services have been 'contracted out' (see Chapter 6). These services include the care of the elderly and chronically sick, refuse collection, and catering and cleaning in public institutions. Recent legislation has gone some way to meet these criticisms. The Health Service Commissioner can now investigate complaints relating to services provided through the internal market created by the NHS and Community Care Act 1990 (s 7(2) Health Service Commissioner Act 1993). The Deregulation and Contracting Out Act 1994 extends the Parliamentary and Local Commissioners' jurisdiction to contracted out functions of central and local government.

The awesome growth in quangos since the 1980s has meant that many public functions slipped out of the ombudsmen's grasp. The Parliamentary and Health Service Commissioners Act 1987 has now extended their jurisdiction to most, but not all, of these bodies.

9.5   The ombudsman process

In this section we trace the steps that have to be followed when complaining to either the Parliamentary Commissioner, health service or local ombudsmen, highlighting the most controversial features. The first point to make is that the process can take a long time: all the ombudsmen have backlogs of cases waiting to be dealt with. In 1993 the PCA and the health services ombudsman took an average of 11 months to complete an investigation, and the local ombudsman took nearly 17 months. Initial screening took about three weeks.

If a person is aggrieved by the maladministration of a central government body, he cannot complain to the *Parliamentary Commissioner* directly: only complaints referred to the PCA office by an MP will be considered. The MP need not be the complainant's own constituency MP. This so-called 'MP filter' is regarded by most commentators (but not all) as a major weakness in the institution of the Parliamentary Commissioner.

9.5.1   The MP filter for the Parliamentary Commissioner

The bar on direct access to the PCA needs to be set into an historical context. Following the English Civil War and the constitutional settlement of the 17th century (see Chapter 3), Parliament became the supreme law-making body. The Bill of Rights 1689 included the promise of the 'redress of all grievances' by Parliament but today no one any longer believes that Parliament alone can redress all grievances. The sheer volume of work is now too much. There is a need for an impartial grievance procedure open to all. Yet the 1689 Bill of Rights has cast a long shadow. Parliament is still seen, or at least sees itself, as the forum for the redress of grievances. The 1967 Act gave Britain an ombudsman, but only if citizens went to an MP first. The ombudsman system is therefore firmly attached to Parliament, rather than the people: the PCA is a creature of Parliament rather than a citizens' champion, as he is in other democracies. The problem is that at present Parliament is failing in its role as protective buffer between the people and a powerful executive. The Parliamentary Commissioner is harnessed to a Parliamentary system that itself needs reform. MPs find it increasingly difficult to hold ministers to account for their actions now that so many public services are run by executive agencies and unelected quangos.

A large proportion of the work of MPs is taken up dealing with particular problems of their constituents on matters such as council housing, immigration status, problems with schools and entitlement to social security benefits. Most MPs have regular 'surgeries' when people can call in to see them and overall MPs receive over 3 million letters a year from members of the public, many asking for help dealing with public authorities. Many, if not most, MPs see this sort of case work as of central importance: it keeps them informed of how government is treating people and can provide early warning

9.5.2   MPs' constituency case work

of controversial problems such as the work of the Child Support Agency. The leading study of how MPs handle complaints is by Richard Rawlings, 'The MPS Complaints Service' (1990) 53 MLR 22 and 149. We'll return to his findings later.

In the mid-1960s when the possibility of establishing an ombudsman in England was first mooted, many MPs were opposed to it, fearing that it would undermine their relationship with their constituents. The Parliamentary Commissioner Act 1967 therefore contained a compromise designed to answer this suspicion: the Parliamentary Commissioner can only investigate complaints forwarded to him by an MP. This 'MP filter' has two main functions.

- First, to give the MP a chance to deal with the complaint herself, eg by writing a letter to the relevant government department. Sometimes this is all that is needed to resolve a problem.

- Secondly, it emphasises the fact that the Parliamentary Commissioner is a servant of Parliament. This needs to be central to any discussion of the efficacy and need for reform of the PCA. There is a continuing debate about whether the Parliamentary Commissioner should be an adjunct to MPs and their constituency casework, or whether he should be a more independent complaints commissioner serving and responding to the public directly.

It is also sometimes suggested that the MPs have a role in weeding out unmeritorious complaints, or complaints about matters which fall outside the Parliamentary Commissioner's jurisdiction. In reality this does not happen as many MPs seem not to understand what types of complaints the Parliamentary Commissioner is able to investigate; a large proportion of complaints referred to the PCA by MPs have to be rejected by the Commissioner's office on the ground that they fall outside his jurisdiction as set down by the 1967 Act.

Drewry and Harlow carried out research into how MPs were using the Parliamentary Commissioner in the mid-1980s: see (1990) 53 MLR 745. They found that every year about 70% of MPs refer between one and six complaints to the PCA. Interestingly, over 26% of MPs had received a request from a person living in another MP's constituency to pass a complaint on to the Parliamentary Commissioner. There was considerable uncertainty as to what an MP should do in such circumstances. Drewry and Harlow conclude that the office of the PCA 'is held in low esteem' both by MPs and the public.

This view is confirmed to some extent by Rawlings' study of the constituency case-work of MPs: see (199) 53 MLR 22 and 149. Indeed, he shows that MPs sometimes have to monitor ombudsmen investigations themselves to ensure that investigations are conducted thoroughly and effectively.

The Parliamentary Commissioner in fact receives more complaints directly (which he has to reject) than he receives from MPs. The Commissioner was so concerned about this, that in 1978 he introduced machinery whereby, with permission of the complainant, he would pass on the complaint to an MP, who in turn could pass it back to the PCA to investigate.

The debate over direct access to the Parliamentary Commissioner continues. In 1977 a report by JUSTICE (a lawyers' pressure group) called *Our Fettered Ombudsman* recommended direct access as did the 1988 JUSTICE/All Souls Review of Administrative Law. The Parliamentary Commissioner himself would also like to see direct access. In his 1993 report, he again complains about the obstacle of the MP filter:

> 'That hurdle is not required before an approach is made to me as Health Service Commissioner. It applies to almost no other national Ombudsman throughout the world. I remain of the view that the filter serves to deprive members of the public of possible redress.'

However, not everyone accepts the need for the removal of the MP filter. Carol Harlow has argued against this and has challenged the assumptions that underlie the calls for direct access (for instance in 'Ombudsmen in Search of a Role' (1978) 41 MLR 446 and Chapter 7 of Harlow and Rawling's *Law and Administration*). She is not keen to see a huge increase in the number of cases investigated by the Parliamentary Commissioner which would be likely to occur if the MP filter were to be removed.

In contrast to the Parliamentary Commissioner, the health service ombudsman and the local ombudsmen allow complainants direct access. In the early years of the local ombudsmen there was a requirement that complaints had to be referred by a councillor, but this was removed by the Local Government Act 1988, since when the public have been able to approach the local ombudsmen directly. This led to a dramatic rise of 44% in the number of complaints received; now over 83% of complaints are made directly rather than via a local councillor. This strongly suggests that the removal of the MP filter for the PCA would result in a considerable increase in work for that office.

9.5.3   Direct access to the other ombudsmen

9.5.4   The ombudsman filter

Once a complaint has been received by one of the ombudsman's offices, the first task is to determine whether it falls within that ombudsman's jurisdiction and whether it shows a prima facie case of maladministration. As we will see, a very large proportion of cases are rejected at this stage because the subject matter falls outside the jurisdiction of the relevant ombudsman or the complaint is not about 'maladministration'.

The ombudsman's office also has to consider whether the aggrieved person should be taking legal proceedings against the public body or should be using any available appeal mechanism. As you can see from the complaints listed above (paras 9.3.1-9.3.3), 'maladministration' often involves rudeness, incompetence, failures in communication and insensitivity on the part of public authorities and their employees. In such cases there would be no grounds for the complainant to apply for judicial review; there was no illegality, irrationality or procedural impropriety. But at other times the complaint of 'maladministration' may also give grounds for some sort of legal challenge. Careless administration, eg losing documents, could possibly give the basis for suing for negligence. A public body's inordinate delay in complying with a statutory duty might give grounds for judicial review. This can cause problems. All the main ombudsmen are precluded from investigating complaints of injustice caused by maladministration if the complainant has a legal remedy available. For example, s 5(2) of the Parliamentary Commissioner Act 1967 provides:

'5(2) - Except as hereinafter provided, the Commissioner shall not conduct an investigation under this Act in respect of any of the following matters, that is to say –

(a) any action in respect of which the person aggrieved has or had a right of appeal, reference or review to or before a tribunal constituted by or under any enactment or by virtue of Her Majesty's prerogative;

(b) any action in respect of which the person aggrieved has or had a remedy by way of proceedings in any court of law:

Provided that the Commissioner may conduct an investigation notwithstanding that the person aggrieved has or had such a right or remedy if satisfied that in the particular circumstances it is not reasonable to expect him to have resort or have resorted to it.'

The ombudsmen have tended to interpret this restriction on their powers to investigate cases with a good degree of flexibility. Sir Cecil Clothier, a former Parliamentary

Commissioner, said that 'where process of law seems too cumbersome, slow and expensive for the objective gained, I exercise my discretion to investigate the complaint myself' (HC 148 (1980/1)).

If the complaint does pass the initial screening, then the complaint is investigated. The ombudsmen's method is inquisitorial rather than adversarial. This will normally involve a person from an ombudsman's office interviewing the aggrieved person to hear his or her account of the events alleged to constitute 'maladministration'. The civil servants, local government officers etc in the public body will also be interviewed.

9.5.5 The investigation

The Parliamentary Commissioner has quite extensive powers. He can compel people to give evidence under s 8 of the 1967 Act. Any obstruction of his investigation may be referred to the High Court for punishment as for contempt. An investigation cannot be stopped by a minister. Nor can the Parliamentary Commissioner be restricted by claims based on the Official Secrets Act, any statutory restriction or public interest immunity. However, Cabinet documents can only be seen if certified by the Prime Minister or the Cabinet Secretary.

If the investigation has failed to produce an informal negotiated settlement of the complainant's grievances, then staff in the ombudsman office produce a written report. A copy is sent to the aggrieved person, the public body which has been investigated, and the MP or any councillor who referred the complaint.

9.5.6   The report

The public body has an opportunity to respond to the report. Central government departments almost invariably assent to the Parliamentary Commissioner's findings and, where this has been recommended, they pay compensation to the victim of the injustice caused by maladministration. There are, however, very real problems with non-compliance with local ombudsman reports by some local authorities. Following the Local Government and Housing Act 1989, local councils which refuse to take satisfactory action following adverse reports from the CLA are required to publish a statement in a local newspaper at their own expense. This can cost more than the sum that the CLA had recommended as compensation! Thirteen such statements were published in 1992-93. The 1989 Act also created Monitoring Officers to follow up cases where redress has been refused. These reforms have resulted in some improvement, but non-compliance remains a problem for the Local Commissioners.

9.5.7   The response to the report

In the Citizens's Charter of 1991 (on which see para 9.7.2 below), the government stated:

'... if difficulties continue we will take the further step of introducing legislation to make the Local Ombudsman's recommendations legally enforceable, as those of the Northern Ireland Commissioner already are.'

| 9.5.8 | The ombudsman reacts |

In fact none of the ombudsmen are keen on the idea of court enforcement proceedings because they fear that the threat of the courts could harm the cooperative relationships they usually enjoy with public bodies. This view was supported by the JUSTICE/All Souls Review only with regard to the PCA: with regard to the CLA, were real problems of non-compliance exist, it was recommended that the disappointed complainant should be able to apply to the county court for relief.

The final stage in the 'ombudsman process' is for the ombudsman to react to the public body's response: as we have just noted, none of the ombudsmen have any powers to enforce their findings, whether it be that the public body give an apology, revoke a decision or pay compensation. The ombudsmen rely on persuasion and publicity to encourage compliance.

That the Parliamentary Commissioner is a servant of Parliament is emphasised by the fact that he makes quarterly and annual reports to Parliament. Sometimes special reports are made on investigations of particular importance, such as the one into the Barlow Clowes affair (discussed below). The Commissioner's close association with Parliament is further enhanced by the existence of a Select Committee on the Parliamentary Commissioner for Administration (consisting of backbench MPs) which scrutinises the work of the ombudsman, liaises with the office, and produces its own reports on the PCA and the HSC. The Health Service Commissioner submits reports to the Secretary of State for Health, who must then lay the report before Parliament.

9.6   The Barlow Clowes affair

Having sketched out what typically happens during the course of an ombudsman investigation, we can now go on to look in more detail at one particular investigation – that of the Barlow Clowes affair.

| 9.6.1 | The background |

Barlow Clowes Ltd was set up in 1973 by Elizabeth Barlow and Peter Clowes; it was a brokerage business selling relatively secure gilts-based investments. Put very simply, the company acted as middleman, investing customers' money on their behalf, in the hope of gaining a profit. Any profit would go to the investor who supplied the money, and the company would claim a fee for its efforts.

Following government deregulation of the money-markets, Barlow Clowes prospered and expanded in the 1980s. An important part of government policy was to open the markets to small investors; rather as the Conservatives had worked to extend home-ownership, so they encouraged ordinary people to take their chances in the City of London. Barlow Clowes specialised in services for such people; all its advertising in the popular press was aimed at small, inexperienced investors. Many investors dealt directly with Barlow Clowes, but many also used financial intermediaries with whom Barlow Clowes portfolios were a popular product for their small investors. The intermediaries often made no effort to spread the risk of individual investments, putting all of an individual's life savings into Barlow Clowes. The typical profile of a Barlow Clowes investor was of a Conservative voter of modest means and advancing age, who wished to invest so as to gain financial security in old age.

The investors 'knew' their savings would be safe. All of Barlow Clowes' brochures and letterheads were stamped with the words 'licensed by the DTI' (Department of Trade and Industry). This department had a system of inspection of financial institutions, and if the company passed muster, it was given a licence and required, by the DTI, to publicise this in its literature and on letterheads.

In June 1988 Barlow Clowes went into liquidation following a demand by the Securities and Investment Board (a regulatory body) that they be wound up. Barlow Clowes owed a total of £190 million to 18,900 clients and investors. Instead of investing money in safer government securities, it had invested £100 million in high risk ventures. Large funds had been removed from Britain and taken offshore to Jersey, where financial controls are weaker. Mr Clowes had been able to lead a luxurious life-style, which included the purchase of property and yachts. As early as December 1984, the Jersey funds were £3.65 million less than obligations. The DTI had failed to notice the existence of the Jersey partnership and the department's procedures were inadequate to reveal this capital shortfall. This happened despite warnings from the accountants, Touche Ross. Despite having licensed Barlow Clowes for 13 years, the DTI had no useful mechanism for monitoring its licensee.

Following nearly 200 requests from MPs, the Parliamentary Commissioner began what was to be the 'most complex, wide-ranging and onerous investigation' he had undertaken. It was contended that actions or omissions of the DTI in connection with its surveillance and licensing of Barlow Clowes under the Prevention of Fraud (Investments) Act 1958, had caused them to sustain financial loss.

9.6.2	The Report of the PCA	The report of Barlow Clowes by the Parliamentary Commissioner found five areas of maladministration by the DTI, including licensing errors and failure to monitor the company. The DTI was also responsible for an unnecessary delay in acting that resulted in further losses. The Parliamentary Commissioner strongly recommended compensation be paid by the DTI.
9.6.3	The government's response	The initial government response to the report in 1988 was defensive, reminding the Parliamentary Commissioner that all investments involved risks. It refused to accept the report unreservedly (see Observations by the Government of the PCA, HC 99 (1989-90)). The Secretary of State for Trade and Industry (Lord Young) refused to compensate investors.

The Parliamentary Commissioner was not the only source of pressure on the government. The media condemned the whole affair, calling it a 'scandal on a grand scale'. *The Times* wrote of 'amateurish arrangements' and the *Financial Times* of 'tunnel vision' at the DTI. A highly effective pressure group, the Barlow Clowes Investors' Group, campaigned with the media, putting considerable political pressure on the government. By the end of 1989, Nicholas Ridley, the new Secretary of State for Trade and Industry, agreed that compensation should be paid.

Ridley made a statement to the House of Commons on 19 December 1989. He said that 'in the exceptional circumstances of this case and out of respect for the office of Parliamentary Commissioner' he would make substantial ex gratia payments amounting to over £150 million.

Why the change of heart by the government? There was more than one reason. The media and the Investors' Group had embarrassed the government. Also, the Select Committee on the PCA voiced strong concern regarding the government's reaction to the scandal. The final factor in the government's change of heart was the publication of the PCA's thorough and condemnatory report. Even so, this was not to be a complete victory for the PCA. The government refused to accept legal liability for the lax regulation by the DTI: payments were ex gratia and only paid out of 'respect' for the Parliamentary Commissioner. Ordinary MPs were furious, but powerless. They described the DTI as 'feckless' and 'incompetent' and asked who in government would take responsibility for this 'negligence on a vast scale' and the subsequent cost to the taxpayer. No one took legal or political responsibility; but the investors were compensated.

The Parliamentary Commissioner won a victory of sorts. However powerful political pressure by the Investors' Group, the media, MPs and the Select Committee all played a vital role. The Barlow Clowes affair highlights some of the weak areas in the ombudsman system.

- The PCA's report need not be accepted by the government, although the Barlow Clowes affair shows that the government will often not dare ignore a report entirely.

- One of the criticisms made by the government of the Report was that the Commissioner had mistakenly questioned the merits of decisions by the DTI, rather than mere maladministration. There is no easy dividing line between policy and operation in public services, and too strict an interpretation of the Commissioner's remit could unduly restrict his discretion.

- An important point is that the jurisdiction of the PCA is so narrow that the other personnel involved in the scandal could not be investigated. The limitations set out in Schedule 2 to the Parliamentary Commissioner Act 1967 excludes the Bank of England, the Stock Exchange, FIMBRA, and the intermediaries, accountants and solicitors, all of who were involved and probably at fault. This meant that the public purse bore the burden of the compensation payments, whereas various private bodies (including the Stock Exchange) and the self-regulatory body, FIMBRA, were neither investigated nor did they contribute financially. This partial investigation by the PCA therefore left many questions unanswered and was unable to provide adequate recommendations to protect investors in the future. It is government policy to encourage the self-regulation of financial institutions, thereby leaving this important area of business without a truly independent investigator.

You may want to read the two-part article by Gregory and Drewry, 'Barlow Clowes and the Ombudsman' [1991] PL 192 and 408.

In many ways 'ombudsmen' are a growth area, with many private sector industries such as banking and insurance deciding to set up investigative complaints mechanisms for their customers. The public sector ombudsmen, by contrast, are looking less successful. As we have noted, the Parliamentary Commissioner is held in low esteem by many MPs and has a very low public profile. Things are little better for the local ombudsmen whose reports are often flouted by local authorities. All the ombudsmen have backlogs of cases waiting to be investigated, a product of inadequate resources. Some cynics argue that the ombudsmen were never really intended to work effectively, merely to give the illusion that grievances could be redressed. But if there is to be reform, what should it try to achieve?

9.7.1   Redressing individual grievances or improving administration?

One fundamental choice that may have to be made is between the ombudsman as 'fire-fighter' and 'fire-watcher' (to use Harlow's terminology). The former clears up the mess and tackles problems as they occur (responding to individual grievances), the latter looks to the future and attempts to prevent problems arising by improving administrative systems. Harlow has argued that the Parliamentary Commissioner is not equipped to deal with numerous small complaints; we have a Rolls Royce service which is put to best effect by giving a quality service, rather than dealing in quantity. Harlow therefore opposes direct access to the PCA. She chooses to emphasise the effect that the ombudsman can have on improving administration: 'a complaint is primarily a mechanism which draws attention to more general deficiencies'.

To boost his powers, Harlow suggests that the Parliamentary Commissioner should have power to investigate and intervene on his own initiative. In a report in 1978, the Select Committee on the PCA recommended that the Parliamentary Commissioner should be able to carry out a systematic investigation of a particular area of the administration, if a tally of individual complaints pointed to a general problem. This was firmly rejected by the government on the grounds that it was not necessary and would distract the Parliamentary Commissioner from investigating individual complaints (January 1979, Cmnd 7449).

For Harlow the desirable output of the Parliamentary Commissioner's office should be a limited number of high-quality reports which result from investigations initiated by himself or MPs. These reports would have a beneficial effect upon the administration, which could learn from past mistakes and thereby improve future performance. The bulk of citizens' complaints should be tackled by MPs, or at a local level, or by specialist agencies, such as tribunals. The Parliamentary Commissioner is all too aware of the need for this type of 'fire-watching'. Of some of his reports, he writes that 'these should be read by public servants. They should learn from others' similar errors.' He believes that there should be a publication of guidance for public servants, as there already is by the local ombudsmen. The Parliamentary Commissioner is concerned not just to redress individual grievances, but also to benefit all in similar positions. For instance, the report on the Disability Living Allowance fiasco resulted in compensation for individuals and altered procedures to prevent further injustice in the future. The Commissioner writes that 'individual redress, though vital, is only part of the story' for there is also an 'external audit of the quality of service being delivered'. Unlike Harlow, the PCA himself does not fear that the removal of the MP filter would weaken the PCA's fire-watching function.

The local ombudsmen were enabled by s 23 of the Local Government and Housing Act 1989 to produce a Code of Guidance called 'Devising a Complaints Procedure for Authorities'. Since this has been produced, many more complaints are dealt with internally by local government. The local ombudsmen now view a failure by a local authority to establish a proper internal complaints procedure as, in itself, amounting to maladministration.

Another possible reform is to raise the public profile of the ombudsmen. Some commentators argue that the Parliamentary Commissioner is too much an 'invisible ombudsman'. He does little or nothing to advertise himself. The wide publicity enjoyed as a result of the investigation into the Barlow Clowes affair was followed by a rise in the number of complaints received; for a while before 1990 complaints had been declining. Compare this with Austria. Their ombudsman (the Volksanwaltschaft) goes out on circuit, a sort of assize, and he advertises his intention of sitting in a particular location. He advertises on television, where he explains and reports on cases recently resolved. His office has a well-publicised direct telephone line for the public, and the complainant pays only a Schilling for the call, regardless of the real cost. The Irish ombudsman also travels around his country and the Commonwealth ombudsman of Australia advertised himself on milk-bottle tops by arrangement with the suppliers! In *When Citizens Complain*, Lewis and Birkinshaw argue that there is an urgent need for a different culture in the PCA: they believe that he is too much an adjunct to Parliament, too much of an insider. They call for the PCA to have greater visibility and accessibility.

If ombudsmen are to be primarily about redressing grievances, the question needs to be asked whether there are not better

9.7.2   Still more informal mechanisms?

ways for providing justice outside courts and tribunals. The publication of the government White Paper *The Citizen's Charter – Raising the Standard* (Cm 1599) in July 1991 appears to give encouragement to 'speedy and informal' grievance redressing. The Charter has four basic aims. Its proposals will 'work for better quality in every public service'; 'give people more choice'; 'make sure that everyone is told what kind of service they can expect to receive'; and 'make sure that people know what to do if something goes wrong'. In relation to procedures for complaints and redress against public bodies, the emphasis is on internal complaints machinery:

'When things go wrong, there must be a swift and simple way of putting them right ... it is usually best to resolve complaints on the spot. The more centralised and remote a complaints procedure is, the likelier it is to be slower, more expensive and less "user friendly".'

When internal complaints procedures fail, the Charter recognises that 'there must be an external route for taking things further'. A new grievance redressing mechanism was to be created. The White Paper had proposed 'lay adjudicators', who would be volunteers, use common sense and deal with 'small problems'. By the end of 1994, not a single lay adjudicator had been appointed. The Office of Public Service and Science, which has overall responsibility for the Citizen's Charter, says that there are no plans for any in the future, though it is possible that some may be appointed. It was felt that lay adjudicators would prove to be just another tier with which the complainant had to deal. Instead, the public information leaflets on various public services produced under the auspices of the Citizen's Charter often refer complainants to the relevant ombudsman if the complaint has not been addressed. Overall, the Citizen's Charter programme looks set to rely heavily upon the ombudsman system. Indeed, it is the policy of the Office of Public Service to attract complaints.

The Parliamentary Commissioner himself recognises his partnership with the Citizen's Charter programme. In his 1993 report he states that he communicates with the Office of Public Service and uses the 'Charter Targets' (performance levels to which the various public services set and aspire to achieve) to help him, taking account of failures to meet targets.

It seems that the Citizen's Charter is affecting the role of the ombudsmen in various ways. If in the future the Charter results in growing numbers of 'small problems' being referred to ombudsman, then the vision of the fire-watcher role for the Parliamentary Commissioner may be compromised.

The Ombudsman system is a method of redress of individual grievances which does not necessitate using the courts. The work of the ombudsmen can be used to improve the administration of services to the public.

The public sector ombudsmen are:

- The Parliamentary Commissioner (PCA Act 1967).

- The Health Service Commissioner (NHS Reorganisation Act 1973; HSC Act 1993).

- The Commission for Local Administration (Local Government Act 1974).

- The Prisons Ombudsman (Woolf Report 1992, set up 1994).

There are also ombudsmen for handling complaints in various service industries, some of whom are part of a statutory regulatory framework.

The Parliamentary Commissioner and local ombudsmen investigate injustice as a result of maladministration, and do not review the merits of a decision. All ombudsmen have public access except for the Parliamentary Commissioner, for which there is an MP filter.

The public sector ombudsmen, and especially the Parliamentary Commissioner, have a low public profile and a poor reputation amongst some MPs. The Ombudsmen receive very few complaints as a proportion of the population.

The ombudsman system should be reviewed in the political and social context of the UK. The Citizen's Charter has affected the work of the ombudsmen.

Summary of Chapter 9

Commissioners for Maladministration ('Ombudsmen')

Complaining to one of the ombudsmen differs from challenging a government decision or omission in court or before a tribunal: their techniques are inquisitorial and investigative rather than adjudicatory; complainants do not usually use a lawyer; and the outcome of an ombudsman investigation will merely be 'recommendations'.

The main ombudsmen operating in the public sector are:

Who are the ombudsmen?

- The Parliamentary Commissioner for Administration (dealing with complaints about central government departments and some other bodies);

- The Health Service Commissioner (complaints about the National Health Service);

- The Commission for Local Administration (complaints about local authorities).

    In addition there are numerous ombudsmen to deal with complaints in private sector industries such as banking and insurance. Some of these have been set up by statute (eg the Legal Services Ombudsmen); others are merely 'voluntary', set up by the industry itself.

The public sector ombudsmen investigate cases where it is alleged a person has suffered 'injustice' as a result of 'maladministration'. The latter term includes bias, neglect, inattention, delay, incompetence, ineptitude, perversity, turpitude and arbitrariness.

What type of complaints do they investigate?

The statutes setting up the public sector ombudsmen place restrictions on the types of situations in which investigations of alleged maladministration can be carried out. The ombudsmen should avoid questioning the 'merits' of a decision and the Health Service Commissioner cannot investigate complaints which involve the clinical judgment of doctors or nurses. Complaints have to be received within 12 months of the day the person aggrieved first had notice of the problem.

Scope of the investigations

The ombudsmen process

When a complaint is made to the ombudsmen it may go through the following stages.

- A person wishing to complain to the Parliamentary Commission must have the matter referred by an MP. This 'MP filter' is controversial and many people advocate its abolition. Complaints can be made directly to the other ombudsmen.

- Which ever ombudsman's office receives the complaint will have to determine whether it falls within its jurisdiction (as determined by the statute setting up that ombudsmen) and whether the complaint is about 'maladministration'. A large proportion of complaints are rejected at this stage.

- If the complaint is accepted then an attempt will normally be made to reach an informal settlement. Many complaints are resolved without there having to be any formal investigation or report.

- There may have to be an investigation. Officials from the relevant ombudsman's office will interview the decision-makers and the complainant and will often also look at background files.

- After completing the investigation, the ombudsman (or one of his staff) will write and publish a report. If injustice caused by maladministration is found, then recommendations will be made. These may include that the aggrieved person be compensated and that the administrative system be improved in specified ways.

- The body complained about decides whether or not to accept the recommendations.

Evaluating the ombudsmen

In order to evaluate the success of the ombudsmen, and whether reform is needed, you ought to consider what their primary rule is (or should be). Is their primary role that of redressing individual grievances? Or should it be improving the quality of administrative decision-making?

Chapter 10

Judicial Review Procedures: Leave and Standing

This chapter and the next one are about the High Court procedures governing applications for judicial review. In other law degree subjects, like contract and tort, little if any attention is paid to the nuts and bolts of litigation procedures, yet most public law courses and textbooks study them. Why? There are at least two reasons:

- First, judicial review procedures are controversial and topical; they have been the subject of major Law Commission reports twice in less than 15 years. Few other areas of law can boast this degree of interest and concern.

- Secondly, it is possible to learn as much about the values underlying administrative law by examining the procedures as by looking at the substantive 'grounds' of judicial review (illegality, irrationality and procedural impropriety). On one level procedure is, of course, about which forms to fill in when and what to do with them. But lurking not very far below this dull, dry surface are issues of constitutional importance. Court procedures determine *access to justice*. There is not much point in a legal system creating constraints within which public officials must work, or giving citizens legal rights, if these things cannot be enforced effectively through the courts.

If you were advising the government of a country adopting a new constitution (eg in Eastern Europe or South Africa) about the sorts of procedures that could be enacted to regulate access to the courts in relation to public law cases, you could have one or more of the following goals in mind:

- **User-friendly procedures**

  One objective may be to make access to justice as cheap, informal and as free from technicalities as possible. There could be generous time limits within which people could challenge government decisions. You might allow *any* person who considers an unlawful decision has been made to challenge it, even if that person's legal rights or interests were not closely affected. Ideally you will want litigation to be determined by the courts reasonably swiftly and avoid backlogs of cases and delays.

10.1 Why are court procedures important?

10.2 Procedures for whom?

- **Protecting public bodies**

  Another set of goals for a system of public law procedures may be to offer protection to government institutions from vexatious or unmeritorious legal challenges. You might fear that cranks and busybodies will exploit the rules for their own ends, or that pressure groups or companies may use litigation tactically in order to delay and obstruct the work of government. These sorts of goals may conflict with attempts to make the whole procedural system user-friendly to aggrieved citizens, and so compromises will have to be made.

- **Helping the courts deal with the caseload**

  Another objective may be to assist the court administrators and judges actually deal with the caseload. The procedural system should therefore enable the courts to determine cases swiftly – maybe even at the price of being less thorough than they could be.

  The judicial review procedures in England exhibit some characteristics of each of these three broad sets of goals. Following a report by the Law Commission in 1976, there was a streamlining of the process. The aim expressed at the time was to make access to the courts easier for citizens. In the years that followed there was certainly a rapid increase in the numbers of people applying for judicial review, from less than 400 in 1981 to over 2,000 in 1993. In spite of this apparent 'success', though, many commentators argue that the worthy goals of the new procedural rules – to improve access – have in fact been subverted by the courts. Professor Wade, for instance, has said that the 1978 reforms have been stood on their head: what was designed to benefit citizens has been used by the judges to give undue protection to public bodies and to help the courts deal with the caseload. As you read this chapter and the next, bear this in mind. Rules concerning who can apply for judicial review, when, and how, are not neutral regulations; they embody various, often conflicting, values.

10.3 What is 'review'?

Before going any further, something needs to be said about what is meant by saying that a decision or action is subject to judicial 'review'. (Chapters 12 onwards will examine the scope and grounds of judicial review in much more detail.) Applying for judicial review is not the same as *appealing* against a decision. On a review, the court is only interested in the question whether or not a public body's decision is legally valid, not whether it was a 'good' decision on the merits of the case. As an illustration, suppose parents express a preference as to which state school their child will attend, a right they have under s 6 of the Education Act 1980. The local authority proposes to allocate the child to another school. The parents appeal to the special statutory tribunal set up by the Act, but it agrees with the local authority. If the parents apply for judicial review of the local authority and/or the tribunal, the judge may well come to the conclusion that their decisions were very harsh and that, had he been a member of the tribunal, he would have allowed the child to go to the parents' chosen school. However, this will not be legally relevant to the judicial review. The parents will have to show, for example, that the authority/tribunal failed to follow proper procedures (eg they denied the parents the right to make representations) or that they took into account something legally irrelevant (eg the fact that the parents belonged to an unpleasant political party). The only time the court will come close to looking at the substance of the decision is if the parents allege that the decision is unreasonable in the *Wednesbury* sense, ie so outrageous in its defiance of logic or accepted moral standards that no reasonable person could have made it. This ground rarely succeeds.

Shortly we will zoom in on several particular aspects of the judicial review procedure, but first it will be useful to stand back and sketch out the whole procedure from beginning to end. The procedural rules of courts perform a very practical and important task for barristers and solicitors: they specify the steps which must be followed in order to get from (a) a client sitting in an office with problems to (b) having his or her case argued in front of a judge.

10.4   Overview of the procedural nuts and bolts

The procedural rules of the High Court are set out in a statutory instrument made under powers conferred by the Supreme Court Act 1981 on a committee of judges and representatives of the Law Society and Bar Council – so much for the separation of powers! The Rules of the Supreme Court (RSC) are published annually with helpful commentaries in two volumes called the *Supreme Court Practice* but known colloquially as The White Book (for obvious reasons). The RSC are divided into over a hundred 'orders' which deal with various aspects of litigation in the different divisions of the High Court and the Court of Appeal. The procedural rules for applications for judicial review are mostly in Order 53. This in turn is broken down into a number of rules.

10.4.1   Rules of Court

To start an application for judicial review of a decision of a public body an applicant must fill in a form known as Form 86A. (You can find a copy of this form at the end of this

10.4.2   Filling in Form 86A

chapter; it would be helpful to tear it out and have it in front of you.) Most Form 86As are in fact completed by barristers as a considerable degree of specialist legal expertise is needed to avoid the many pitfalls that exist. The form needs to set out the facts of the applicant's case and his/her legal submissions. An affidavit (ie a formal written statement) must also be sworn by the applicant verifying that the facts in the Form 86A are true.

These documents are then sent to the High Court with a fee of £10. Order 53 r 4 requires that all of this to be done 'promptly and in any event within three months' of the decision or action complained about'. This is not long, especially considering that an applicant has to realise that his/her problem is a legal one, find a solicitor who recognises that judicial review is appropriate and possibly apply for legal aid to fund the litigation. An application may fail on the ground that the applicant failed to make it 'promptly' even within the three-month period: see *R v Swale Borough Council ex p Royal Society for the Protection of Birds* (1990).

| 10.4.3 | Obtaining leave |

Normally in litigation, once a person submits pleadings to the court and pays a fee, these can be served on the defendant and litigation begins. Not so in judicial review. Section 31(3) of the Supreme Court Act stipulates that all applications must first be vetted by a judge in what is called the 'leave stage' before they can be served on the government department or other public body. Only if the judge is satisfied that the applicant has a proper case will permission be given for the case to proceed any further. Some people think that this preliminary vetting by a judge is a constitutional monstrosity; we will look at in more detail below.

The leave stage also gives the applicant an opportunity to ask for an interim injunction to 'hold the ring' and preserve the status quo until the full hearing is over. For example, an applicant challenging the decision of the Home Office to deport her will ask for an order preventing the deportation taking place until the judicial review is finally determined (which will take at least several months).

| 10.4.4 | The respondent's reply |

Assuming leave is granted, the respondent government body has 56 days to put in a formal written reply to the Form 86A disputing any facts and answering the applicant's legal submissions.

| 10.4.5 | The full hearing |

After this, the application is set down for the full hearing (and the applicant must pay another £60 in court fees). There is a considerable backlog of cases waiting to be heard and so it will not be unusual for a person to have to wait 18 months. During the wait, negotiations often take place between the parties and many applications are settled out of court. The full hearing is in open court before a single judge or sometimes a Divisional Court consisting of a Lord Justice and a puisne judge. Counsel for the applicant makes submissions (based on the grounds set out in the Form 86A) and counsel for the public body then responds. It is highly unusual for any witnesses to be called to give evidence or to be cross-examined. Judgment is then given.

Even if the applicant's barrister wins all the legal arguments at the hearing, there is no guarantee that the decision will be set aside or the public body's actions declared unlawful. All remedies are discretionary and may be withheld by the court for a number of reasons, such as that the remedy would serve no useful purpose, or the applicant delayed making the application and to grant relief would be detrimental to good administration or would prejudice the rights of third parties (see s 31(6) Supreme Court Act).

10.4.6   Remedies are discretionary

Assuming a remedy is granted, the only practical effect will often be that the public body is required to consider its decision again, this time steering clear of the procedural impropriety etc which invalidated it in the first instance. The actual outcome may well be the same, eg the licence to trade is still refused. This can be a shock and disappointment for an applicant who thought she had 'won' her case. Where the judgment is against a central government department, the government may decide to introduce legislation to overturn or modify the general effect of the judgment (and this is perfectly proper given the principle of Parliamentary sovereignty).

10.4.7   After the case

Having taken this overview of the ord 53 judicial review procedure we can now swoop down and look in more detail at several aspects of it. In the rest of this chapter we will look at the following.

- How Form 86A can be used as a checklist when answering problem questions.

- The leave stage.

- The rule that only people with 'sufficient interest' in a decision can seek judicial review of it.

If in your examination you will have to tackle a problem question on judicial review, Form 86A can act as a good checklist for the things you will need to consider and advise on. It is a good idea to work systematically through the form, imagining that you have to complete it. You will not necessarily want to present your answer in this order, but it will help you make sure you don't overlook any major issues.

10.5   **Form 86A as a framework for advising**

- **Who is the applicant going to be?**

  The first part of the form asks for the applicant's name. This may be straightforward but, especially if a pressure group is involved, there may be a problem with standing. The Supreme Court Act and Order 53 stipulate that only an applicant with 'sufficient interest in the matter to which the application relates' can use the judicial review procedure. (This is discussed in more detail below.)

- **Identify all the decisions/actions to be challenged**

  There may be several decisions, each capable of being challenged on different grounds of judicial review. Also, only certain sorts of decisions are subject to judicial review; this is a very complex area of law considered in Chapter 11.

- **Relief sought**

  Give some thought to the order you will want the court to make at the conclusion of the full hearing if your client is successful. The options are:

  (a) a declaration stating what the law is and how it applies to the facts of the case;

  (b) certiorari, an order quashing a decision and remitting it back to the decision-maker to reconsider it;

  (c) a mandatory injunction (or order of mandamus) requiring the respondent to do something, particularly to carry out a statutory duty imposed on it; and/or

  (d) a prohibitory injunction (or order of prohibition) preventing action being taken.

  Damages may also be claimed on the Form 86A but an applicant will only be awarded these if it can be shown that the public body committed a recognised tort such as negligence or trespass. English law gives no right to damages for administrative action which is unlawful only in the sense that it contravenes one of the grounds of judicial review (illegality, procedural impropriety or irrationality).

- **Grounds on which relief is sought (including an outline of any propositions of law, supported by authorities)**

  In many ways this is the most important part of the form. It differs from pleadings in civil litigation (eg contract and tort disputes) because it requires the applicant to put his 'cards on the table' – state what his legal submissions are – from the very outset. (Pleadings in civil cases are confined to statements of the material facts and it is only quite close to the trial that the parties must disclose their legal arguments.) This part of the form will therefore contain propositions of law – often under the headings of illegality, procedural impropriety and irrationality – plus cases/legislation as authority for them. There is not much space on the form and in practice the grounds will often be set out on several pages attached to it.

If you look at the top of Form 86A, you will notice that everything takes place in the Queen's Bench Division (QBD) of the High Court. There is no specialist Administrative Law Division (in contrast, for example, to the Family Division). Some people have argued that there ought to be, but on the whole there is acceptance of the Diceyan principle that 'every man, what ever be his rank or condition, is subject to the ordinary law of the realm and amenable to the jurisdiction of the ordinary tribunals'.

10.6   Which court?

There is, however, something in the QBD called the Crown Office which deals with the administration of judicial review applications. And only certain High Court judges are let loose on judicial review cases; there are currently 18 'nominated' judges chosen by the Lord Chief Justice. Although they may only spend a few weeks a year specialising in public law (the rest of the time they do other QBD work and go on circuit round the country hearing murder trials and other serious crimes) they do develop some expertise.

Judicial review is entirely London-based. Even if a resident of Newcastle is challenging the validity of a decision of that city council, all the legal proceedings will have to take place in the High Court in the Strand.

Notice, also, the rather odd title given to the cases: *R v [Government Department etc] ex p [Citizen etc]*. As with criminal prosecutions, applications for judicial review are nominally brought by the Crown ('R'), in this context on behalf of (*ex p –* ie, *ex parte*) the aggrieved citizen. This emphasises the fact that there is a public interest in the case; it is not purely a private dispute between the applicant and the respondent public body.

Those, then, are the main features of Form 86A. The form's first main function is that it initiates the leave stage and so we now turn to look at this process. (If leave is granted, the Form 86A will then be used as the basis for counsel's legal submissions at the full hearing.)

Form 86A is the 'notice of application for leave to apply for judicial review'. The requirement that a citizen must first ask the permission of a judge before he is allowed to commence a judicial review challenge to a government body is imposed by

10.7   The leave stage

s 31(3) of the Supreme Court Act and ord 53 r 3. It is deeply controversial; some people (including Professor Sir William Wade) think that it is wrong that if you want to challenge the decision of a public body you have to get the permission of a High Court judge before you can start legal proceedings. About half of all the 2000 or so applications for leave are refused every year.

10.7.1 How are leave applications dealt with?	Order 53 r 3(3) gives the applicant a choice as to how to apply for leave. It can be done entirely on paper, in which case the judge looks only at the Form 86A and the applicant's affidavit (often at home or at weekends). Alternatively, an oral application can be made in open court when counsel for the applicant will be given up to 20 minutes to address the judge and persuade him to grant leave. Two important characteristics of the leave stage are that (a) the judge normally hears only the applicant's account of events and the law, not the respondent's; and (b) the process is usually very summary, ie decisions are made on a quick perusal of the documents or after hearing brief submissions from counsel. It is possible that these features result in 'good' applications being turned away.
10.7.2 Why are leave applications refused?	There is no comprehensive official list of the criteria which the judge should apply when considering whether to grant or refuse leave. Recent research has shown that, partly as a result of this, there is an astonishingly wide variation in the proportion of cases granted leave by different judges: some judges refuse 75% whereas other refuse less than 25%. (For a full analysis see Sunkin, Bridges and Mészáros, *Judicial Review in Perspective* (1993).) This is clearly a cause for concern.

Section 31 of the Supreme Court Act and ord 53 state that leave should be refused on two grounds:

- The application has not been made 'promptly and in any event within three months'. The judge has a discretion, however, to grant leave even if the time limit has been exceeded. This often happens, leaving the parties to argue about issues to do with delay at the full hearing.

- The applicant does not have standing, ie 'a sufficient interest in the matter to which the application relates' (considered in more detail below). Again, however, this is rarely a reason for refusing leave and the House of Lords has said that the issue should normally be left to be argued out at the full hearing: see *R v Inland Revenue Commissioners ex p National Federation of the Self-Employed and Small Businesses Ltd* (1982).

The Supreme Court Act and ord 53 therefore gives little guidance. Research by Le Sueur and Sunkin discovered that the following were some of the most frequently given reasons for refusing leave (see [1992] PL 102, 120).

- The application was in some way 'unarguable'. A few applications for leave are made by cranks and this is what Lord Scarman had in mind when, in the *National Federation* case, he said that the leave stage 'enables the court to prevent abuse by busybodies, cranks and other mischief makers. I do not see any further purpose served by the requirement for leave.' At other times, however, arguability means something quite different and the judges seem to require to be satisfied that the case is likely to be won by the applicant if it proceeds to the full hearing. Given that the application is made either in writing or at most with 20-minute oral submissions and the respondent is not present at this stage, it is often very difficult to predict this, especially if a case involves complex facts or law as many do. Another problem with the arguability criteria is that some judges take it to mean that leave should be refused if there is a first instance authority against the applicant; but this is probably too harsh a test. If applied too widely it would prevent the development of the grounds of judicial review.

- Judicial review is not the correct procedure, eg because the applicant should have appealed to a tribunal instead. Judicial review is regarded as a remedy of last resort and applicants are expected to have exhausted all other appeal mechanisms etc before resorting to ord 53 proceedings. Leave is also refused on the ground that the decision challenged is not one of 'public law'; this is considered in more detail in the next chapter.

- The application is made too soon, eg during rather than at the end of the deliberations by a statutory disciplinary tribunal. Generally a person is expected to wait for a final decision to be made and not jump in too soon with a judicial review challenge. In reality, the fact that applications are premature is as frequent a reason for refusing leave as the fact that they were not made promptly (though only the latter problem is expressly addressed by s 31 and ord 53).

- A final important type of reason sometimes given for refusing leave is that it would not be in the public interest to do so. The judges have earmarked certain types of decision as ones which should not routinely be subject to judicial review on the grounds that this would be detrimental to good administration. These include: (a) the refusal of entry to the UK by the immigration authorities on the grounds that they do not believe the person is a genuine visitor (*R v Secretary of State for the Home Department ex p Swati* (1986)); and (b) decisions of local authorities not to house people who claim to be homeless (*Puhlhofer v Hillingdon Borough Council* (1986)). Only if cases in these categories raise 'exceptional' issues of 'principle' will leave be granted. These cases are open to criticism for several reasons, for example, that it is wrong that some people (such as the homeless) are subject to more a stringent test at the leave stage than others.

If the leave application is made on paper and is refused, the applicant is allowed a second bite of the cherry and can make an oral application in open court. Every year a handful of cases go one step further, with the applicant taking the leave application to the Court of Appeal, as happened in the important Datafin case discussed in the next chapter.

10.7.3 **What is the leave stage for?**	The leave stage is often described as a 'filter' process and we have used the term 'preliminary vetting'. But this does not really explain why the procedure exists. The leave stage probably performs three main functions (which can sometimes conflict):

- The leave requirement protects government bodies from having to respond to unmeritorious judicial reviews. This seemed to be the view of Lord Diplock in *National Federation* where he said its purpose was 'to remove the uncertainty in which public officers and authorities might be left as to whether they could safely proceed with administrative action while proceedings for judicial review of it were actually pending even though misconceived.' In other words, public authorities can know within four months or so of any decision or action that there will be no challenge and they do not have to take any steps themselves to deal with vexatious and unmeritorious challenges.

- The leave stage helps the courts cope with the ever-growing judicial review caseload. Lord Donaldson MR in *R v Monopolies and Mergers Commission ex p Guinness plc* (1990) said that the 'public interest normally dictates that if the judicial review jurisdiction is to be exercised, it could be exercised very speedily and, given the constraints imposed by limited judicial resources, this necessarily involves limiting the number of cases in which leave to apply should be given'. As we have already noted, the leave stage effectively disposes of half the judicial review caseload without the need for full hearings. Some writers have suggested that it is constitutionally inappropriate for judges to be involved in allocating resources in this way. It is probably also mistaken to think that, in the absence of a leave stage, all judicial review cases would go as far as a full hearing: as in other areas of law it is highly likely that many, perhaps most, would be settled by out-of-court negotiations between the parties long before this time.

- It has also been suggested that applying for leave is beneficial to applicants because it 'provides a remarkably quick, cheap and easy method of obtaining the view of an experienced High Court judge as to whether the application has any merit' (Lord Woolf). In other words, the leave hurdle should not be viewed as an unpleasant hurdle over which applicants have to jump, but as a service for aggrieved citizens. Leave applications are normally determined within a few weeks (or much sooner if the matter is urgent) and at £10 (plus lawyers' fees) are good value. If leave is refused, at least everyone knows where they stand quite soon; if granted, this is likely to improve the applicant's bargaining position. Indeed, it is arguable that the leave stage is a victim of its own success and by its cheapness and speed actually encourages people to 'have a go' whereas, if they knew they would have to pay the other side's costs if they lost (the normal position in litigation) they would not do so.

10.7.4 Does the leave stage need to be reformed or abolished?

Some people have argued that the leave requirement ought to be abolished because it is wrong, as a matter of principle, that a procedural hurdle exists which makes it more difficult for a citizen to obtain justice against government bodies than against fellow citizens. This is the view of Professor Wade and also of the JUSTICE/All Souls Committee in 1988. They have suggested that vexatious and unmeritorious judicial reviews should be dealt with in the same way as tort and contract cases, where the defendant must take the initiative and go to court to ask for the action to be 'struck out' on the ground that it discloses no cause of action. The usual response to this proposal is that it is unrealistic: the government is unlikely to agree to any amendment of s 31 of the Supreme Court Act which would make departments more open to challenge. Also, it may damage the interests of applicants as a whole: remember that almost half of leave applications are refused. If all or most of these cases were allowed to proceed to a full hearing the backlog and delays might be even greater than they are now. For applicants with good cases this might mean 'justice delayed is justice denied'.

In October 1994 the Law Commission published a report called *Administrative Law: Judicial Review and Statutory Appeals* (Law Com No 226/HC 669). It concludes that it is 'essential to filter out hopeless applications for judicial review by a requirement such as leave'. The report recommends that the leave stage be re-named the 'preliminary consideration'. This would not merely be a cosmetic change, it argues, but would remove the perception that a citizen seeking judicial review is at a considerable disadvantage compared with a person suing in contract or tort. The report also recommends that most preliminary considerations take place with the judge looking only at the Form 86A rather than having a hearing in open court.

Another change seen as desirable was a reformulation of the 'test' applied by the judges: rather than asking whether there was an arguable case, the threshold should be that 'unless the application discloses a serious issue which ought to be determined it ought not be allowed to proceed to a substantive hearing'.

The Law Commission also recommends that Form 86A be modified in order to give the judge more information at the 'preliminary consideration' (as the leave stage would be called). There should be a box on the form for the applicant to explain whether any alternative remedies was available, whether it has been pursued and the stage it has reached. (Remember that judicial review is seen by the courts as a remedy of last resort and applicants are expected to have used any formal appeal mechanisms that exist before using ord 53 proceedings.) The judges should also have the power to make a 'request for information' at the preliminary consideration by sending a form to the respondent public body, asking whether the applicant had been given an opportunity to make representations before the public body made its decision and details of any internal reviews of the decision challenged by the applicant.

Some of these recommendations can only be implemented by amending s 31 of the Supreme Court Act 1981 as they are too far-reaching to be put into effect merely by modifying ord 53. Nor is it clear that the government will accept all these recommendations, though, given their relatively uncontroversial nature, the best guess is that it will. It may well be several years, however, before they are put into practice.

10.8 Who can apply for judicial review?

So far in this chapter we have looked at Form 86A and how this initiates an application for leave. Order 53 and s 31(3) of the Supreme Court Act 1981 stipulate that an applicant must have 'standing' (also known as *locus standi* or 'sufficient interest'). In the words of the statute:

> 'No application for judicial review shall be made unless the leave of the High Court has been obtained in accordance with the rules of court; and the court shall not grant leave to make such an application unless it considers that the applicant has a sufficient interest in the matter to which the application relates.'

Following the *National Federation* case, it is however more usual for the question of standing to be postponed until the full hearing if the applicant is thought in other respects to have good grounds for obtaining judicial review. This is because it is a mixed question of fact and law and normally cannot be determined during the summary leave procedure.

Let us consider an example. A company wants to open a sex shop (retail premises selling pornographic material) and under English law must first obtain a licence from a local authority under s 2 of the Local Government (Miscellaneous Provisions) Act 1982. Suppose a licence is granted subject to the condition that the shop may only open for two hours a day between 3 pm and 5 pm. Which of the following do you think ought to be permitted to apply for judicial review (assuming they have good grounds)?

- Should the company be able to challenge the imposition of conditions (eg on the grounds that they are Wednesbury unreasonable)? Where an administrative decision has a very direct, adverse effect on a person, it seems fairly clear that such a person (including a company) should have standing to make an application.

- What about the owner of the premises next door to the proposed sex shop who might claim, for example, that she was not properly consulted?

- The local residents' amenity group?

- A national pressure group with no local ties which campaigns against the sale of pornography?

  Some people think that all of these should be entitled to commence applications for judicial review; others would want to limit it to the first two or three cases.

In every branch of law there are rules delimiting the people who may bring legal action against another. (In contract there is the privity rule and in negligence a variety of mechanisms including the rule that only certain people are owed a duty of

10.8.1   Why is a requirement of 'standing' necessary?

care.) There has therefore to be some rule in relation to judicial review, even if it is a very wide one that any person can seek judicial review of any allegedly unlawful decision. The advocates of strict rules of standing put forward several arguments, including the following:

- It is a way of rationing judicial review; a requirement of *locus standi* helps keep some cases off the court list so helping other applicants and saving judge and court time. (But, as we have already noted, lack of standing is rarely a ground for refusing leave and is a matter normally dealt with at the full hearing.)

- Standing rules prevent the purely tactical use of judicial review. Pressure groups and others in no 'real' sense affected by a decision can be barred from using the proceedings just to delay and obstruct the public body's proposed action.

- It is undesirable to have individuals or groups setting themselves up as 'private Attorneys General' and using the courts to enforce what they see as the public interest.

- In the *Rose Theatre* case (considered below), Schiemann J said that the purpose of standing rules was to reduce uncertainty and chaos and the need to discourage over-cautious decision-making by public bodies.

- An alternative to making the standing rules more liberal would be to create a public official with responsibility for initiating judicial review whenever it was in the public interest and no other person seemed likely to do so. Several people have made proposals along these lines, including Lord Woolf's suggestion for a Director of Civil Proceedings.

People who prefer a more open system of access to the courts make these points:

- A legal system is discredited and the rule of law weakened if an allegedly unlawful decision is immune from challenge in the courts just because there is none with a 'sufficient interest' in the matter (as in the *Rose Theatre* case).

- There are situations where an individual does have standing because his interests are directly affected, but he is reluctant to risk the expense and stress of commencing legal proceedings. It would make sense in such cases to permit a pressure group to seek judicial review on his behalf. An example of this is where a nuclear power station is granted a licence by the government (allegedly unlawfully) to carry out tests which put people living nearby at risk; it is argued that a body such as Greenpeace ought to be able act for them.

- Another situation where pressure groups should be given standing is where many individuals are affected by an allegedly unlawful decision, but each only to a trivial extent and so may not want to bother. For example, the Department of Social Security may be underpaying 100,000 people welfare benefit by 5p a week. Here it might be appropriate to allow a pressure group such as the Child Poverty Action Group to seek judicial review.

The 'sufficient interest' formula used in s 31(3) of the Supreme Court Act gives a considerable degree of discretion to the judges. Judges, like the academic writers, disagree over the relative merits of 'open' or 'closed' systems of access to judicial review. This was reflected in the House of Lords's decision in the *National Federation* case, where a well-respected and influential pressure group set up to promote the interests of small businesses sought judicial review of a decision of the Inland Revenue to grant an 'amnesty' to casual print workers in the newspaper industry who for many years had used false names (such as Mickey Mouse) to avoid paying income tax. As a quid pro quo for the newspaper owners and workers regularising the position, the Inland Revenue agreed not to demand back taxes from the employees. The National Federation thought that this was unfair (their members were always being hounded by the tax authorities) and unlawful. The majority of the House of Lords held that the National Federation did not have sufficient interest to seek judicial review of the tax affairs of other citizens. Lord Diplock dissented on the point:

> 'It would in my view be a grave lacuna in our system of public law if a pressure group, like the Federation, or even a single public-spirited taxpayer were prevented by outdated technical rules of *locus standi* from bringing the matter to the attention of the court to vindicate the rule of law and get the unlawful conduct stopped.'

The *National Federation* case did little to clarify this area of law and, as we have noted, stated that questions of standing should normally be dealt with at the full hearing rather than the leave stage. The continuing uncertainty can be illustrated by two recent first instance decisions:

- *R v Secretary of State for the Environment ex p Rose Theatre Trust Company Ltd* (1990) (by Schiemann J).

10.8.2   The meaning of 'sufficient interest'

- *R v Secretary of State for the Environment ex p Greenpeace Ltd (No 2) (1994)* (by Otton J).

10.8.3   *Rose Theatre*: a narrow approach

In *Rose Theatre* a group of actors and archaeologists formed a company to act as a pressure group to campaign for the preservation of the foundations of the Rose Theatre, where some of Shakespeare's plays had been first performed. These had been unearthed during the building of a new office block in London. The group asked the Secretary of State to intervene and declare the site an ancient monument under powers given to him by the Ancient Monuments and Archeological Areas Act 1979. When he refused, the group sought judicial review. Leave was granted and the issue of standing was left to the full hearing before Schiemann J. Counsel for the Secretary of State submitted that even if the group were correct in their argument that the minister had misinterpreted his duties under the Act, nevertheless the company set up by the campaigners should not be granted judicial review.

Schiemann J held that the Secretary of State had not acted unlawfully in refusing to declare the theatre remains an ancient monument. He *then* went on to consider the question of standing. (Should this not have been dealt with first?) The company, he held, did not have sufficient interest to allow it to be an applicant. Applying *dicta* from the majority speeches in the *National Federation* case, he said that a group of people, none of whom had standing individually, could not confer standing on themselves by forming a company. Nor could the fact the minister had agreed to hear and respond to representations from the group give them standing. Schiemann J believed that there were good reasons for having standing rules: they reduced uncertainty and chaos and discouraged over-cautious decision making by public bodies. (The Law Commission later suggested in a Consultation Paper that this was not a very good reason and that such problems were adequately dealt with by the requirement that the applications be made promptly and in any event within three months). Schiemann J conceded that his decision meant that *nobody* had sufficient interest to challenge decisions under the Ancient Monuments Act, but this did not worry him: it was an inevitable consequence of the Supreme Court Act's requirement that applicants have 'sufficient interest'. The decision was much criticised and Schiemann J took the very unusual step of defending his decision by writing an academic article: see [1990] PL 342.

10.8.4   *Greenpeace (No 2)*: a broader approach

In 1993 Greenpeace applied for judicial review of a decision of the Inspectorate of Pollution to vary British Nuclear Fuel plc's licence so allowing the testing of a new nuclear reprocessing plant (THORP) at Sellafield in the north of England. As in the

Rose Theatre case, leave was granted but the question of standing was raised at the full hearing in front of Otton J.

It was held that the Inspectorate had not misinterpreted its powers to vary licences under the Radioactive Substances Act 1960 and so Greenpeace lost. Otton J did, however, hold that Greenpeace had standing – an important victory of principle for the pressure group. Otton J made the following points.

(i) Greenpeace UK had over 400,000 supporters in the UK and about 2,500 were in the Cumbria region where THORP was situated. It would be to ignore the blindingly obvious for the court to disregard the fact that those people were inevitably concerned about, and had a genuine perception that there was a danger to, their health and safety from any additional discharge of radioactive waste even from testing. There was no doubt that the issues raised in the application were serious and worthy of determination by the court.

(ii) If standing were denied to Greenpeace, those it represented might not have an effective way of bringing the issues before the court. There would have to be an application either by an individual employee of BNFL or a near neighbour. In that case it was unlikely that either would be able to command the expertise which was at the general disposal of Greenpeace. Consequently a less well-informed challenge might be mounted which would stretch unnecessarily the resources of the court and which would not afford the court the assistance it required in order to do justice between the parties. Further, if the unsuccessful applicant had the benefit of legal aid it might leave the Inspectorate of Pollution and BNFL without an effective remedy in costs. Greenpeace had experience in environmental matters, it had access to experts in relevant realms of science, technology and law and was able to mount a carefully selected, focused, relevant and well-argued challenge.

(iii) The nature of the relief sought also had to be taken into account. In *National Federation* the House of Lords expressed the view that if *mandamus* were sought that would be a reason to decline jurisdiction. Here the main remedy was certiorari, (an order merely quashing the minister's decision) which Otton J thought was less stringent than *mandamus* (and order requiring a public actively to do something).

(iv) Otton J warned that it must not be assumed that Greenpeace (or any other interest group) would automatically be afforded standing in any subsequent application for judicial review in whatever field it (and its members) may have an interest. This would have to be considered on a case by case basis at the leave stage and, if the threshold was crossed, again at the substantive hearing as a matter of discretion.

(v) The decision of Schiemann J in *Rose Theatre* would not be followed. Suffice to say that the circumstances were different, the interest group had been formed for the exclusive purpose of saving the Rose Theatre site and no individual member could show any personal interest in the outcome. In any event, Schiemann J's decision on the locus standi point (as in the present case) was not central to his decision, Otton J held.

The *Greenpeace* case shows how allowing pressure groups to commence judicial review proceedings may be of help to both the judges (who can be assisted by their technical and legal expertise) and, to some extent, also to respondents (who, if they win, will at least be able to recover their costs from a pressure group whereas they could not from a legally-aided individual). A broader approach to standing is therefore not necessarily disadvantageous to government.

10.8.5	Trends in local standing

So far we have noted that the formula 'sufficient interest in the matter to which the application relates' used in s 31(3) of the Supreme Court Act 1981 gives a judge a considerable degree of discretion. Some have chosen to interpret this narrowly (eg Schiemann J in *Rose Theatre*); others more broadly (eg Otton J in *Greenpeace (No 2)*). What, then, are the general trends? Broadly speaking, it can be said that the courts have *tended* recently to take an increasingly liberal approach to standing. This can be illustrated by two recent cases.

In *R v Secretary of State of Foreign and Commonwealth Affairs ex p Rees-Mogg* (1994), Lord Rees Mogg, a former editor of *The Times*, was held to have sufficient interest to challenge the decision to ratify the Maastricht Treaty on the basis of his 'sincere concerns for constitutional issues'.

Secondly, in *R v Secretary of State for Foreign and Commonwealth Affairs ex p World Development Movement Ltd* (1994) a pressure group was held to have standing to challenge the Foreign Secretary's decision, taken contrary to advice by senior civil servants, to make a grant to the government of Malaysia to build a hydro-electric power station on the Pergau River. The court held that the project was economically unsound and so the grant was *ultra vires* s 1(1) of the Overseas Development and Co-operation Act 1980. The WDM is a well-respected pressure group with over 7,000 members and has official consultative status with United Nations bodies. However, it was accepted that none of its individual members had any direct personal interest in the grant made under the 1980 Act (and so were is a rather different position to the Greenpeace members, some of whom were directly affected by THORP because they lived in cumbria) and that its motivation was altruistic (like the *Rose Theatre* group). Nevertheless, the court held that the WDM did have standing. In coming to its decision, the court placed weight on a number of factors:

- the importance of vindicating the rule of law;
- the likely absence of any other responsible challenger;
- the nature of the breach of duty against which relief was sought; and
- the prominent role of the WDM in giving advice, guidance and assistance with regard to aid.

The court in these two cases did not say that *Rose Theatre* had been wrongly decided, but they clearly indicated that there is little judicial sympathy for Schiemann J's restrictive approach.

In its 1994 Report on Judicial Review (Law Com 226), the Law Commission considered what, if any, changes needed to be made to the current law on standing. The report noted that the 'fluid nature of the requirement of sufficiency means that it is uncertain what precisely is required' and also the trend towards liberalisation in cases like *Greenpeace (No 2)*. The Commission recommends a 'two track system' of standing be adopted. Applicants whose personal rights or expectations have been affected by a decision would be in the first track and they will have standing.

10.8.6   Law Commission recommendations

The second track would be for situations where the court 'considers that it is in the public interest for an applicant to make the application'. This would cover situations where individuals or groups seek judicial review in respect of matters which affect the public generally (eg cases like *R v Secretary of State for Social Security ex p Child Poverty Action Group* (1988) discussed below) and challenges by groups rather than specific individuals where a decision affects a particular individual (eg cases like *Royal College of Nursing v DHSS* (1981) considered below). The court would have a broad discretion to decide whether or not to grant standing in the 'second track' bearing in mind factors such as the importance of the legal issue raised.

If the government accepts these recommendations it may be necessary to amend s 31 of the Supreme Court Act 1981 before they can be put into effect. This may take several years.

10.8.7	Advising on issues of standing

The *National Federation, Rose Theatre* and *Greenpeace (No 2)* cases show how judges can differ in their approach to deciding whether or not a person has 'sufficient interest'. This makes it a tricky issue to advise on. If you have to tackle a problem question on standing it is worthwhile considering – perhaps even mentioning – some of the following points.

- Section 31(3) gives the court a great deal of discretion.

- Questions of standing will, despite words to the contrary in s 31(3), normally be dealt with at the full hearing rather than the leave stage.

- The issue of standing is one of mixed fact and law. The courts often arrive at their conclusions after very detailed analysis of the statutory framework in which the decision was taken: see, eg *Rose Theatre* and the House of Lords's decision in *R v Secretary of State for Employment ex p Equal Opportunities Commission* (1994).

- The question of standing goes to the jurisdiction of the court to hear the application. In other words, a respondent cannot just agree that an applicant has standing – it is always a question for the court (*R v Secretary of State ex p Child Poverty Action Group* (1988)). This may be legally correct because s 31(3) makes it a matter of jurisdiction. But why should a court turn away two parties who agree that there is a serious issue to be tried?

- It is sometimes suggested that the standing test will vary according to the type of remedy which the applicant is seeking, eg it will be less stringent if only a declaration is sought than if the applicant is asking for certiorari to quash or mandamus.

- In *National Federation* it was suggested that the degree of 'seriousness' of the alleged unlawful decision was relevant to the issue of standing, eg whether it was a one-off or recurring. (Can this be right in principle?).

- If a person has a financial interest in the decision, this will almost always give him standing. It is not, however, necessary for the applicant to show that he personally had any legal *right* greater than any other citizen. But if he had no right than there must be a least a legal rather than a purely moral duty on the public body before the courts can interfere by way of judicial review (see *R v Secretary of State for Defence ex p Sancto* (1993).)

- The position of taxpayers is not as straightforward as might be suggested by *National Federation*. Although it is true that as a general rule being a taxpayer gives no standing to challenge the way in which another taxpayer has been treated by the Inland Revenue or decisions about how tax is spent, this is not an invariable rule. In *R v HM Treasury ex p Smedley* (1985) a tax payer was held to have locus standi to challenge decision of the government to agree to pay a financial contribution to the EC. (This case is very difficult to explain satisfactorily.) Also, a tax payer has been held to have standing to challenge the Inland Revenue's method of assessing a rival's profit: *R v Attorney General ex p ICI* (1987). ICI's argument was not that it was being over-taxed but that Shell, Esso and BP were being under-taxed. The Inland Revenue contended that ICI had no standing but the court held ICI did and it won the case. Perhaps the case can be distinguished from *National Federation* on the basis that there were only four companies paying the special tax in question and so the profits of each were directly affected by decisions taken about others.

- In the context of local government, being a council tax payer gives a person locus standi to challenge decisions of a local authority because a 'fiduciary duty' is owed by a council to its council tax payers.

- The problems with pressure groups do not really arise where the group is directly representative of individuals each of who would have had standing, (as in *Royal College of Nursing v DHSS* (1981) where the RCN challenged a government circular about the lawful role of nurses in carrying out abortions. The difficult case is where there is an organisation (eg the National Federation of Small Business or the Rose Theatre Trust group) wanting to challenge a decision but no individual member has suffered damage or has an interest over and above the general public. In several cases the courts have said that an aggregate of individuals, each of whom does not have interest, cannot of itself have an interest.

Judicial Review Procedures: Leave and Standing

A good way to work out what needs to be said about a judicial review problem question is to imagine that you are filling in Form 86A (the form which is used to commence an application for leave). (see pp176-177).

- Who is the applicant? Has he/she/it got 'sufficient interest'?

- Identify all the decisions/actions/omissions to be challenged. Consider whether the decision is a 'public law' one (on which, see Chapter 11).

- Work out what the appropriate form of relief is (*certiorari*, prohibition, *mandamus*, injunction, declaration).

- State the grounds on which relief is sought 'including an outline of any propositions of law, supported by authorities'.

Supreme Court Act 1981 s 31(3) and ord 53 require applicants to obtain the leave of the court before a public body's decision can be reviewed. This is controversial. The Law Commission has recommended that this initial screening be called 'preliminary consideration' rather than 'leave'.

The purpose of the leave stage is not spelt out in the legislation. It can be said that it exists to:

- protect public bodies;

- assist the court cope with the increasing case load; and

- help applicants know whether or not they have a good case (which may make their negotiating position stronger).

Supreme Court Act 1981 s 31(3) and ord 53 stipulate that only a person 'with sufficient interest in the matter to which the application relates' can apply for judicial review. The issue is usually dealt with at the full hearing rather than the leave stage.

The formula 'sufficient interest' gives the judges a great deal of discretion. Some have interpreted the standing requirement to exclude pressure groups (see eg *Rose Theatre Trust Company*) whereas other courts have permitted pressure groups to bring challenges (see eg *Greenpeace (No 2)*). The trend is for the courts to be increasingly liberal in their approach to standing.

The Law Commission has recommended that the courts ought to be able to take into account whether it is in the public interest for an applicant to make an application for judicial review even though he is not directly affected.

In the High Court of Justice
Queens Bench Division
Crown Office List

Crown Office Ref

CO

In the matter of an application for Judicial Review

The Queen - v -

Ex parte

**Notice of application for leave to apply for Judicial Review
Order 53 rule 3(2)**

This form must be read together with Notes for Guidance obtainable from the
Crown Office

To the Master of the Crown Office, Royal Courts of Justice, Strand, London WC2A 2LL

The Applicant:
Name
Address

Description

Judgement, order,
decision or other
proceeding in
respect of which
relief is sought, and
the date thereof.

Relief sought:

(Grounds for the
relief should be
set out overleaf)

Signed   Dated

Name and address of the
applicant's solicitors, or,
of no solicitors acting, the
address for service of the
applicant.

Applicant's Ref.

Telephone No.

Fax No.

Grounds on which relief is sought

Include an outline of any propositions of law, supported by any authorities.

If there has been any delay, include the reasons here.

Grounds must be supported by an affidavit which verifies the facts relied on.
Where grounds have been settled by Counsel they must be signed by Counsel.

Chapter 11

Judicial Review Procedures: The Public/Private Divide

This chapter examines the problem which textbooks often refer to in rather abstract terms as the 'public/private divide'. In fact, this difficult area of law is, at heart, about very practical issues: the sorts of decisions which can be challenged in judicial review proceedings. Two propositions of law will be dealt with.

- If you're challenging a public law decision of a public body, you *have* to use the Order 53 procedure (the so-called exclusivity principle).

- You can *only* use Order 53 to challenge the validity of 'public law' decisions.

  There is sometimes a tendency to merge these two rules, and although they are interrelated, it really is much better to keep them separate.

In the previous chapter we described the RSC Order 53 procedure and noted that it was introduced in 1978 following a report by the Law Commission. Order 53 created a single, flexible, unified procedure by which an applicant could mix and match any remedies (*certiorari*, prohibition, *mandamus*, declarations, injunctions and even damages) to suit his case.

Prior to 1978 there were distinct procedures, eg different time limits and standing rules, for each of these remedies; it was a technical minefield. But practitioners had a choice as to what sort of remedy they could try to obtain for their clients (and therefore which procedure to use).

- First, they could opt for one of the public law remedies (called for various historical reasons 'prerogative orders'), ie *certiorari*, prohibition or *mandamus*.

- Alternatively, they could seek a declaration or injunction.

  If a solicitor opted for one of the prerogative orders it was necessary to obtain the leave of the court (just as in Order 53 today) and the time limits for challenge were quite short – three to six months depending on which particular remedy was sought. To get a declaration or injunction, however, the procedure was quite different. These remedies were obtained by ordinary writ action (as in contract and tort litigation). There was no requirement of leave and much longer time

11.1 Introduction

11.2 The exclusivity principle

11.2.1 The position before 1978

limits. Many of the leading administrative law cases were in fact actions for declarations or injunctions rather than applications for a prerogative order, eg *Ridge v Baldwin* (1964) and *Padfield v Minister of Agriculture, Fisheries and Food* (1968).

In its 1976 report, the Law Commission envisaged that lawyers would continue to have the option of using writ actions to get injunctions and declarations after the introduction of the new Order 53 procedure, even though these remedies would then be available under the new application for judicial review.

Paragraph 4 states:

'Public law issues concerning the legality of acts or omissions of persons or bodies do not arise only in applications to the Divisional Court for prerogative orders. They may be the direct subject of an ordinary action for a declaration or an injunction ... In the light of our consultation, we are clearly of the opinion that the new procedure [ord 53] we envisage ... should not be exclusive in the sense that it would become the only way by which issues relating to the acts or omissions of public bodies could come before the courts.'

The judges, however, thought otherwise.

11.2.2   *O'Reilly v Mackman*

In 1982, the House of Lords – without referring to the passage from the Law Commission's 1976 report – held that it was 'an abuse of the process of the court' for a person to seek a declaration by way of a writ action when he was challenging a public law decision of a public body. The person *had* to apply under Order 53. Lawyers would no longer have any option.

The facts were these. Following a riot in 1979 at Hull prison, a number of prisoners, including Mr O'Reilly, were subject to a disciplinary hearing in front of a prison Board of Visitors. Afterwards, O'Reilly claimed that the hearing had been unfair and in breach of the rules of natural justice because he had not been given a proper opportunity to present his case. His lawyers sought a declaration in the High Court, using the writ procedure (as in *Ridge v Baldwin*).

The reason given by the House of Lords for striking out O'Reilly's statement of claim was that the new Order 53 procedure provided decision-making bodies with certain procedural protections:

- the leave stage;

- 'cards on the table' about legal submissions from the outset;

- no automatic discovery (but this was available on application);

- no oral evidence, so keeping hearings shorter; and

- the requirement of promptness and in any event within three months.

Lord Diplock said that the whole purpose of these protections would be defeated it a person could use the writ procedure to obtain a declaration to challenge public law decisions. (The new Order 53, as we saw in the Chapter 10, allowed applicants to ask for a declaration under the judicial review procedure). Professor Wade's response to *O'Reilly* was little short of apoplectic. He argues that this decision is a serious setback for administrative law:

> 'It has caused many cases, which on their merits might have succeeded, to fail merely because of the choice of the wrong form of action. It is a step back towards the time of the old forms of action which were so deservedly buried in 1852. It has produced great uncertainty as to the boundary between public and private law since these terms have no clear and settled meaning ... the House of Lords has expounded the new law as designed for the protection of public authorities rather than of the citizen.' (*Administrative Law*, 6th ed, pp 677-678).

Compare this with the views of his old sparring partner, Lord Woolf. He argues that without the safeguards, the public would go unprotected. If there were no procedural safeguards, the courts would be much more cautious in developing grounds of judicial review such as legitimate expectation and the duty to give reasons and extending existing grounds, such as procedural fairness, to new situations. The result would be that far from the citizen being in a better position, he would be in a worse position because the law would not have developed as rapidly as it has. (See *Protecting the Public: the New Challenge* p 233). You must not, suggests Woolf, lose sight of the fact that public law is designed to protect the public as a whole, not just individual citizens with particular grievances.

In the years that followed *O'Reilly v Mackman*, a number of exceptions have been developed in the case law.

In *Wandsworth London Borough Council v Winder* (1985), the council passed a resolution raising the rents of council houses. Mr Winder, a tenant, refused to pay the new sum, and possession proceedings were commenced against him in the county court. He argued that the council's resolution was unlawful. The council tried to strike out his defence on the basis that he could not raise such a public law issue other than by Order 53. The House of Lords disagreed, holding that

11.3   Exceptions to the exclusivity principle

11.3.1   Public law issues as a *defence* in private law litigation public law issues could be raised by way of a defence in private law cases. It was not an abuse of process because the tenant was merely trying to defend himself. The same principle applies to criminal prosecutions, as shown by *Director of Public Prosecutions v Hutchinson* (1990) where women anti-nuclear missile campaigners successfully challenged the validity of Greenham Common by-laws in their defence in criminal proceedings started in a magistrates' court.

For Woolf, these cases are an undesirable dilution of the rule in *O'Reilly v Mackman*. He cannot see why Mr Winder should be in a better position if he waits to be sued for the rent than if he applied for judicial review of the decision at the proper time. But you may think that a distinction is needed. It would not really be sensible to insist, for instance, on the Greenham women having two separate and parallel proceedings – one for judicial review and the other to defend themselves in the criminal courts – when a single court was prepared to deal with all the issues. Also, there was no reason for the Greenham women to challenge the by-law in question, or even to have heard of its existence, before it was used to prosecute them. Had they had to use Order 53, it would surely be unfair prevent them from arguing that the by-law was invalid on the grounds that they had failed to challenge it 'promptly and in any event within three months'.

11.3.2	Exclusivity principle does not apply if you have private law (as well as public law) rights

A second important exception to the exclusivity principle emerged from *Roy v Kensington & Chelsea and Westminster Family Practitioner Committee* (1992). Dr Roy, a general practitioner, claimed he was entitled to a full basic practice allowance in accordance with a statutory instrument, but the family practitioner committee refused to pay, alleging that he had been out of the UK for periods of time and had been employing a locum. The doctor's lawyers issued a writ (rather than an application for judicial review) seeking a declaration and payment of the sums he claimed due to him. Lawyers for the committee, relying on *O'Reilly v Mackman*, sought to strike out parts of his claim, arguing that he should first challenge the committee's decision by judicial review and only if he won could he commence an action for payment of the sums due. The House of Lords held that there was no abuse of process. Lord Lowry said that there were two ways of looking at *O'Reilly*:

• The 'narrow approach'

  The exclusivity rule applies to *all* proceedings in which public law decisions are challenged, subject to some exceptions when private law rights are involved.

- The 'broad approach'

  O'Reilly applies only when private law proceedings were not at stake. (The prisoners in *O'Reilly* had no private rights.)

His Lordship preferred the broad approach, but said that he did not need to choose. There were many indications in favour of a liberal approach: the Law Commission's 1976 report, and the litigation in *Wandsworth v Winder*, had included private law rights. Lord Lowry's conclusion in *Roy* was that:

> '... unless the procedure adopted by the moving party is ill-suited to dispose of the question at issue, there is much to be said in favour of the proposition that a court having jurisdiction ought to let a case be heard rather than entertain a debate concerning the form of the proceedings.'

In its Consultation Paper No 126 (July 1993), the Law Commission noted three fundamental criticisms of the rule. First the exclusivity rule 'automatically' gives protection to public authorities without taking account of the real administrative inconvenience that might, or *might not*, be caused if a litigant could sidestep the Order 53 procedure. Secondly, no sharp distinction can be drawn between 'public' and 'private' rights. Thirdly, public authorities are not given similar procedural protections when they are sued in contract or tort – so why do they need them in respect of judicial review?

11.4   Reform of the exclusivity principle

In its 1994 Report (No 226), the Law Commission concluded that:

> '... the present position whereby a litigant is required to proceed by way of Order 53 only when (a) the challenge is on public law and no other grounds, i.e. where the challenge is solely to the validity or legality of a public authority's acts or omissions and (b) the litigant does not seek either to enforce or defend a completely constituted private law right, is satisfactory.'

In other words, the report supported the 'broad' approach outlined by Lord Lowry in *Roy*. It seems likely that the judges will gladly pick this up. In *Equal Opportunities Commission v Secretary of State for Employment* (1994) – where the House of Lords declared statutory provisions treating part time workers less favourably than full timers contrary to European Union law – Lord Lowry added this as a footnote to his speech:

> 'I feel bound, however, to add (as can perhaps be inferred from my speech in *Roy*) that I have never been entirely happy with the wide procedural restriction for which *O'Reilly v*

Mackman is an authority, and I hope that the case will one day be the subject of your Lordships' further consideration.'

The Law Commission Report also recommended that Order 53 be altered to allow people who begin actions by writ to have their cases transferred into Order 53 when appropriate; at the moment this can only happen the other way round.

11.5	Order 53 can only be used to challenge the validity of 'public law' decisions

So far this chapter has been about people – Mr O'Reilly, Mr Winder, Dr Roy, Ms Hutchinson – who were keen to *avoid* having to using Order 53. If you've been following the argument, it should now be clear why this was so: the Order 53 procedure, while giving protections to public bodies, often operates harshly against the aggrieved citizen because of its time limit, the leave requirement, etc. The second proposition we need to look at is this: Order 53 proceedings can *only* be used to challenge the validity of public law decisions. The following cases are about people who *wanted* to use Order 53, but it was argued that they could not do so. At first sight it might seem very strange why anyone would *want* to use a procedure which seems to have so many disadvantages for the applicant. As we will see shortly, the explanation is that where the applicant has no cause of action in private law (eg for breach of contract) there is often no alternative but to try judicial review. It's Order 53 or bust.

11.6	Public law decisions

In a series of cases the courts have laid down a rule that only 'public law' decisions are susceptible to judicial review. The policy justifications for this are only very occasionally spelt out by the courts. One is that this is another way of rationing judicial review and scarce judicial resources. Another is that it would be unfair to expect small organisations (such as university sporting clubs) to have to comply with the decision-making standard demanded by the grounds of judicial review principles which were developed over the years to control abuse of power by the state. The third justification is theoretical: as can be seen in Chapter 12, the basis of the court's jurisdiction to judicially review public bodies is the *ultra vires* doctrine. Put very simply, this means that the task for the courts is to make sure that public bodies act within the powers given to them by Parliament. Yet, private bodies are not, by definition, created by Parliament.

It is sometimes said that the issue is about which 'bodies' are subject to judicial review but this is a very misleading way of putting the problem. A great many decisions made by *clearly* public bodies, such as the Home Office, are *not* amenable to judicial review challenges, eg a decision as to which supplier to buy paper clips from or a decision to relocate an individual employee from London to Basingstoke. What matters is not really the status of the organisation but the *type* of decision that is made. Unfortunately, it is quite difficult to state in any simple way which decisions are, and which are not, susceptible to judicial review.

A good starting point is to imagine a spectrum of different sorts of decisions – all of which, it is alleged by the people involved, were taken unfairly (eg they weren't allowed to make representations before the decision was taken).

11.6.1 A spectrum of decision making

- At one end, a decision by an immigration officer to refuse a person entry into the UK taken under powers conferred by the Immigration Act 1971.

- At the other, the committee of a university hang-gliding society expels a member.

The first causes no difficulty for the law and the courts will allow judicial review (assuming there isn't any tribunal to which the person should first appeal). This is because the source of the decision is statutory – clearly a 'public' power. The second case also seems straightforward. The Hang-gliding society is just a members' club. The source of the committee's power is contractual. There is no 'public' element here and the expelled member will have to sue in contract (eg breach of an implied term that members will not be expelled contrary to the principles of natural justice) if she wants to challenge the decision. If the aggrieved person had been someone who wanted to join the club, there would of course not be any contract yet; this is a more difficult situation and will be considered below.

The difficulty for the courts has been what to do about situations which fall between the two ends of this spectrum. There are a considerable number of bodies which carry out regulatory functions but which are not set up by statute. Examples include self-regulatory organisations in the financial services industry (LAUTRO, FIMBRA etc), the Advertising Standards Authority, Press Complaints Commission and many sporting bodies such as the Jockey Club and the Football Association. Such bodies have often draconian powers to ban people from earning a living in a particular business or from participating in other activities. The question for the courts is whether their decisions should be subject to judicial review. A variety of tests have been developed.

In the early days of Order 53 the courts applied a quite mechanistic test and asked, in effect, only if the particular decision which was to be challenged was made under statutory powers (or after *Council of Civil Service Unions v*

11.6.2 Source of power test

Minister for the Civil Service (1984) the prerogative). In other words: what was the source of the decision taker's power?

An illustration of this is *Law v National Greyhound Racing Club Ltd* (1983). The club disciplined one of its members, a trainer. He brought an ordinary action for a declaration that the club was in breach of contract; there was an implied term that a licence would be taken away only on fair and reasonable grounds. The club argued that, because of the exclusivity established by *O'Reilly v Mackmon* principle , the trainer had to use Order 53. The Court of Appeal said this was wrong as the club was a private 'domestic' body and the trainer's licence derived solely from a contract between him and the club. Although the public might be affected by the club's decision, that was not relevant.

11.6.3   Functions test

Prompted by the growth of self-regulatory organisations during the 1980s, the courts abandoned the test based solely on the source of power and devised a more sophisticated approach which rested on the nature of the 'function' being performed by the decision taker when he made the decision or the nature of its consequences. The leading case is *R v Panel on Take-overs and Mergers, ex p Datafin plc* (1987). The Panel on Take-overs and Mergers is a self-regulatory organisation concerned with ensuring 'fair play' during take-overs and mergers of companies in England. It is an unincorporated association consisting of 12 members nominated by bodies such as the CBI, the Bank of England and the Institute of Chartered Accountants.

Datafin plc was involved in a take-over bid. The Panel made certain decisions which the company believed to be unlawful, in particular it refused to investigate a complaint. How could Datafin challenge this decision? It applied for leave to apply for judicial review; the judge applied the 'source test' and held that clearly the Panel could not be subject to judicial review because it was not exercising statutory powers. The leave application was renewed to the Court of Appeal which held that the Panel was subject to judicial review because the source of a decision-maker's power was not always conclusive of the issue.

What powers did the Panel have? This question caused the Court of Appeal to scratch its collective judicial head. The Panel clearly had no statutory or prerogative powers. Nor was it in a contractual relationship with those it sought to regulate. Its power derived merely from their consent. Lloyd LJ devised a test:

'... the source of the power will often, perhaps usually, be decisive. If the source of the power is a statute, or subordinate legislation, then clearly the body will be subject to judicial review. If, on the other end of the scale, the source of power is contractual ... then clearly [the body] is not subject to judicial review ... But between these two extremes there is an area in which it is helpful to look not just at the source of the power but at the nature of the power. If the body in question is exercising public law functions, or if the exercise of its functions have public law consequences, then that may be sufficient to bring the body within the reach of judicial review. It may be said that to refer to "public law" in this context is to beg the question. But I do not think that it does.'

In other words, to work out whether a decision can be challenged in Order 53 proceedings it may be necessary to ask three questions:

- What was the source of the decision-makers power? (The old test which in most cases still provides the conclusive answer.)

- What functions was the decision maker carrying out?

- What were the consequences of the decision?

At the time some commentators predicted that this meant that there was now virtually no limit to the reach of judicial review, but this has not been the case. *Datafin* has, however, created considerable uncertainty and spawned a morass of case law. There have been several judicial attempts to refine the rather fluid language used by Lloyd LJ and a number of mini-tests have emerged.

- Is the decision maker exercising monopolistic powers? If yes, this will indicate a reviewable decision.

- Did the applicant consensually submit to the decision-maker's authority? If yes, this suggests not reviewable, though not in the particular circumstances of the *Datafin* case itself.

- A 'but for' test: if the decision-making body did not exist, would the government have set up a similar one? If so, this indicates reviewability.

- Is the decision one in the nature of a 'governmental function'? If so, it is more likely to be reviewable.

- Is there 'statutory underpinning' for the decision? If yes, then review is more likely. Although the Panel was not a statutory body, the government had designed the financial services legislation on the assumption that it existed.

It is impossible to review all the case law in the area, so just two cases – against bodies regulating sports – will be examined.

<table>
<tr><td>11.6.4</td><td>The aftermath of Datafin</td></tr>
</table>

In *R v Football Association Ltd ex p Football League* (1993) the FA, the guardian of the laws of the game and governing body for soccer in England, wanted to set up a new premier league. The FA was a company set up in 1903. The Football League was the most important of the 2,000 leagues approved by the FA. The League did not like the fact the sport's regulatory body was planning to set up its own league in competition to that of the League's. The League believed that the proposals were unlawful and sought judicial review.

Rose J held that the FA was not subject to judicial review. It did have virtually monopolistic powers and its decisions were of great importance – including decisions which affected members of the public. But the source of its powers were contractual. It was distinguished from the *Datafin* because here there was no 'statutory underpinning' or any potential government interest in the matter. If the FA ceased to exist, a commercial concern (eg a TV company) would step in, rather than government. Rose J also commented that to apply to the governing body of football the principles honed for the control of the abuse of power by government and its creatures would involve a quantum leap. It would also be a misapplication of scarce judicial resources.

In *R v Jockey Club ex p Aga Khan* (1992) a horse belonging to the Aga Khan was disqualified from a race by the disciplinary committee of the Jockey Club, a body with a Royal Charter that for many years has regulated racing in Britain. His Excellency applied for judicial review (the third attempt by someone to attempt to review the Club in a few years). The Court of Appeal unanimously held that the Jockey Club was not subject to judicial review, though each of the judges had somewhat different reasons for arriving at this conclusion.

The Master of the Rolls accepted that, given the importance of the racing industry, the government would intervene to regulate it if the Jockey Club did not exist. The other members of the court, Hoffman and Farquharson LJJ, did not agree with this point.

All three judges held that there had been consensual submission to the jurisdiction of the Club in this case; while it was true that if the Aga Khan wanted to race horses in Britain he had no choice but to submit to the Jockey Club's jurisdiction, 'nobody is obliged to race his horses in this country and it does not destroy the element of consensuality' (*per* Farquharson LJ). This clear statement overrules some doubts about this test voiced by Simon Brown J in cases such as *R v Chief Rabbi ex p Wachmann* (1991) where he had held that this criterion was only relevant as a pointer to non-reviewability where submission was truly a matter of choice such as in an arbitration agreement.

Possibly the most important aspect of the *Aga Khan* case are the statements to the effect that the nature of the decision maker's power has not only to be 'public' but also 'governmental'. It is not entirely clear what this means, but several commentators have suggested that this 'shows a return to a primarily "source-based" test: a concentration on the provenance of the power (contract) and its nature (non-governmental)' (Herberg et al (1993) 46 CLP Annual Review, p 111).

The Court of Appeal also expressly left open the question of whether a decision of the Jockey Club affecting a person who was not a member would be subject to judicial review or not. In such a case the aggrieved person, who, for example, might have been refused membership, would have no alternative remedy in private law for breach of contract.

Judicial Review Procedures:
The Public/Private Divide

The Order 53 procedure is the so-called exclusivity principle. The justification for preventing people seeking injunctions or declarations using the writ procedure is that this would deny public bodies the procedural protections they are given under Order 53:

To challenge the validity of a public law decision of a public body, the Order 53 procedure must be used

- the requirement of leave;

- the applicant's 'cards on the table' from the outset;

- no automatic discovery of documents;

- no oral evidence at the court hearing; and

- the requirement that applications be made promptly and in any event within three months.

There are two main exceptions to the exclusivity principle:

- public law issues can be raised as a defence in private law litigation (eg *Wandsworth v Winder*); and

- where a person has private law as well as public law rights (eg *Roy*).

A number of different tests have been used to determine whether a decision is susceptible to judicial review. Today it is necessary to ask the following:

Order 53 proceedings can only be used to challenge the validity of 'public law' decisions

- What was the source of the decision-maker's power? If it is statutory, then it is probably reviewable.

- What functions was the decision-maker carrying out? If these were 'public law' functions, as in *Datafin*, then the decision is probably reviewable.

- What were the consequences of the decision? If the consequences were 'public law' ones, again the decision is probably reviewable.

Chapter 12

Introduction to the Grounds of Judicial Review

This chapter examines two fundamental issues. First, we take a preliminary look at the 'grounds' of judicial review (which will be examined in much more detail in the next five chapters), and consider how they might be categorised. Secondly, we take a step back, and ask what it is that gives unelected judges the power to review the decisions of public bodies at all – in other words, we look at the 'theoretical underpinnings' of judicial review.

12.1   Introduction

The 'grounds' of judicial review are the arguments which a lawyer can put forward as to why a court should hold a public body's decision to be unlawful. They can be categorised in various ways. If you look at the contents pages of the standard textbooks on judicial review/administrative law, you will notice a startling lack of uniformity; the same material is divided up in quite different ways, with different chapter headings and sub-headings.

12.2   The grounds of review

To some extent the differences are merely terminological and organisational. In one sense, it does not matter whether the courts' power to review a decision for reasonableness comes under a chapter labelled 'Abuse of Discretion', or labelled 'Unreasonableness', or labelled 'Irrationality'. On the other hand, the differences of terminology should not be ignored altogether. For one thing, it is necessary to be aware that someone else (a judge, or an academic) may be using a word in a different sense to that which you expect. This is even the case with regard to quite central concepts such as 'illegality' (considered further below) where differences in meaning can cause spectacular misunderstandings.

Further, changes in vocabulary can be a sign of more substantive shifts in the nature of the ground of review in question. For example, the gradual shift of vocabulary from 'natural justice' to 'fairness' (a process still not complete), coincided with a relaxation of many of the previous rigidities of the doctrine, and a recognition that it could apply to areas previously considered out of bounds to procedural intervention. This is so even though, today, many judges use the terms 'natural justice' and 'fairness' entirely interchangeably. Similarly, the move away from the phrase 'Wednesbury unreasonableness' and the adoption of the term 'irrationality' (still not universally accepted), may highlight a change in the nature of that ground of review; we examine this in more detail in Chapter 17.

For now, it is useful to set out the terminology which we have adopted in this book. We have followed the well-known division of the grounds of review enunciated by Lord Diplock in the *GCHQ* case (*R v Minister for the Civil Service ex p Council of Civil Service Unions* (1985)). Lord Diplock divided the grounds of review under three heads:

'Judicial review has I think developed to a stage today when without reiterating any analysis of the steps by which the development has come about, one can conveniently classify under three heads the grounds upon which administrative action is subject to control by judicial review. The first ground I would call 'illegality', the second 'irrationality' and the third 'procedural impropriety'. That is not to say that further development on a case by case basis may not in course of time add further grounds. I have in mind particularly the possible adoption in the future of the principle of 'proportionality' which is recognised in the administrative law of several of our fellow members of the European Economic Community; but to dispose of the instant case the three already well-established heads that I have mentioned will suffice.'

To get an overview of what follows in the next three chapters, it is worth briefly considering each of these 'heads' or 'grounds' of review in turn.

12.2.1   Illegality

In the *GCHQ* case, Lord Diplock gave a very brief definition of 'illegality':

'By illegality as a ground for judicial review I mean that the decision-maker must understand correctly the law that regulates his decision-making and must give effect to it.'

Lord Diplock's meaning is best illustrated by a simple example. If a decision-maker is given the power to decide between options (a), (b), and (c), then he would be acting outside his powers if he were to chose option (d); he would be acting outside the 'four corners' of his jurisdiction. Within the ground of illegality may also be classified the requirements that a decision-maker shall not 'fetter' his discretion (by deciding how to exercise it in advance of the decision), or unlawfully delegate his discretion (by giving the power of decision to another person). We will look at all these different aspects of illegality in the next chapter.

12.2.2   Procedural impropriety

It is more convenient to take Lord Diplock's second and third grounds in reverse order. By 'procedural impropriety' Lord Diplock sought to include those heads of review which uphold procedural standards to which public decision-makers must, in certain circumstances, adhere. These include the duty to give a fair hearing to a person affected by a decision (which we examine in Chapter 14), and the duty not to be affected by bias (Chapter 15). It also includes, as we shall see, the obligation not to disappoint a legitimate expectation (dealt with in Chapter 16).

In the *GCHQ* case, Lord Diplock explained the term 'irrationality' as follows:

> 'By "irrationality" I mean what can by now be succinctly referred to as "*Wednesbury* unreasonableness" (*Associated Provincial Picture Houses v Wednesbury Corporation*). It applies to a decision which is so outrageous in its defiance of logic or of accepted moral standards that no sensible person who had applied his mind to the question to be decided could have arrived at it. Whether a decision falls within this category is a question that judges by their training and experience should be well equipped to answer, or else there would be something badly wrong with our judicial system.'

12.2.3   Irrationality

Whether or not this is an adequate, or indeed an accurate, definition of the power will be considered in Chapter 17. For now, it is merely worth noting that under this head comes what may be characterised (in spite of judicial protestations to the contrary) as review of the *merits* of the decision (however limited a scrutiny of the merits that may turn out to be). An important issue here is the extent to which the decision should be measured against the yardstick of *substantive principles* of judicial review. Advocates of such an approach argue that these substantive principles include the doctrine of proportionality, referred to by Lord Diplock in the passage above as a possible fourth ground of review, as well as other principles such as legal certainty and consistency.

12.3   A caution

We should re-emphasise that these categories are not set in stone. They are mere 'chapter headings' for the grounds of judicial review (*per* Lord Donaldson MR in *R v Secretary of State for the Home Department ex p Brind* (1990)). Furthermore, the grounds are themselves divided into sub-categories which are often more convenient to use as tools in the day to day task of establishing whether the decisions of public bodies infringe the principles of judicial review. For example, a sub-category such as the rule against the 'fettering of discretion', which we have located under 'illegality', could justifiably be placed under 'procedural impropriety' – or conceivably under 'irrationality'.

However it is identified, the content of the rule is the same, and as a matter of day to day practicality it will be applied in the same way however it is regarded.

For an alternative approach to the classification of the grounds of review, you might want to have a look at the position in Australia, where the grounds have been codified by the (Australian) Administrative Decisions (Judicial Review) Act 1977 (as amended) ss 3-7 (which are set out in Appendix 8 of the JUSTICE-All Souls Review of Administrative Law in the United Kingdom (1988)). Rather than attempting to classify the different grounds of review under 'chapter headings' like illegality or irrationality, the statute sets out in s 5(1) a long list of grounds (nine basic ones) upon which an applicant may rely.

12.4	**The basis of the courts' power to intervene**	From where do the courts derive their power to review the decisions and actions of ministers, elected local authorities, and other public bodies? The question may at first glance seem unnecessary; after all, in other areas of law (eg contract or tort) the answer to this sort of question is taken for granted – or the question is not asked at all. But in public law, this apparently 'theoretical' question often arises in the most 'practical' contexts; it is of central importance to an understanding of the present day scope and limitations of judicial review. So it's important to spend some time looking at the traditional answer to the question posed – and at some alternative answers.
12.5	**The traditional analysis: the *ultra vires* doctrine**	The traditional explanation of the courts' power to intervene can be stated briefly, if crudely. The twin doctrines of the sovereignty of Parliament and the rule of law, which have been examined earlier in this book, require that a body or person exercising statutory powers can only exercise those powers which have been given, either expressly or impliedly, by Parliament. Statutory bodies (such as local authorities) cannot create their own power. The courts, in judicially reviewing an action of a public body, are merely adjudicating upon the exact limits of a particular allocation of power; ie checking whether the public body has been given the power to act as it did.
12.5.1	An 'inherent' jurisdiction	Ultimately, the courts' power to perform this 'checking' role is not itself conferred by any statute (how could it be – since how would the law which purported to confer the 'checking' role on the courts itself be 'checked'?) – although it has of course been recognised by statute (most importantly by s 31 of the Supreme Court Act 1981, which regulates the application for

judicial review). The courts' power simply rests, as in any other area of law such as contract, tort, or the criminal law, upon the fact that society generally accepts that the courts possess this role (because the courts have always had it, or because we continually consent to their having it, or because judges have the power to enforce it, or for one of a number of different reasons which a legal philosopher could provide). The courts' power to intervene is often referred to as the courts' 'inherent jurisdiction'.

But the important feature of judicial review, so the traditional theory goes, is that the courts' power is *limited* to this 'checking' role. A court in judicially reviewing a decision of a public body does not have the right to re-take the challenged decision, or to hear an appeal from the decision. Its role is simply to ensure that the public body has not acted outside its powers or (to put it another way) to check that the body has not acted *ultra vires* – the ubiquitous latin phrase so often used by the courts.

12.5.2   System of review v system of appeals

There is therefore a fundamental distinction between a system of *judicial review* and a system of *appeals*. On an appeal, the court can concern itself with the merits of the decision under challenge. In judicial review, the court is concerned merely to check the *legality* of the decision which the public body has made – whether the decision is *ultra vires* or *intra vires*. If the court finds that the public body has exceeded its powers – has acted *ultra vires* -then it has the power to quash the decision, or to require the public body to act in accordance with a duty placed on it by the law, but it does not ordinarily have the power to re-take the decision itself, or to exercise the discretion in the way which it, the court, thinks would be best. The reason that it does not have this power is simple: Parliament has conferred the discretion upon the public body in question, not upon the court. The court merely has the role of supervising the exercise of power by the public body. For this reason, the courts' power to intervene by way of judicial review is sometimes described as the courts' *supervisory jurisdiction* (derived from the idea that the court is supervising the exercise of public power). This is distinct from the *appellate jurisdiction* that the courts exercise in other areas.

12.5.3   The concept of jurisdiction

Another piece of terminology which is frequently used – some might say all too frequently – is the concept of *jurisdiction*. In essence, jurisdiction simply means power; the limits of the jurisdiction of a public body are the limits of its power. A public body which acts *ultra vires* may also be described as acting 'outside its jurisdiction'. When it does so, it commits what is known as a *'jurisdictional error'* – ie an error which takes it outside its jurisdiction. Thus the ultra vires doctrine and the concept of jurisdiction are closely linked; according to the ultra vires doctrine, a court can only intervene by way of judicial review if a jurisdictional error is established. How far this is theory is actually consistent with practice will be examined below.

12.5.4 Summary of the *ultra vires* doctrine

A useful recent summary of the traditional theory of the courts' power of review is contained in the judgment of Lord Browne-Wilkinson in the House of Lords decision *R v Hull University Visitor ex p Page* (1993):

> 'Over the last 40 years the courts have developed general principles of judicial review. The fundamental principle is that the courts will intervene to ensure that the powers of public decision-making bodies are exercised lawfully. In all cases, save possibly one, this intervention ... is based on the proposition that such powers have been conferred on the decision-maker on the underlying assumption that the powers are to be exercised only within the jurisdiction conferred, in accordance with fair procedures and, in a *Wednesbury* sense ... reasonably. If the decision-maker exercises his powers outside the jurisdiction conferred, in a manner which is procedurally irregular or is *Wednesbury* unreasonable, he is acting *ultra vires* his powers and therefore unlawfully.'

This passage is particularly useful because it shows how the traditional theory explains each of the different grounds of judicial review, which we looked at in para 12.2 above.

12.6 Problems with the traditional analysis

The *ultra vires* doctrine does not, however, provide a neat explanation for the whole of judicial review. There are a number of problems with the theory:

- It is artificial in some situations

  Lord Browne-Wilkinson, in the passage from *ex p Page*, quoted above, explained that the traditional theory is based on the 'underlying assumption' that powers given to a public body were only intended to be exercised in accordance with fair procedures, etc. But is this realistic? For example, in relation to natural justice, it may be unconvincing to claim that Parliament intended that a public body exercising a particular power should give a fair hearing before it takes the decision. Parliament may not have thought (insofar as Parliament can 'think'!) about the question of a prior hearing; it may even have assumed that no prior hearing would be required. A similar criticism can be levelled at the justification of judicial review for irrationality. In each case, the objection goes, it is entirely artificial to claim that the court is merely 'supervising' the exercise of power by the public body; or that the court is merely ensuring that the body only exercises the power in accordance with the wishes of Parliament. When the court reviews a decision for breach of the principles of natural justice, it does not do so (the objection runs) because it has looked at the legislation and decided that Parliament impliedly included the principles of natural justice in the legislation. Instead, the court simply asserts that the principles of natural justice are important, and that the decision-maker has failed to live up to them. This last sentence is the seed of the alternative theory, to which we shall return shortly.

- Existence of 'error of law on the face of the record'

  You may have noticed that Lord Browne-Wilkinson stated (in the above quotation from his speech in *ex p Page*) that intervention by way of judicial review can be explained by the traditional theory 'in all cases, save possibly one'. The exception to which he was referring is review for 'error of law on the face of the record.' This power – which is today certainly anomalous, and probably entirely obsolete – is indeed a major headache for supporters of the *ultra vires* doctrine. Put simply, a decision may be reviewed under this head if the court detects an error of law which appears 'on the face of' (ie 'obvious on') the record of the decision of the tribunal or other public body. If such an error exists, then the court can review the decision *even if* the error is not one which is *ultra vires* the decision-maker (ie even if it is not an error which takes the decision-maker outside its jurisdiction). For practical purposes, as we shall see, the existence and ambit of error of law on the face of the record is not important today, but the significance from our perspective is that:

  (a) error of law on the face of the record, even if now obsolete, has been well established for a long time (see eg *R v Northumberland Compensation Appeal Tribunal ex p Shaw* (1952); and

  (b) it is entirely inconsistent with the *ultra vires* doctrine, and with traditional theory of judicial review, because a decision may be struck down under this head even if the decision-maker has not acted outside its jurisdiction.

- The courts' ability to review the exercise of prerogative powers

  So far, we have been considering judicial review of statutory powers; powers which derive, at least ultimately, from legislation. But, as we saw in Chapter 7 (para 7.6), the courts are also able to review the exercise of prerogative powers: *R v Criminal Injuries Compensation Board ex p Lain* (1967), reaffirmed in *R v Minister for the Civil Service ex p Council of Civil Service Unions* (1985)). This is not easily explainable in terms of the *ultra vires* doctrine. How, for example, can the doctrine justify the ability of the courts to hold that an exercise of the prerogative is *Wednesbury* unreasonable? Where the power to make the decision originated in statute, the doctrine would hold that there is a presumption that Parliament did not intend the decision-maker to exercise it unreasonably. However, this explanation is not available in the case of the prerogative, because no one 'confers' the power on the person exercising the prerogative (certainly not Parliament). That person (whether the sovereign, or a minister) cannot be 'presumed' not to want to allow him- or herself to exercise the power unreasonably. Thus, the critics argue, the traditional theory fails to explain the fact that the prerogative is judicially reviewable.

- The courts' discretion to refuse a remedy

  Finally, the *ultra vires* doctrine is hard to reconcile with the courts' undoubted discretion to decline to grant a remedy to an applicant for judicial review, even once a ground of review has been established. If one applies the *ultra vires* doctrine strictly, then where the court finds that a public body had no power to act as it did, it should logically find that the purported decision was a *nullity* (ie was void and of no effect), because it is as if a decision had never been made. Where a decision is held to be *ultra vires*, it should automatically follow that the court holds it to be void. But if that were the case, how is it that the court has a discretion not to grant a remedy? Once it has found that a ground of review has been made out, then there is no valid 'decision' for the court to decide not to overturn. It would therefore appear that the traditional theory is not consistent with the existence of the discretion to refuse to grant a remedy.

12.7   A new theory of judicial review?

An alternative theory emerges from the above objections. It starts from the premise that the courts have now become more confident of their constitutional role, which is to uphold the rule of law. The courts no longer need to resort to the fiction of 'jurisdictional error' to strike down a defective decision; they do not need to pretend that Parliament did not 'intend' to allow the decision-maker to act as it did. Instead, the courts have the power to strike down errors of law (whether due to failure to give a fair hearing, irrationality, or whatever) simply because they have asserted the power do so, and because that abrogation of power is generally accepted in our society.

This view has been well expressed by Dawn Oliver, ('Is the *ultra vires* rule the basis of judicial review?' [1987] Public Law 543). She suggests that 'judicial review has moved on from the *ultra vires* rule to a concern for the protection of individuals, and for the control of power....' (p 543). And she concludes:

> 'Notwithstanding the supremacy of Parliament, the courts impose standards of lawful conduct upon public authorities as a matter of common law, and it is arguable that the power to impose such standards is a constitutional fundamental ... In place of the *ultra vires* rule a doctrine is emerging that, in the public sphere, the courts in exercising a supervisory jurisdiction are concerned both with the *vires* of public authorities in the strict or narrow sense ... and with abuse of power. If abuse of power is established, the courts may properly intervene (p 567).'

So on this view, the courts' power to intervene (in cases of 'abuse of power', at least) is justified not by reference to the presumed intention of Parliament, but by the courts' own self-asserted constitutional right to interfere when they detect abuse of power. Judicial review has, it is said, outgrown the need to rely upon fictions like the *ultra vires* doctrine.

We will see some of the practical implications of this debate in the next few chapters. It's important to remember, however, that the *ultra vires* doctrine is not dead and buried. Indeed, it remains the conventional explanation for at least most of judicial review (as illustrated by Lord Brown-Wilkinson's recent endorsement of the doctrine in *ex p Page*) – even if the theory needs to be modified to take into account objections of the sort set out above.

Introduction to the Grounds of Judicial Review

The grounds of review are the bases on which the court can hold that a public body's decision is unlawful. They may be divided up in a number of different ways; the most convenient is to follow the approach of Lord Diplock in the *GCHQ* case (*R v Minister for the Civil Service ex p Council of Civil Service Unions* (1985)), where he separated the grounds under three headings:

The grounds of review

- Illegality

  In essence, this is the principle that 'a decision-maker must understand correctly the law that regulates his decision-making and must give effect to it'. Under this head may also be included the requirements that a decision-maker must not *fetter his discretion* (by deciding how to exercise it in advance of the decision), nor unlawfully *delegate his discretion* (by giving the power of decision to another person).

- Procedural impropriety

  This covers those heads of review which specify procedural standards to which public decision-makers must adhere. These include:

  (a) the duty to give a fair hearing to a person affected by a decision (which we examine in Chapter 14);

  (b) the duty not to be affected by bias (Chapter 15);

  (c) the obligation not to disappoint a legitimate expectation (Chapter 16).

- Irrationality

  This includes what is sometimes known as *Wednesbury* unreasonableness. To a limited extent, this ground ventures into principles of 'substantive' review – ie into the merits of the decision.

The basis of the courts' power to intervene

The courts' power to review public law decisions is traditionally explained by the *ultra vires* doctrine. This states that a body exercising statutory powers cannot act outside the powers conferred upon it, either expressly or impliedly, by statute. If the body acts outside its powers, then it goes beyond its jurisdiction, and its decision may be reviewed for *jurisdictional error*.

The courts' power to intervene in this way is not conferred by statute; it is part of the courts' *inherent jurisdiction*. The power is (in principle) confined to 'checking' the limits of the decision-maker's power; it is not an appeal against the decision. Thus judicial review is a *supervisory jurisdiction*, not an appellate jurisdiction.

Objections to the traditional analysis

There are a number of objections to the above explanation. It is said that:

- *the theory is artificial* in its reliance on 'presumed' Parliamentary intention;

- it fails to explain the power of the court to review for *error of law on the face of the record*;

- it fails to explain *judicial review of prerogative powers*;

- it is inconsistent with the *courts' discretion to refuse to grant a remedy*.

New theory of judicial review

As a result of these objections, it has been suggested that judicial review does not need to rely upon the 'fiction' of the *ultra vires* doctrine. Instead, the courts may intervene simply because they detect an abuse of power; because of a self-asserted constitutional right to control errors of law, and procedural and substantive abuses of power. However, the *ultra vires* doctrine is still influential (see eg Lord Browne-Wilkinson in *R v Hull University Visitor ex p Page* (1993)). The practical implications of the debate will appear in the next few chapters.

Suggested further reading

On the 'traditional theory' of judicial review:

Wade & Forsyth, *Administrative Law* (7th ed), pp 24-49

Cane, *An Introduction to Administrative Law* (2nd ed), Chap 20

On the defects of that theory and the 'new' theory:

Oliver, 'Is the *ultra vires* rule the basis of judicial review?' [1987] Public Law 543'

Sir John Laws (Chapter 4 in Supperstone and Goudie (eds)), *Judicial Review*

Chapter 13

The Grounds of Judicial Review I: Illegality

As we saw in the last chapter, the basic idea behind the ground of review called 'illegality' is very simple: a public body must act within the 'four corners' of its powers or jurisdiction. If a decision-maker is given the power to choose between (a), (b), and (c), he would be acting illegally if he chose (d).

Let's take a rather more complicated example, which we can follow throughout the chapter.

Parliament decides to pass legislation to control local markets. It enacts a statute called the 'Market Stallholders (Control) Act 1995'. This statute provides that it is unlawful for anyone to trade from a market stall without a licence. The statute sets up a body called the 'Market Traders Licensing Board' ('the MTLB') to issue licences.

Section 2 provides 'the MTLB shall have the power to issue or renew market stall licences to applicants as it sees fit'.

Section 3 provides 'in considering whether or not to issue a licence to an applicant, the MTLB shall consider whether the applicant is a fit and proper person to hold a licence'.

Section 4 provides 'the MTLB shall have power to prevent anyone from trading from a market stall without a licence, and can confiscate equipment used in market trading by any such person'.

In this (fictitious) example, it is easy to imagine a straightforward example of illegality. The MTLB warns Marks & Spencer that it cannot continue trading without a licence, and threatens to confiscate all of its cash tills if it opens its stores on the following day. M & S could challenge this decision on the ground that the MTLB is acting outside its powers; that it is acting illegally. Parliament has not given the MTLB the power to regulate shops, but only to regulate market stalls. The MTLB is threatening to act *ultra vires* (or, in other words, outside its jurisdiction).

In practice, illegality is by far the most common ground of judicial review. The day to day work of a lawyer specialising in public law does not concern abstruse questions as to the meaning of the concept of legitimate expectation, or as to the existence of proportionality, but involves examining and arguing over whether individual Acts of Parliament (like the Market Stallholders (Control) Act) and statutory instruments do, or do not, confer power on a decision-maker to act as it did. This work is first and foremost an exercise of interpretation, not of knowledge of law or of precedent. Every statutory situation is different, and it is not usually very helpful to know what has happened in different situations.

This fact is important to bear in mind in answering judicial review problem questions. You cannot prepare yourself by 'learning' cases in which illegality has been used as a ground of review. Rather, it is important to understand the 'logic' behind the idea of illegality: the different types of reasons that a court may give for concluding that a decision-maker has acted outside its powers. Then you can apply that reasoning to any situation with which you may be confronted. In other words, one must absorb the thinking processes which courts and lawyers typically follow.

The next few sections (13.2 to 13.5) identify some of these 'thinking processes'. Although each is often referred to as a separate sub-ground of review (eg a court will grant judicial review because the decision-maker has been 'influenced by an irrelevant consideration'), you should be able to see how each is merely a 'working through' of the basic idea of illegality — that a body is not allowed to exceed the powers which it has been given.

| 13.2 | **Relevant and irrelevant considerations** | A decision-maker acts illegally if it 'fails to take into account a relevant consideration' – ie it does not consider something which it ought to consider. Let's go back to our example: |

> *The MTLB grants a licence to trade to Albert, who has just been released from prison after serving time for running protection rackets and intimidation. The MTLB decides, in considering whether to grant Albert a licence, to ignore the question of whether he is fit and proper, because it feels that 'he has already been punished enough'.*

This decision could be challenged for failure to take into account a relevant consideration. Section 3 of the Act requires that the MTLB shall, in considering whether or not to issue a licence, take into account whether it thinks the applicant is a fit and proper person to hold a licence. It has failed (indeed, refused) to do so.

In this example, the relevant consideration which the MTLB ignored was actually spelt out in the statute ('shall consider' whether the applicant is fit and proper): it was 'an *express consideration*'. But the decision-maker may also have to take into account relevant considerations which are not actually stated in the statute, but which are merely *implied* by the statutory context. For example:

> *The MTLB's decision to grant Albert a licence is quashed for the reason above. It has to decide his application again (because he still*

wants a licence). This time, it does consider whether he is fit and proper, but in doing so it excludes the evidence of his past convictions, again on the basis that 'he has been punished enough for that'.

This time, the MTLB has followed the letter of the statute: it has considered whether he is fit and proper. But the decision could still be challenged for failure to take into account a relevant consideration – namely, Albert's past convictions. This consideration is not 'express': the legislation does not actually say that the MTLB has to take into account past convictions. But there is surely a very strong argument for saying that in considering whether someone is fit and proper, it must be relevant to consider any recent convictions for serious offences. To ignore such an issue is to ignore an (implied) relevant consideration. Once again, the courts would be likely to quash the MTLB's decision to grant Albert a licence.

There are no clear rules for deciding whether a statute impliedly requires a decision-maker to take a particular consideration into account. In every case, it is a matter of interpretation for the court, looking at the words of the statute, the context, and making certain assumptions or educated guesses about the intention of Parliament.

As the obverse of the above, a decision-maker also acts illegally if it *takes into account an irrelevant consideration.* Once again, irrelevant considerations may be either express in the statute, or implied. An example of an implied relevant consideration may be as follows:

The MTLB refuses a licence to Belinda on the basis that she has red hair.

The MTLB has quite obviously taken into account an irrelevant consideration, even though it is not expressly stated in the Act that 'the MTLB shall not consider the colour of an applicant's hair'. The decision may also be unreasonable (see Chapter 17 below).

In practice, it may not be easy to discover whether or not a consideration has been taken into account by the decision-maker – unless, as in the above example, the decision-maker reveals that it has been influenced by that factor. It may be particularly difficult if the decision-maker does not have a duty to give reasons for its decision (as to which, see Chapter 14 below, para 14.6.5), especially since discovery is rarely ordered in judicial review proceedings (and certainly nothing in the nature of a 'fishing expedition' will be ordered).

13.3   Improper purpose

A decision-maker ought only to use the power given to it by Parliament for the purpose or purposes for which it was given the power. The decision-maker acts *ultra vires* if it uses the power for a different purpose. The classic case in which this doctrine was explained is *Padfield v Minister of Agriculture, Fisheries and Food* (1968). The Minister had a discretion conferred by the Agricultural Marketing Act 1958 to refer complaints about the operation of the milk marketing scheme to a commission. The Minister refused to refer a complaint from a body of milk producers to the commission, because he feared that, if the complaint was upheld, it would undermine the whole milk marketing scheme. The House of Lords held that this decision was unlawful, because he was exercising his discretion not to refer for a wrong purpose: to protect the existing scheme. The statute conferred the power to refer on the Minister just so that such challenges could be made. As Lord Reid (p 1034) put it:

> 'The Minister's discretion ... must be inferred from a construction of the Act read as a whole, and for the reasons I have given I would infer that the discretion ... has been used by the Minister in a manner which is not in accord with the intention of the statute which conferred it.'

A more recent example is *R v Inner London Education Authority ex p Brunyate* (1989). Under the Education Act 1944, local education authorities had power to appoint school governors, and had an (apparently) unfettered power to remove them from office. ILEA decided to remove certain governors because it disagreed with the policies which they were pursuing. The House of Lords held that, construing the statute as a whole, the governors were given an independent function. Therefore, ILEA was acting with an improper purpose in attempting to remove them for a reason which would undermine that independent function.

Once again, working out whether a decision-maker is acting with an improper purpose is a matter of fact in each case, looking at the statutory context. We can look at one more illustration, using our example:

> *The MTLB resolves that in considering licence applications, it will favour 'active followers of an organised religion' in order 'to promote the growth of spiritual awareness in the country'.*

This decision could be challenged on the ground that the MTLB has adopted an improper purpose (promoting spiritual awareness) in exercising its discretion to issue licences. Looking at the statute as a whole, it is clear that this was not one of the purposes for which Parliament conferred the power on the MTLB, rather (from the extract of the statute which we have seen), it would appear that the primary purpose was to ensure that market stalls are run by honest ('fit and proper') people.

Don't be too worried about the precise distinctions between categories such as 'irrelevant considerations' and 'improper purpose' – they tend to run into each other. For example, in the last example above, one could say that the MTLB has acted illegally because it has taken an irrelevant consideration into account (promoting spiritual awareness) rather than saying that it has adopted an improper purpose. It doesn't matter how you describe it; what is important is to identify that the decision-maker has acted outside its powers by exercising its discretion wrongly. A recent example of a case which can be categorised under either heading is *R v Somerset County Council ex p Fewings* (1993) (Council's ban on stag hunting on Council land unlawful).

13.4 Fettering of discretion

If Parliament gives a discretion to a particular public decision-maker, the courts expect that body actually to exercise the discretion. 'Discretion' means, essentially, making a choice between two or more options. So the courts insist that the decision-maker actually makes that choice in each case: ie applies its mind to the different possible decisions which it could make, and chooses between them. The courts will not allow a decision-maker to pre-judge cases, or to bind or 'fetter' its discretion by adopting a rigid policy so that the outcome of individual cases is decided in advance. This is known as the rule against the fettering of discretion.

It is best illustrated by our example.

The MTLB, in a state of shock after being twice overruled in relation to Albert, goes to the other extreme. It decides to adopt a policy, which provides that: 'Any applicant with any criminal convictions (other than driving convictions) cannot be considered fit and proper, and so must be refused a market stall licence.' Albert applies for a licence for a third time and is refused, because of the policy. This time it is he who challenges the decision.

The decision is unlawful. The MTLB has adopted a rigid policy which binds it as to how it decides future cases. Even if that policy was completely reasonable (in this case you may think it is not), it is still unlawful, because it fetters the MTLB's discretion to decide each individual case according to its merits. Albert would succeed in his judicial review.

Of course, in practice, many thousands of public decision-makers make policies which they adopt to help them take decisions; large-scale decision-making would be impossible without them. Indeed, there are obvious advantages to having clear policies in organisations: it promotes consistency between different decision-makers, it speeds up decision making, and it enables senior people in the organisation to communicate to the actual people making the decisions the sort of factors they ought to consider.

The rule against the fettering of discretion does not stop decision-makers adopting policies. It simply insists that such policies should not be applied rigidly, so as to remove any ability to depart from the policy in an appropriate case. A good example of this distinction can be seen in *British Oxygen v Board of Trade* (1971). In this case, the Board of Trade had a discretion to make investment grants for certain purchases. It refused to pay British Oxygen an investment grant for the purchase of a large number of metal cylinders, which cost less than £25 each, because it had a policy of not awarding grants for the purchase of items which individually cost less than £25. British Oxygen challenged this policy as a fetter on the Board's discretion to make grants. The House of Lords decided that the policy did not fetter the Board's discretion. Their Lordships stated that public bodies are allowed to form a policy to deal with a large number of applications, as long as they are prepared to 'listen to someone with something new to say', and to waive the policy in appropriate cases. In other words, one can have a policy, but it must not be 'set in stone'. There was evidence that the Board of Trade did not apply its policy rigidly, and so the House of Lords rejected British Oxygen's case.

An example of a case going the other way is *Stringer v Minister of Housing and Local Government* (1970). A local authority made a written agreement with Manchester University, by which it undertook to discourage development near the site of a large telescope operated by the University – the University was worried that if houses were built nearby, the telescope's operations would be disrupted. Later, a builder's application for planning permission to build houses near the telescope was turned down by the local authority, on the ground (partly) that the development would interfere with the telescope. The builder challenged this decision by way of judicial review, and the court agreed that:

(i) the agreement between the authority and the university was invalid, because it fettered the authority's statutory discretion to consider applications for planning permission on their merits in each case; and

(ii) therefore the particular refusal of planning permission in this case was void also. (In fact, the court also held that an appeal to the Minister, in which he had confirmed the local authority's decision, was valid).

Note that the courts will not necessarily automatically accept a claim by a decision-maker that it has 'kept its mind open' in applying its policy; after all, it is a very easy claim to make. In *R v Secretary of State for Transport ex p Sheriff & Sons* (1986), the Department of Transport had circulated a departmental handbook, in which it was stated that a certain grant would be refused in specified circumstances. This was challenged as an unlawful fetter of discretion. The Secretary of State argued that his department did not really rely on the handbook – that he had kept his mind open. The court rejected this, holding that the handbook was 'so much a part of the Department's thinking' that his discretion was clearly fettered.

It is important to watch out for 'fettering' issues in exam problems – they can be quite easy to miss, especially when the problem also contains a much more obvious ground of review such as a failure to offer a fair hearing. It is worth getting into the habit of mentally checking in each case the scope of the decision-maker's discretion, whether it has been regulated by a policy or usual practice, and if so, whether it has been applied rigidly.

If an Act of Parliament confers a discretion on a particular public body, the courts normally require that the discretion be exercised by that same body. The decision-maker is not normally allowed to delegate that discretion to someone else, because that would be contrary to the intention of Parliament as expressed in the words of the statute. If Parliament had wanted that other person to exercise the discretion, it would have conferred it on them in the first place. For example:

13.5   Delegation of discretion

After the Albert debacle, the MTLB resolves that 'decisions as to the fitness and propriety of all applicants for licences shall be taken by the local police force of the area concerned'. The MTLB refuse Albert's (fourth) application for a licence after the local police state that as far as they are concerned, he is completely unfit and improper.

This decision is invalid, because it is flawed by an unlawful delegation of discretion. Parliament conferred the discretion to decide whether the applicant is fit and proper on the MTLB, not on the police.

Note that the courts will examine who *actually* exercises the discretion, and will not be satisfied merely because the person on whom the discretion has been conferred exercises it in name. If the decision-maker 'acts under dictation', by simply adopting someone else's decision, this is unlawful. On the other hand, a decision-maker is usually allowed to take someone else's view into account. It is a question of judgment in each case which side of the line the decision-maker has fallen. Thus:

The MTLB adjusts its policy, and resolves that the MTLB will itself decide whether the applicant is fit and proper; but that in each case it will seek the view of the local police on that question. It rejects Albert's application once again, after hearing the police's view.

It is impossible to tell from these facts whether the MTLB has acted lawfully or not. If it has merely taken the police's view into account, and decided independently whether or not it agrees with it, then the decision is likely to be valid. However, if it has effectively simply deferred to the police's view, then it has unlawfully acted under dictation. Which of the two is the case might be apparent from the MTLB's records of its decision-making process – otherwise Albert may have an uphill task trying to show that the decision is flawed.

A good example of the distinction in practice is the case of *Lavender v Minister of Health and Local Government* (1970). Here, the Minister of Health and Local Government refused Lavender's application for planning permission to develop land for use as a quarry, after hearing objections from the Minister of Agriculture. The decision was challenged on the ground that the Minister had acted under dictation – he had effectively abdicated his decision to the Minister of Agriculture. The House of Lords held that the Minister was entitled to listen and to pay close attention to the views of the Minister of Agriculture – but that he could not in effect turn the decision over to the Minister of Agriculture because, under the statute, the decision was his alone. On the facts, the House of Lords held that the Minister had wrongly delegated his discretion to the Minister of Agriculture, because he had adopted a policy stating that he would not grant this class of planning application 'unless the Minister of Agriculture is not opposed'.

Remember that some statutes expressly allow the decision-maker to delegate the decision to someone else. Obviously, in that case, the decision-maker is allowed to delegate, and the rule against delegation has no effect (save, of course, that the decision-maker can only delegate to those whom the statute allows it to). Further, the courts may sometimes be prepared to *infer* that a statute permits delegation – ie the statute contains an implied right to delegate. However, since there is a presumption against delegation, the courts will only find that this is the case if the implication is clear.

13.5.1   The *Carltona* principle

In one exceptional situation, the general presumption against the delegation of discretion is reversed. Where a discretion is conferred upon a government Minister, the courts presume, in the absence of evidence to the contrary, that the Minister is allowed to delegate the discretion to officials in his department – even though the statute does not expressly say so.

The *Carltona* principle takes its name from the well-known case of *Carltona v Commissioner of Works* (1943). An official in the Ministry of Works wrote a letter to Carltona Limited requisitioning the building which Carltona occupied. Carltona challenged the decision to requisition on the basis that while the letter was written (and the decision taken) by an official, the statute gave the power to requisition only to the Minister. But the Court of Appeal held that there was a presumption that the Minister was allowed to delegate the decision to officials in his department. In part, this decision was simply a recognition of the fact that it would be physically impossible for the Minister personally to discharge all the decisions given to him by statute. But the court also pointed out that because of the doctrine of ministerial responsibility, the Minister was responsible to Parliament for what happened in his department (whether he was delegating to people who were too junior, and so on), and therefore there was an additional safeguard in cases of this sort which would not be present in a normal case of unauthorised delegation. The officials in a Minister's department are sometimes called his 'alter ego': ie they are effectively treated as being part of the Minister, so that (in one sense) no delegation takes place at all.

The *Carltona* principle is still alive and well today; it is sometimes suggested that it is a dangerous principle which allows excessive delegation (particularly as the doctrine of ministerial responsibility may not be as effective as it used to be, or was assumed to be). In *R v Secretary of State for the Home Department ex p Oladehinde* (1990), for example, the question was whether the Secretary of State had the power to delegate to immigration inspectors the power to deport aliens. Oladehinde argued that Parliament could never have contemplated that such an extreme delegation would occur; he said that the statute contemplated that decisions might be taken by Home Office officials (as well as by the Secretary of State), but not by immigration inspectors. However, the House of Lords held that since immigration inspectors are civil servants, they therefore came under the *Carltona* principle. The principle applied because there was nothing in the statute to exclude it (either expressly or impliedly). The delegation was therefore lawful.

At this stage, we must step back again, and re-focus on 'illegality' as a ground of review in more general terms. It is necessary to look at some new complications.

Up till now, in the example which we have been following through, the errors which the MTLB has been making have on

13.6   Errors of law and fact

the whole been errors of law. For example, in refusing to consider Albert's criminal record, or taking account of Belinda's red hair, the MTLB has not been making mistakes of fact, but has been misinterpreting the extent of its powers: making errors of law. But a body may sometimes be judicially reviewed for making factual errors as well as legal errors. For example:

MTLB confiscates Cassandra's stall because it discovers that she is trading without a licence. In fact, Cassandra claims that she does have a licence, but that her registration number was accidentally missed off the MTLB's record of licensees.

Cassandra could review the MTLB's decision to confiscate her stall for error of fact: in mistakenly believing that she was unlicensed.

However, the courts are fairly reluctant to get involved in reviewing alleged errors of fact. For one thing, the courts may know much less than the decision-maker about the factual issues in question (especially in 'specialist' areas) – if the court intervenes, who is to say that in fact the decision-maker did not get the fact right, and the court wrong? Secondly, the powers of the courts to help it get to the true facts are very limited. Courts on judicial review applications rarely hear live witnesses, and very rarely order cross-examination (although they have the power to do so), and they are also reluctant to order a party to produce documents ('discovery'). Once again, therefore, the original decision-maker may be better placed to discover the true facts than the court. Finally, the courts are very nervous about the sheer number of cases which might result if they entertained judicial reviews every time someone alleged that a decision-maker had got a fact wrong. They are concerned that to do so might effectively turn a system of 'review' into a system of appeals. For example:

The MTLB is considering whether to renew David's licence after allegations that he has been selling alcoholic drinks from his stall without the necessary separate drinks licence. After hearing evidence from Oliver that he bought alcoholic drinks from David's stall and hearing David deny it, the MTLB find the allegations proved, and refuse to renew David's licence on the basis that he is not fit and proper.

Could David review the decision of the MTLB on the basis that it committed an error of fact in finding that he had sold alcoholic drinks to Oliver? If so, how would the court decide whether the MTLB had or had not made a mistake? In fact, David probably could not obtain judicial review for such an alleged error.

Compare these difficulties with the courts' attitude to errors of law. When an error of law is alleged, the court can at least be confident that it has the necessary expertise to decide the question, and it has a procedure specially designed to help it do so (eg disclosure of legal arguments very early, in the Form 86A). Further, the court has the leave stage to help it filter out cases where the alleged error of law is simply not arguable (by contrast ,it is very difficult to weed out bad factual arguments at the leave stage). For all these reasons, the courts are far more reluctant in judicial review applications to interfere with findings of fact than with findings of law.

The result of the above is that the courts have to make two sets of distinctions. Firstly, the courts have to distinguish errors of law (which, subject to para 13.7 below, are always reviewable), from errors of fact (which may or may not be reviewable). Secondly, the courts have to distinguish reviewable errors of fact ('jurisdictional errors of fact') from non-reviewable errors of fact ('non-jurisdictional errors').

Both of these distinctions are of extreme complexity, and in a typical constitutional and administrative law course you will not be expected to know a vast amount about the area. Nevertheless, it is important to understand the problems which make the area so difficult.

A good illustration of the difficulties which the distinction between errors of law and errors of fact can cause can be seen by going back to our first example: the MTLB's threat to stop Marks & Spencer trading for not having a licence. There, the question at issue was whether the words 'market stall' in the legislation include a shop, or a department store. The answer is, pretty obviously not – but for present purposes, the important point is, is the question of the interpretation of 'market stall' a question of fact or law? On the one hand, it seems to be a question as to what ordinary people understand by the term; one might ask: Is the stall outside? Is it temporary? etc. On the other hand, the court has to interpret the wording of the statute: it has to ask what meaning Parliament intended to attribute to the words 'market stall' in the legislation. Is this not a question of law?

13.6.1   Errors of law versus errors of fact

Judges have introduced the concept of 'mixed questions of law and fact' to deal with cases in this grey area. Thus one question ('does an M & S store come within the definition of 'market stall'?) may include questions of fact (what are the characteristics of an M & S store?) and questions of law (what did Parliament intend by the phrase 'market stall'?). But you should not assume that any question as to the meaning of a word in a statute is necessarily a question of law; in *Brutus v*

Cozens (1973) it was suggested that when a word in a statute is intended to bear its 'ordinary' everyday meaning, then its interpretation in any particular case is a question of fact, not law.

13.6.2   Reviewable and non-reviewable errors of fact

When are the courts prepared to review decisions for alleged errors of fact? Once again, there are no easy answers. A cynic would say that the reason that this issue (and the previous issue, about the distinction between fact and law) are so confused is because the courts are result-driven: they decide whether or not they want to intervene, and then start trying to think of a reason to justify that conclusion. The result is inconsistent and confused decisions.

However, trying to simplify a confused area, one can say:

• Normally, the courts will not review a decision simply because an applicant alleges that the decision-maker has made a mistake of fact. Questions of fact are for decision-makers, not for the reviewing court.

Thus David (above) cannot review the MTLB just because he says it made a mistake in finding that he sold alcoholic drinks.

• However, when the decision-maker's entire power to decide (or 'jurisdiction') depends on it making a finding of fact, then that finding of fact is reviewable (sometimes called a 'precedent fact'). A decision-maker cannot increase its power by mistakenly thinking that it has a power to decide something which it does not. As Lord Wilberforce put it in *Zamir v Home Secretary* (1980), in some cases:

'... the exercise of power, or jurisdiction, depends on the precedent establishment of an objective fact. In such a case it is for the court to decide whether that precedent requirement has been satisfied.'

To go back to our example: The MTLB's power to take action against M & S depends upon it making a finding of fact that M & S's stores are 'market stalls'. If the correct answer is that the stores are not market stalls, then the MTLB has no power to act against M & S. The MTLB cannot, by mistakenly finding that a store is a market stall, give itself extra powers. So the courts will intervene to strike down such an error, because the fact in question is a 'jurisdictional fact' – a fact on which the MTLB's jurisdiction depends.

Another example of a jurisdictional error of fact is contained in the case of *White and Collins v Minister of Health* (1939). A local authority had power (by statute) to acquire land compulsorily – but not if the land was part of a park. A landowner objected that a particular Order was invalid because the local authority had mistakenly failed to realise that the land in question was part of a park. The Court of Appeal held that it could review the decision on that basis.

- The court will also entertain a challenge for error of fact (even if not a jurisdictional fact) where it is alleged that there is *no evidence* to support the finding of fact at all (it is occasionally suggested that the test is, or should be, no substantial evidence: *Secretary of State for Education and Science v Metropolitan Borough of Tameside* (1977). This is sometimes seen as part of review for unreasonableness/irrationality (how can one reasonably reach a finding of fact with no evidence to support it?). It is, for obvious reasons, not easy to establish.

13.7   Are all errors of law reviewable?

We have seen how the courts will only review some errors of fact. We have noted that the courts are, for various reasons, much more reluctant to review errors of fact than errors of law. The question then arises – are there any errors of law which the courts will not review?

In the past, this was yet another highly complex area. There were lots of cases suggesting that something called a 'non-jurisdictional error of law' did exist – ie an error of law that the courts would not review – a point of law which the decision-maker had the final authority to determine, whether rightly or wrongly. Unfortunately, there were almost no cases actually identifying what such errors of law were, and no one was able to produce a satisfactory definition so that one could identify them in the abstract.

The position has now been reached where in all but a few exceptional circumstances, one can assume that all errors of law are jurisdictional errors. That means that whenever a public decision-maker makes an error of law, the court automatically has power to judicially review the decision, without having to worry about whether or not the error 'goes to jurisdiction'. This has major advantages for you as a student. When you are faced with a problem question raising a possible error of law, you still have to analyse it to work out whether there is in fact an error of law, but once you are satisfied that there is, you can go straight on to consider whether or not the courts are likely to grant a remedy. In other words, you can usually entirely ignore the whole debate about jurisdictional versus non-jurisdictional errors. And if you look at 99% of recent reported cases, you will see the courts doing exactly that: ignoring the jurisdictional/non-jurisdictional debate. It is simply assumed that if there is an error of law, it is reviewable by the courts on judicial review.

The one main exception to this happy assumption is where you are dealing with an 'ouster clause': a statutory provision which tries to oust the power of the court to review the decision. We deal with this difficult topic in Chapter 18 below, and also consider there whether the distinction still has some life where one is trying to review not an administrative decision-maker or tribunal, but an inferior court. There are also a few anomalous situations where the jurisdictional/non-jurisdictional distinction is still relevant, which you may come across – the most prominent being in relation to the powers of university visitors, where the House of Lords recently reaffirmed the distinction (*R v Hull University Visitor ex p Page* (1993)). The case can be explained as resting on the historically exclusive jurisdiction of university visitors.

13.8   A practical approach to errors of law

To conclude what is a fairly complex area, the good news is that in an ordinary case, most of the problems are ignorable or bypassable. Most errors are errors of law. If you are dealing with an error of law, then you can assume that, once the error is established, the decision is reviewable. To work out whether there is an error of law or not, you need to have in mind the logical tests which we have labelled relevant/irrelevant considerations; improper purpose; fettering and delegation of discretion.

Errors of fact are rarer. Although the dividing line between errors of law and fact is hard to define, hopefully in most cases you will, like the 'David' example above, be able to spot them relatively easily. Once you spot an error of fact, you need to think carefully about whether it is a fundamental or 'jurisdictional' fact – ie one on which the body's entire power depends. If so, it is reviewable. If not, it is probably not reviewable, unless there is 'no evidence' to support the finding of fact.

The Grounds of Judicial Review I: Illegality

Illegality rests on the fundamental principle that a public body can only act within its powers or 'jurisdiction'. The courts have developed a number of 'reasoning processes' by which they may conclude that a decision-maker has acted outside its powers. These are:

Types of illegality

- Acting outside the 'four corners' of the statute (where the decision-maker simply does something which it has no power to do).

- Failing to take into account a relevant consideration. The relevant consideration may be either actually set out in the statute ('express') or merely implied.

- Taking into account an irrelevant consideration, which again may be either express or implied.

- Adopting an improper purpose (eg *Padfield v Minister of Agriculture*).

- Fettering of discretion. While it is legitimate for decision-makers to adopt policies to help them take decisions (as in *British Oxygen v Board of Trade*), it is unlawful for anyone exercising a discretion to apply a policy rigidly (*Stringer v Minister of Housing and Local Government*).

- Delegation of discretion. A decision-maker must exercise a discretion conferred on it unless authorised to delegate that discretion to another. It must exercise that discretion in substance as well as in form; in other words, it must not act under dictation from another body (*Lavender v MHLG*).

  However, under the *Carltona* principle a discretion conferred upon a government Minister may be exercised by an departmental official, even if the statute does not so provide:

  Carltona v Commissioner of Works (1943)

  R v Secretary of State for the Home Department ex p Oladehinde (1990)

Whereas errors of law are always reviewable (for present purposes), errors of fact are not. It is therefore necessary to distinguish errors of law from errors of fact. In this complicated area, a good rule of thumb is that the interpretation of a word in a statute is a question of law

Public decision-makers may be reviewed for errors of fact as well as law

(unless, possibly, the word is intended to bear its ordinary everyday meaning (*Brutus v Cozens*)).

Most errors of fact are not reviewable

Summarising a difficult area, one can say that an error of fact is only reviewable if:

- the issue of fact is 'fundamental' to the decision-maker's power to decide (a 'precedent fact'); see *Zamir v Home Secretary* (1980); and *White and Collins v Minister of Health* (1939); or

- there is no evidence to support the finding of fact at all.

All errors of law are reviewable (normally)

By contrast, given the recent developments in the law it is safe to assume that all errors of law are reviewable (because all such errors are 'jurisdictional'). There is a possible exception to this convenient rule in the context of ouster clauses, which we examine in Chapter 18 below.

Chapter 14

The Grounds of Judicial Review II: Fair Hearings

14.1 Introduction

The courts may review a public body's decision on the ground of 'procedural impropriety' if the decision-maker has failed to meet required standards of fair procedure. It is very difficult to define precisely what is meant by the word 'procedure' in this context, but in essence, it concerns *the way in which the decision is reached* rather than the *actual decision itself* (in contrast, the grounds of review known as illegality and irrationality both generally look, in different ways, at the actual decision). Over the years, the courts have built up detailed rules setting out what is required of decision-makers procedurally in different circumstances – in other words, what procedures they have to follow in order to ensure that their decisions comply with the requirements of 'fairness'.

Different types of decisions, and different decision-makers, have to conform to different standards of procedural propriety. At one extreme, almost all decision-makers are required not to be biased when taking decisions. On the other hand, only some decision-makers are required to offer a person likely to be affected an oral hearing before taking a decision. The crucial skill which you therefore have to develop is to be able to recognise what the courts are likely to require by way of procedural fairness in any given situation. This is not an easy task because there are few fixed rules to guide you. Over the past few years, the courts have increasingly emphasised that what is required of a decision-maker is simply what is 'fair in the circumstances' – and they have emphasised that 'fairness' is a flexible concept. This means that in order to predict what the courts might require in any particular situation with which you are faced, you have to be aware:

- of what the courts have done in similar situations in the past; and

- of the general principles which the courts follow in applying the 'fairness' concept,

    so that you can be alert to differences between your case and past cases, and thus have an idea as to how the courts might react to your situation.

14.2 Terminology: a brief history

It is easy to get confused by the different terms used by judges and academics in this area. As is so often the case in judicial review, the terminology is far less important than the actual concepts. But you need some awareness of differences in terminology, because the labels are of more than merely historical interest. A wide variety of terms is still used today.

Traditionally, the requirements of procedural fairness have been known collectively as *'the rules of natural justice'*. This phrase reflects the courts' original explanation of the source of the doctrine: that it was not invented by judges, but reflected 'natural' or even god-given laws of fairness. (In one 18th century case, Fortescue J even traced the doctrine back to Old Testament roots!) The rules of natural justice were traditionally categorised under two headings, each known by a latin tag:

- The principle *audi alteram partem* (meaning 'hear the other side'), encompassed the group of rules that required a decision-maker to offer a hearing, either written or oral, to an affected individual before a decision was taken;

- The principle *nemo judex in causa sua* (or 'no man a judge in his own cause') covered the rules which ensured that a decision-maker was not biased, and should not appear to be biased, in coming to a decision.

These rules were slowly developed by the courts, relying heavily on analogies with court procedures. In other words, the courts looked at the procedural protections which a person would be entitled to in court (such as a right to an oral hearing, a right to call witnesses, a right to be represented by a lawyer, a right to cross-examination, and so on) and applied similar rights to persons affected by decisions of public bodies who were entitled to natural justice.

In the 1970s, this rather rigid approach was softened, as the courts began to state that the rules of natural justice were not necessarily uniform in different situations; that what was required in each case was simply whatever 'fairness' demanded. There was then a long debate in the late 1970s and early 1980s about whether there was any difference between 'natural justice' and 'fairness'. The answer today is, probably not. The best evidence of this is the number of judges who simply talk about 'the requirements of natural justice or fairness' without even attempting to distinguish them. One can still use the language of 'natural justice' (and plenty of judges and lecturers do), as long as one remembers that it is a much more flexible concept than it was 20 years ago.

In the *GCHQ* case (1984), Lord Diplock proposed that rather than the term 'natural justice' or 'procedural fairness', we should use the term 'procedural propriety'. He explained that:

'I have described the third head as 'procedural impropriety' rather than failure to observe the basic rules of natural justice or failure to act with procedural fairness towards the person who will be affected by the decision. This is because susceptibility to judicial review under this head covers also failure by an administrative tribunal to observe procedural rules that are expressly laid down in the legislative instrument by which its jurisdiction is conferred, even where such failure does not involve any failure of natural justice.' (p 411)

We have adopted Lord Diplock's categorisation here. Under the heading of 'procedural impropriety', therefore, there are three broad areas which must be examined. Don't worry if this is not the same classification that your lecturer uses; as we've already said, the concepts should be the same, even if the labels are different! Our headings are:

- The right to a fair hearing. A fair hearing may be required *either* by statute, or by the common law (the latter being what is known as the rules of natural justice or fairness). This is dealt with in this chapter.

- The rule against bias (dealt with in Chapter 15).

- The doctrine of legitimate expectation (dealt with in Chapter 16). This is the idea that decision-makers ought, where possible, to fulfil expectations which they have, by their actions, aroused in affected individuals.

14.3   A framework for thinking about the right to a fair hearing

There are a huge number of cases dealing with the right to a hearing: this is the most litigated area of procedural impropriety. Most of the cases deal with different aspects of the same basic question: in the circumstances of the individual case, has the applicant any entitlement to procedural protection before the decision is taken, and if so, what protection can he or she demand? We have broken this question down into three separate elements:

- *When* is a fair hearing *prima facie* required? (see para 14.4);

- Is there any reason why the *prima facie* entitlement to a hearing should be *limited* or *defeated*? (see para 14.5);

- If a some sort of hearing is required, *what* procedural protection can the applicant actually demand? (see para 14.6).

14.4   When is a fair hearing required?

The question of when a fair hearing is required is certainly the most difficult of the three issues. Let us go back to the example which we followed in the last chapter.

Alice applies to the MTLB for a market stallholders licence. She has never had one before. She fills in a short application form, and sends it to the MTLB. Some time later, she gets a letter from the MTLB turning down her application on the ground that the MTLB believes that she is not a fit and proper person. The MTLB states that its decision is final, and that it will not listen to further representations.

Alice wants to know if she can challenge this decision because the MTLB has not given her an opportunity to make representations. She says she would have liked to make oral representations, or, failing that, to put in representations in writing. Has she got a good ground of challenge on the basis that the MTLB has failed to give her a fair hearing?

14.4.1 'Judicial/ administrative' and 'rights/privileges'

In answering this question, the first golden rule to remember is, don't trust any cases decided before the mid 1960s! Until that time, the courts used to insist that to be entitled to a fair hearing, you would have to show that the decision-maker was a 'judicial body' (ie it had the characteristics of a court or tribunal) rather than an 'administrative body'. You would also have had to show that the decision in respect of which you sought the hearing was one which concerned your legally enforceable rights, rather than merely your 'privileges' or 'expectations'.

In Alice's case, although she might be able to show that the MTLB was a 'judicial body' (depending on the MTLB's precise character), she would not be able to show that the decision concerned any legally enforceable 'right'. She has no right to a licence – only a hope of a getting one. So, under the old law, Alice would have had no right to a hearing.

14.4.2 Rigid distinctions swept away

These distinctions have now been swept away. In many ways, the law is now closer to what it was in the mid to late 19th century, before these rigid distinctions arose (you may well come across the case of *Cooper v Wandsworth Board of Works* (1863), which is still (in broad principle) good law). The case that really confirmed the death of these old distinctions between judicial/administrative bodies and rights/privileges was the landmark decision of *Ridge v Baldwin* (1964). Ridge was the Chief Constable of Brighton, until he was dismissed from his post without a hearing by the local authority (which had the power to dismiss him 'at any time' if in its opinion he was 'negligent in the discharge of his duty, or otherwise unfit for the same'). His dismissal followed a corruption trial at which he was acquitted, but where the judge had made various criticisms of him. Ridge challenged his dismissal on the ground that he should have been given an opportunity to make representations to the local authority, defending himself against the allegations made against him. The local authority argued (following the old case law) that since Ridge had no 'legal right' to his position, he had no entitlement to a hearing before dismissal.

The House of Lords found that Ridge should have been given a hearing before being dismissed. Lord Reid held that *whenever* a decision by a public authority resulted in a person being deprived of his employment, or resulted in his reputation being significantly diminished, that person ought to be given a chance to make representations before the decision was taken. It was irrelevant whether the person had a 'right' to his position or whether it was merely a 'privilege'. In a case a few years later (*Re H K (an infant)* (1967)) it was confirmed that the effect of *Ridge v Baldwin* was also to sweep away the judicial/administrative distinction: in other words, Ridge would have been entitled to a hearing even if the local authority were not acting 'judicially' (this was not clear from the judgments in *Ridge* itself). In *Re H K*, the court for the first time talked of the requirement 'to act fairly'.

Ridge and *Re H K* together are so important because they opened up for debate the question of whether a hearing is required in any particular situation, irrespective of its formal categorisation. They did not, of course, provide a complete answer to that question, beyond suggesting that a hearing would be required when livelihood or reputation was significantly put at risk by a decision (as in *Ridge v Baldwin*), or where a fundamental right like the right to enter the county by immigration was at issue (as in *Re H K*).

Those decisions do not, however, help us in our example. Alice's existing livelihood has not been put at risk, because we know that she has never traded in the past. It could be argued that a finding that she is not fit and proper does significantly affect her reputation, but if no one else knew of the MTLB's decision, this is doubtful.

To decide, therefore, whether Alice is entitled to a hearing, it is necessary to look for authorities dealing with situations which are more similar. This is the same process that you have to go through each time you are confronted with a new situation to which you are not sure whether the rules of procedural propriety apply. In this case, we need to look for authorities on licensing decisions.

Licensing is an important function of government and self-regulatory bodies. In many walks of life, people are required to obtain a licence in order to engage in their desired activity –

14.4.3   Fair hearings and licensing decisions

whether following a particular profession or trade, broadcasting, or professional sport. The most important case in this area is probably *McInnes v Onslow-Fane* (1978). McInnes sought a boxing manager's licence from the British Boxing Board of Control. He had held a licence in the past, but not for several years before this application. The Board refused to grant him a licence without giving him an oral hearing, and without disclosing to him the basis of their decision. McInnes challenged this decision, claiming that the Board had acted in breach of natural justice and unfairly. In his judgment, Sir Robert Megarry VC divided up licence cases into three categories:

- The first category consisted of *'revocation cases'*: where someone holding an existing licence has it revoked for some reason. In that type of case, he held, the person should normally be offered a fair hearing before being deprived of the licence.

- At the opposite end of the spectrum were *'application cases'* – where a person who doesn't hold an existing licence applies for one. Here, he held, there would not normally be any obligation on the decision-maker to offer a hearing.

- Thirdly, the judge identified a category which he called 'expectation cases' but which, for reasons which we will deal with later, it is better to call *'renewal cases'*, where someone has held a licence which has expired by passage of time, and he or she applies for it to be renewed. The judge did not have to decide on this last category, but suggested that it was 'closer to the revocation cases' – ie closer to the situation where a hearing would be required.

On the facts, the judge found that McInnes came within the 'application' category, because he did not hold an existing licence, and therefore he was not entitled to a hearing or to know the case against him.

Although *McInnes* is as good a starting point as any in the context of licensing cases, it is not the last word on the subject. It is a little misleading in suggesting that classes of case can be divided up in the abstract, when in fact, as judges have subsequently emphasised, all depends on what is 'fair' in the particular circumstances. Since the *McInnes* decision it has become clearer that 'renewal cases' are indeed closer to 'revocation cases' - ie that unless there is a very good reason to the contrary, a person applying to continue a licence which has expired is entitled to a hearing before he or she is refused (see, for example, *R v Assistant Metropolitan Police Commissioner ex p Howell* (1986)). It has also become clearer that even in 'application cases', where the applicant has never held a licence before, there may be a limited right to a fair hearing. After all, a person can be as badly affected by being rejected in a 'first time' application as when losing an existing permit; she may be prevented from following a trade or vocation which she had set her heart on. In *R v Huntingdon District Council ex p Cowan* (1984), an applicant was refused an entertainments licence (after a first-time application) without being told of various objections which the Council had received, and without being given a hearing. The court held that the applicant should as a minimum have been informed of the nature of the objections made, and have been given a chance to reply in writing.

On this basis, we might advise Alice as follows:

Since Alice has not previously held a licence, she falls into the category known as 'application cases' which Megarry VC in *McInnes* suggested would not normally attract an entitlement to a hearing. However, the *Huntingdon* case suggests that even in this situation, a hearing may sometimes be required. Since the MTLB has turned Alice down on a very serious ground – that she is not fit and proper – without giving her any opportunity to comment (on an issue which she might well be expected to have something relevant to say), it is likely that a court would find that the MTLB has acted unfairly here. However, she is probably not entitled to an oral hearing, but only to be told of the objections against her and to have the opportunity of submitting written representations.

This is how you might deal with one particular situation; you should try to build up a picture from your lectures and textbooks as to what the courts have done in other factual contexts. What is most important is to try to develop an 'instinct' as to how the courts are likely to react. This is partly a matter of common sense. For example, it is fairly obvious why Megarry VC drew a distinction between application cases and revocation cases in *McInnes*. In a revocation case, an applicant may be losing his or her livelihood (or at least an important right) by being deprived of a licence. A first time applicant, on the other hand, has no existing rights to lose. Further, the class of people in the 'revocation' situation is limited (only those people who already have licences can be deprived of a licence), so the number of people to whom the authority might have to give a hearing is restricted. By contrast, the class of 'first time applicants' is potentially entirely unlimited. What would happen if the courts held that every applicant for a licence had to be given an oral hearing, and then one million people applied? The system would break down. It is important to realise that judges are influenced by practical considerations of this sort.

14.4.4	Summary of entitlement

To summarise the position today, we can suggest some general principles, always remembering that they are not rules, and that the answer is dependent upon what is fair in each individual case.

- As a very general rule, the courts tend to require that a fair hearing be given *whenever* an applicant's rights or interests are adversely affected in any significant way by a decision, unless there is good reason not to require a hearing.

- This general rule does not apply in the 'legislative' context – eg where an individual may be significantly affected by a proposed statutory instrument. Here, the courts incline against any right to a hearing (*Bates v Lord Hailsham* (1972)), although the position is not so rigid as it once was.

- Otherwise, if an applicant is deprived of a private law 'right', then a hearing is almost certainly required before the decision is taken.

- If an individual is by reason of the decision to be deprived of his or her livelihood, or a significant part of it, then a fair hearing is very probably necessary before the decision is taken.

- If an individual's reputation will be seriously affected by the decision, or if the individual's interests will otherwise be seriously affected, then a fair hearing is very probably necessary.

14.5   Restrictions on entitlement to a hearing

Even in a case where, by following the above analysis, you might expect an applicant to be entitled to a fair hearing, there are a number of reasons why that entitlement may be excluded. Below we list some of the more common reasons why this may happen. This list should not be regarded as rigid, or the last word on the subject; it is simply a collection of some of the reasons that the courts have given for holding that applicants have no entitlement to a fair hearing even though they might fall into a class which would normally be entitled. In addition, it is important to remember that the court in judicial review cases always has a general discretion not to grant a remedy, even where a ground of review, such as failure to grant a fair hearing, is made out. Some of the restrictions on entitlement listed below are sometimes used by the courts in this different way – as reasons why a remedy should not be granted. For present purposes, however, the distinction is not particularly important.

A statute may expressly exclude the right to a hearing in particular circumstances. Where this happens, the courts must give effect to the statute because, like the rest of the common law, the rules of natural justice are subservient to the will of Parliament. Express statutory exclusion therefore presents no difficulties.

14.5.1 Express statutory exclusion

In theory, implied exclusion is no different from express exclusion. If the way in which a statute is worded implies that Parliament must have intended that the right to a fair hearing be excluded (even though the statute does not actually say so), then the courts must give effect to that implied intention, and exclude any right to a hearing. However, in practice the courts are very reluctant to interpret a statute in this way, because the right to a fair hearing is regarded as of fundamental importance. The courts are more likely to be persuaded that Parliament intended to exclude natural justice if the legislation provides for *some* procedural protection (eg the right to make written representations); the court may then presume that the words of the Act impliedly exclude *greater* protection (eg the right to an oral hearing). But even in this situation, the courts may still supplement the statutory procedures with natural justice. In *Re Hamilton; Re Forrest* (1981), the court was faced with a decision of magistrates to commit Hamilton to prison, without giving him a hearing (and in his absence), for failing to pay sums due under a court order. The magistrates thought that they did not have to give him a hearing because Hamilton was already in prison for other offences, and the relevant legislation only required a hearing 'unless ... the offender is serving a term of imprisonment'. However, the House of Lords found that the legislation only exempted the magistrates from giving prisoners an oral hearing, and held that natural justice required that Hamilton be given an opportunity to make written representations.

14.5.2 Implied statutory exclusion

If a hearing, or the disclosure of information, would be prejudicial to the public interest then the court may refuse to grant a remedy whatever ground of judicial review is established; ie illegality or irrationality as well as breach of natural justice. The best example is the *GCHQ* case (1985), where the House of Lords held that the trade unions were in principle entitled to consultation before the ban on trade union membership was promulgated, but that on the facts this entitlement was defeated by an argument relying on national security: that if the government had consulted the trade unions before instituting the ban, this would have risked precipitating the very disruption to services that the ban was intended to avoid.

14.5.3 Where a hearing, or disclosure of information, would be prejudicial to the public interest

14.5.4	**In an emergency**	If a public body has to act very urgently, then it may be exempted from offering a hearing before taking the decision. A good example is *R v Secretary of State for Transport ex p Pegasus Holidays (London) Ltd* (1988), where the court held that the Secretary of State's decision to suspend the licences of Rumanian pilots without first giving them a hearing was justified in circumstances in which he feared an immediate threat to air safety (the pilots had failed a Civil Aviation Authority test). Note that there will normally still be a duty on the decision-maker to offer the individual a fair hearing as soon as possible after the decision – as and when time permits.
14.5.5	**Where it is administratively impracticable to require a hearing**	As we have already seen, administrative impossibility may be a reason for the courts finding that there is simply no prima facie entitlement to a fair hearing (remember the example of the 1 million licence applications, in para 14.4.3). But it may also, in rare cases, prompt the courts to refuse to grant a remedy even where there is a prima facie right to a hearing. So in *R v Secretary of State for Social Services ex p Association of Metropolitan Authorities* (1986), the court held that even though the Secretary of State had failed in his statutory duty to consult before making certain regulations, it would not quash the regulations (although it did grant a declaration) because by the time of the court's decision the regulations had been in force for some while, and it would cause great confusion to revoke them at that stage. The judge also took into account the fact that the regulations were a form of delegated legislation, which the court is always more reluctant to overturn.
		It is only in very exceptional circumstances that the court will refuse to quash a decision on this ground. Usually, the maxim 'justice and convenience are not on speaking terms' applies. It may be inconvenient for a decision to be quashed, but this is not a good reason for allowing an *ultra vires* decision to stand.
14.5.6	**Where the unfair decision has been 'cured' by a fair appeal**	What if an individual is wrongly denied a fair hearing, but there is then an internal appeal to an superior body which hears the case properly? Does the fair appeal 'cure' the unfair hearing? This is a difficult issue. On the one hand, it might be said that if a person is entitled to a hearing and to an appeal, then he or she is entitled to expect each to be fair, not merely the appeal. On the other hand, the individual has at least received one fair hearing (the appeal), and natural justice would not of itself normally require that there be more than one hearing.
		The general rule is that both the hearing and the appeal must be fair. The reason for this is that a fair appeal may be no substitute for a fair hearing: it is often easier to convince

someone of your case first time round, rather than persuading someone to change a decision on appeal; the burden of proof may be different on appeal; the appeal may not re-open issues of fact, etc.

However, where the appeal is a 'full' one (ie it is effectively a re-hearing of the original hearing), then the appeal may 'cure' the unfair hearing so that the individual cannot quash the decision on judicial review. In *Lloyd v McMahon* (1987), the House of Lords were faced with a situation where a district auditor had surcharged local authority councillors for deliberately failing to set a rate, after a 'hearing' which the councillors alleged was in breach of natural justice (because he had only offered them an opportunity to make written representations rather than an oral hearing). The councillors had made use of a statutory appeal to the High Court, which had rejected their appeal. The House of Lords held that, the district auditor had not in fact acted unfairly in not offering an oral hearing, but further held that even if that failure was unfair, it was 'cured' by the statutory appeal to the High Court, because the appeal was a full rehearing of the matter, rather than simply an appeal; there was 'no question of the court being confined to a review of the evidence which was available to the auditor' (Lord Keith) (see also the Privy Council decision in *Calvin v Carr* (1980)).

Similar issues arise where the decision alleged to be unfair is only preliminary to subsequent decision before which a hearing will be given. Although there are a number of confusing cases, the test is essentially the same as before: has any real unfairness been caused by the fact that the applicant has not been granted a fair hearing at the preliminary stage?

14.5.7   Where the decision is only preliminary to a subsequent decision before which a hearing will be given

On various occasions, courts have suggested that an applicant is not entitled to a fair hearing if the court thinks that the procedural error made 'no difference' to the decision reached, or where, because of the bad conduct of the applicant or for some other reason, the court thinks that it would be 'futile' to grant a remedy because the decision-maker would inevitably come to the same decision a second time.

14.5.8   Where the error made 'no difference' to the result, or where a hearing would be futile

Both these lines of reasoning have in common the fact that the court is looking beyond the defect in procedure, and is taking into account the actual merits of the case. This is normally regarded as the cardinal sin of judicial review – the court is not meant to second-guess the decision-maker, by deciding what would have been the result if the decision-maker had acted properly! The courts therefore normally refuse to go along with this type of argument. To take an example:

Alice (in the example in para 14.4 above) takes your advice and seeks judicial review of the decision to refuse her application without a hearing. The MTLB admits that it should have given her an opportunity to make written representations, but puts evidence before the court to show that Alice is a notorious thief and confidence trickster, and therefore would be a completely unsuitable person to hold a licence. The MTLB argues that the court should not quash its decision because its error (the failure to entertain written representations) did not affect the result. Given her bad character, she could say nothing in her representations which could lead the MTLB to make a different decision. Making us take the decision again, say the MTLB, would be futile.

The answer to this is that it is not for the court to judge whether or not the MTLB would necessarily come to the same decision. The role of the court is to quash the decision, if a ground of review is made out, and to remit the case back to the MTLB for it to re-take the decision with an open mind.

Having said this, you may well come across a few 'rogue' decisions where the courts have, in effect, committed the cardinal error and accepted the 'futility' argument. For example, in *Glynn v Keele University* (1971), the court refused to overturn a disciplinary decision in respect of a university student, even though the court found that the hearing was defective. This was because the offence (nude sunbathing!) merited a severe penalty 'even today', and all that was lost was a chance to plead in mitigation. And in *Cinnamond v British Airports Authority* (1980), the Court of Appeal upheld an order excluding six minicab drivers from Heathrow airport, even though BAA had wrongly failed to give the drivers a hearing, because (as Lord Denning put it), the past records of the six were so bad (convictions, unpaid fines, flouting of BAA's regulations) that they could not expect to be consulted over the decision, and there was therefore no breach of natural justice.

However, these are isolated cases. More representative of the law is the well known dictum of Megarry J in *John v Rees* (1970):

> 'As everybody who has anything to do with the law well knows, the path of the law is strewn with examples of open and shut cases which somehow, were not; of unanswerable charges which, in the event, were completely answered; of fixed and unalterable determinations that, by discussion, suffered a change. Nor are those with any knowledge of human nature ... likely to underestimate the feelings of resentment of those who find that a decision against them has been made without their being afforded any opportunity to influence the course of events.' (at p 402)

So far in this chapter, we have spoken in general terms of 'fair hearings'. We need now to consider what precisely is meant by the phrase. Assuming that an entitlement to a fair hearing does exist, what procedural rights can the applicant actually expect? The answer depends, as always, upon what fairness requires in the individual circumstances of the case. Once again, the best way to get a 'feel' for what is required in different circumstances is to look at what the courts have done in past cases, and to put that together with the principles on which the courts tend to act. What follows is a 'menu' of different procedural protections, starting from the most basic and widespread, and progressing to rights which are certainly not required in every case.

Whenever an individual has any right at all to be consulted or heard before a decision is taken, he or she will almost inevitably also have a right to disclosure of the case to be met, or the basis upon which the decision-maker proposes to act. The courts have recognised that it will often be meaningless to give someone a right to make representations if they do not know the case against them, because they will not know to what issues to direct their representations. As Lord Denning MR put it, 'If the right to be heard is to be a real right which is worth anything ... [an applicant] must know what evidence has been given and what statements have been made affecting him' (*Kanda v Government of Malaya* (1962)).

An example of a case where the decision-maker failed to make proper disclosure is *Chief Constable of North Wales v Evans* (1982). Here, a probationer police constable was required to resign by the chief constable following various allegations as to his 'unsuitable' lifestyle, of which he was not informed at the time he was effectively dismissed. Most of the allegations turned out to be untrue or very misleading. The House of Lords held that the chief constable had acted in breach of his duty of fairness in not putting to Evans the adverse factors on which he relied.

There are, however, limits on the right to disclosure. Public decision-makers are not normally obliged to disclose every relevant document to an affected individual, as if they were giving discovery in civil litigation. The test is normally whether the individual had sufficient information and material as to the case against him so that he was able to make informed submissions. Further, in some situations the material which the applicant wants to see may be confidential or sensitive. In such cases, the applicant may have to make do with rather less than full disclosure. In *R v Gaming Board ex p Benaim and Khaida* (1970), the applicants re-applied for gaming

14.6 Content of the fair hearing

14.6.1 Disclosure to the applicant of the case to be met

licences. The Board gave them a hearing and indicated the matters which were troubling the Board, but refused their application without indicating the source or precise content of the information upon which the Board relied. The Court of Appeal held that, in the circumstances, it was enough that the applicants were given the general nature of the case against them, sufficient to prepare their representations. The Board did not need to 'quote chapter and verse' against them, nor did it have to disclose information which would put an informer to the Board in peril of discovery, or which would otherwise be contrary to the public interest.

14.6.2	Written representations v Oral hearings; Consultation

Ordinarily, where a hearing is required, then it must be an oral hearing. But in some circumstances, the courts have held that the requirements of fairness are satisfied by an opportunity to submit written representations. For example, in *R v Huntingdon District Council ex p Cowan* (1984) (discussed above in relation to licence applications, para 14.4.3), it was held that in considering an application for an entertainments licence, a local authority was not under a duty to give the applicant an oral hearing; it was sufficient to inform him of objections made and to give him an opportunity to reply in writing. Part of the reason for this, as noted above, is the sheer impracticality of insisting on oral hearings in circumstances where there is an entirely open-ended category of applicants.

In general, the requirement that a hearing should be oral is only likely to be relaxed where there is no good reason for any more than written representations. If, therefore, the decision may turn on the applicant's credibility, or on contested evidence of witnesses, then an oral hearing will have to be given. Similarly, where the applicant faces disciplinary charges, or any other decision which will have a serious impact on his reputation, the courts are likely to require the decision-maker to allow the applicant to address it in person.

Many statutes provide that the minister, or other public authority, shall undertake 'consultations' before arriving at a decision. In general, the courts have interpreted this as requiring no more than allowing affected parties to submit written representations (see eg *R v Secretary of State for Health ex p United States Tobacco International Inc* (1991)). The courts will try to ensure, however, that such consultation is more than a mere formality. Thus, in *R v Secretary of State for Social Services ex p Association of Metropolitan Authorities* (1986), Webster J stressed that: 'the essence of consultation is the communication of a genuine invitation to give advice and a genuine consideration of that advice.'

Fairness may require that the decision-maker allow persons affected to call witnesses to give evidence to support their case. This is likely to be so in more 'formal' proceedings, such as disciplinary hearings. The courts have held that tribunals and other decision-makers have a *discretion* as to whether or not to allow witnesses to be called; however, this discretion must be exercised reasonably and in good faith. In this context, the courts will be prepared to intervene to strike down a decision not to allow witnesses to be called not only if they think that the decision is *Wednesbury* unreasonable or irrational (see Chapter 17), but on the much narrower ground that they believe that the decision was unfair and unreasonable. Thus in *R v Board of Visitors of Hull Prison ex p St Germain (No 2) (1979)*, the court struck down as contrary to natural justice the decision of a prison board of visitors at a disciplinary hearing (following a prison riot) not to allow a prisoner to call witnesses because of the administrative inconvenience involved in calling the witnesses – who were fellow prisoners, then at different prisons. The court also (not surprisingly) rejected that argument that the witnesses were unnecessary because the tribunal believed that there was ample evidence against the prisoner.

In other circumstances, the courts may be more respectful of the tribunal's decision not to allow witnesses to be called. In *R v Panel on Take-Overs and Mergers ex p Guinness plc (1989)*, the Court of Appeal stated that it felt the 'greatest anxiety' about the panel's decision not to grant an adjournment to allow witnesses for Guinness to attend. However, the court found it impossible to say that the decision had been wrong, bearing in mind that the panel did not exercise a disciplinary function, and was an 'inquisitorial' rather than 'adversarial' body. The court also took into account the 'overwhelming' evidence in favour of the panel's view.

14.6.3 The right to call witnesses

Essentially, the same principles apply to the right to legal representation and to cross-examination of witnesses as to the entitlement to call witnesses. The tribunal or decision-maker has a discretion as to whether or not to allow an applicant to be legally represented. However, the courts may intervene to strike down a decision not to allow representation if the decision is unfair. Unfairness will almost certainly exist if the tribunal allows one side to be legally represented and not the other. It may also exist, particularly in formal disciplinary proceedings, if the questions at issue are complex and the applicant is not genuinely capable of representing him or herself. Thus in *R v Home Secretary ex p Tarrant (1984)*, the court quashed a disciplinary decision of a prison Board of Visitors

14.6.4 The right to legal representation and to cross-examination of witnesses

for unfairness caused by a failure to allow legal representation. The court set out a number of factors, which together required that representation be allowed: the seriousness of the charge and penalty which the prisoner faced; the likelihood that points of law would arise; the prisoner's capacity to present his own case, and the need for fairness between prisoners, and between prisoners and prison officers. The House of Lords approved the decision in Tarrant in *R v Board of Visitors of HM Prisons, The Maze, ex p Hone* (1988) – but remember that in each case must be considered on its merits; there are other prisoners' discipline cases where the opposite conclusion has been reached, where the charges were straightforward (legally and factually), and where the prisoner was articulate (*R v Board of Visitors of Parkhurst Prison ex p Norney* (1989)).

The question of entitlement to cross-examine witnesses produced by the other side normally (although not always) arises where the parties are legally represented. As a general rule, it can be said that if a witness is allowed to testify orally, then the other side should be allowed to confront the witness by cross-examination. But once again, this is a matter of discretion for the tribunal or adjudicator, and if the tribunal feels that cross-examination will serve no useful purpose, then the court may be slow to disturb that decision. The most important case on this question is *Bushell v Secretary of State for the Environment* (1981), where the House of Lords refused to overturn the decision of an inspector at a public inquiry in relation to a proposed motorway not to allow cross-examination as to the basis of the Department predictions of the environment's future traffic flow. Although the decision can be read as suggesting that cross-examination should not be allowed on 'policy' type issues, it is more accurate to say that the crucial point was that the House of Lords (and the inspector) did not regard the issue of future traffic flow as a *relevant* question for the inquiry to decide; hence, it was reasonable not to allow cross-examination on the point (there is, however, an unanswered question as to why, if this is right, the Secretary of State was allowed to adduce evidence as to traffic flow forecasts at all).

14.6.5   **The right to reasons for the decision**

Whether or not a person affected by a decision has a right to be provided with reasons explaining or justifying that decision is an important and fast-growing topic in public law. It is a topic which can arise, for students, both in the context of a judicial review problem question and in an essay question. It is therefore worth considering the subject in some detail.

Before looking at the current position in English law, it is worth asking whether an entitlement to be given reasons for a decision of a public body is really so important, and if so, why. It is clear that eminent contemporary public law writers do regard an entitlement to reasons as important. As Lord Woolf has said (41st Hamlyn Lectures, *'Protection of the Public - A New Challenge'*, 1990):

> 'I regard the giving of satisfactory reasons for a decision as being the hallmark of good administration and if I were to be asked to identify the most beneficial improvement which could be made to English administrative law I would unhesitatingly reply that it would be the introduction of a general requirement that reasons should normally be available, at least on request, for all administrative actions.'

Professor Wade has stated that the lack of a general duty to give reasons is an 'outstanding deficiency of administrative law'; and that 'a right to reasons is an indispensable part of a sound system of judicial review' (Wade & Forsyth, *Administrative Law* (1994) pp 544, 542). And the JUSTICE-All Souls Committee report 'Administrative Justice, Some Necessary Reforms' (1988) devoted an entire chapter to the duty to give reasons, and concluded by endorsing the 1971 JUSTICE Committee report 'Administration Under Law' that:

> 'no single factor has inhibited the development of English administrative law as seriously as the absence of any general obligation upon public authorities to give reasons for their decisions.'

Why do these writers think the duty to give reasons so important? They do not all share the same view, and it is well worth comparing eg the JUSTICE-All Souls view with Lord Woolf's position. Note particularly that reasons are not only valuable for the individual or individuals who will be affected by the decision; many writers believe that it is also in the interests of the decision-maker itself to give reasons. To summarise greatly, one can categorise the advantages of the duty to give reasons as follows:

- From the affected individual's point of view:

    (a) to satisfy his expectation of just and fair treatment by the decision-maker, both in his particular case and as a decision-making body in general;

    (b) to enable him to decide whether the decision is open to challenge (by way of appeal, further representations, or judicial review).

- From the decision-maker's point of view:

    (a) to improve the *quality* of decision-making (if someone knows that they have to justify their decision, that fact alone may make them take the decision more responsibly, may improve the articulation of their thought processes etc; reasons may therefore be a check on arbitrariness);

(b) to help 'legitimation' of decision-making process: to ensure that the decision-maker is generally regarded as a fair and reasonable body;

- to *protect* the administration from hopeless appeals or other challenges (the idea is that if an individual has a decision explained to him, he may be more inclined to accept it and therefore not challenge it).

Finally, courts and other reviewing or appellate bodies may need reasons in order to assess whether or not the original decision was lawful or correct.

Obviously, some of these arguments in favour of a right to reasons are stronger than others; you may think some of them carry little weight or are even insignificant. And when considering how important it is for English law to include a duty to give reasons, you should bear in mind that there are also significant disadvantages. The most obvious is the extra administrative burden on public bodies; the sheer time and effort involved in justifying every decision to every affected individual. You will notice that Lord Woolf, quoted above, suggests that reasons should be available 'at least on request'; this suggests one way in which the burden might be cut down – but it still leaves decision-makers whose decisions affect a large number of persons potentially exposed to a great administrative burden. Also, some might argue that a duty to give reasons would increase the number of challenges against public bodies, since people will want to challenge reasons which they believe are wrong. That might be no bad thing, if the reasons really are wrong, but it might also expose decision-makers to large numbers of unmeritorious challenges.

One caution at this point: it is very important to distinguish the *right to reasons* for a decision from the right to be informed of the case against one before the decision is taken – the right to *proper disclosure in advance*. The latter is, as we have seen in para 14.6.1, a basic requirement of natural justice, and is quite different from the duty to give reasons, because it relates to the provision of information *before* the decision is taken, rather than after the event. In a nutshell, disclosure is important so that one knows what representations one should make, while reasons are important so that one knows how and why the decision was made.

Ultimately, different people will have different views about the relative strengths of the arguments for and against reasons. Of course, the debate is not simply black and white: either for or against reasons. English law is increasingly attempting to identify those situations where it would be valuable for reasons to be given, and to distinguish those from others where the decision-maker does not have to justify the decision. In considering the case law, it is worth keeping in the back of your mind the general arguments for and against reasons, and 'measuring' the decisions in the cases against your views of the strengths of the different arguments.

- No general duty to give reasons?

   The traditional position in English law has always been that there is no general rule of law (or in particular, of natural justice) that reasons should be given for public law decisions. This view was recently reaffirmed in the important House of Lords case of *R v Secretary of State for the Home Department ex p Doody* (1993). But recent cases – including *Doody* itself – have emphasised that this is only a *general rule*. If fairness requires it in any particular situation, the courts have now begun to insist that decision-makers provide reasons for decisions. Judges have not done this in any organised way; ie they have not laid down a series of propositions which set out in the abstract those categories of case in which reasons are required. Instead, they have developed (and are developing) the law on an incremental basis. The law is therefore uncertain at the moment; indeed, it is beginning to look as if the 'general position' that there is no right to reasons, endorsed in *Doody* only two years ago, is rapidly becoming the exception rather than the rule. Recent cases in which the courts have held that a right to reasons exists include:

   (a) *R v Civil Service Appeal Board ex p Cunningham* (1992): the Court of Appeal held that fairness required that a prison officer be given reasons by the Civil Service Appeal Board for an (unexpectedly low) award of damages for unfair dismissal (the Board, unlike the Industrial Tribunals on which it was modelled, is not required by statute or regulation to give reasons);

   (b) *Doody* (above): the Home Secretary must give reasons for the 'tariff' period to be served by certain life sentence prisoners;

   (c) *R v Harrow Crown Court ex p Dave* (1994): the Crown Court should give reasons for all its decisions (except possibly some interlocutory and procedural decisions);

(d) *R v Lambeth London Borough Council ex p Walters* (1993):
a local authority should give reasons for its decision
on an individual's application for local authority
housing – the judge went so far as to suggest that
there is now usually a general duty to give reasons –
although this probably does not (yet!) represent the
real state of the law.

There are still cases, however, where reasons are not
required to be given. In *R v Higher Education Funding
Council ex p Institute of Dental Surgery* (1994), the court held
that the HEFC was not required to give reasons for its
decision to assess the Institute at a relatively low level in its
comparative assessment of the research of all higher
education establishments. Although the fact that the
decision was one of academic judgment, arrived at by a
panel of experts, did not of itself mean that reasons could
not be required, the court found that given the
'combination of openness in the run-up [to the decision]',
and 'the prescriptively oracular character of the critical
decision', the HEFC's decision was 'inapt' for the giving of
reasons. Even here, however, the court rejected that
argument that the duty to give reasons could be seen as an
'exceptional' one any longer.

In general, one can summarise the present position by
saying that while each case depends on what is 'fair' in the
circumstances, the following factors may dispose a court in
favour of requiring reasons: (1) the decision affects
individuals' 'fundamental' rights (such as liberty); (2) the
decision-maker in question must make a 'formal' decision
– ie after a judicialised hearing; (3) the decision is one for
which the person affected needs reasons in order to know
whether to appeal or seek judicial review; (4) it would not
be administratively impracticable for the decision-maker to
give reasons for each decision.

Where reasons are required, they may usually be brief; the
courts do not readily entertain challenges to the *adequacy* of
reasons. And even where a decision-maker fails to give
reasons for a decision where it is obliged to do so, the court
will not necessarily quash the decision. If it has remedied
the error by providing proper reasons in an affidavit sworn
in judicial review proceedings (or otherwise later notified
the individual of the reasons for the decision), then the
court may well in its discretion decide not to overturn the
decision.

- Reasons to the court

So far, we have examined the circumstances in which the common law requires a public body to give *the person affected* reasons for its decision. A different situation arises where an application for judicial review is made, on any of the grounds of review; does the public body then have to give reasons for its decision *to the court*? While the court cannot compel the decision-maker to justify the decision, it may well be more willing to strike down a decision if no reasons are given for it, even though fairness/natural justice does not require that reasons be given. This is really based on common sense: a decision which the decision-maker does not defend may well be more vulnerable to challenge. In *Padfield v Minister of Agriculture* (1968), the House of Lords went so far as to suggest that if an applicant could establish a *prima facie* case of unlawfulness, then in the absence of reasons the court could infer that unlawfulness was made out. Another example of this line of reasoning is *Cunningham* (above), where Sir John Donaldson MR was prepared to infer, in circumstances where the Civil Service Appeal Board had not attempted to justify to the court an apparently unusually low award of compensation to a prison officer, that the decision was irrational. Of course, this line of cases is not really an example of 'procedural impropriety' at all; it is merely an example of the court effectively shifting the evidential burden onto the respondent. However, it is worth taking into account in this context, because it provides another route by which decision-makers may ultimately be forced to give reasons for their decisions; if not immediately, to the individual, then later, to the court.

The Grounds of Judicial Review II: Fair Hearings

By articulating standards of *procedural propriety*, the courts control the way in which decision-makers arrive at their decisions. This is achieved by a number of different techniques, which we have categorised under three headings:

- the right to a fair hearing (dealt with in this chapter);

- the rule against bias (Chapter 15);

- the doctrine of legitimate expectation (Chapter 16).

The *entitlement to a fair hearing* depends, in essence, upon what fairness requires in any given set of circumstances. This can be broken down into three elements:

A fair hearing is required, in essence, whenever an applicant's rights or interests are adversely affected in any significant way by a decision, unless there is a good reason not to require a hearing.

When **is a fair hearing** *prima facie* **required?**

Some possible reasons as to why the entitlement to a hearing may be restricted are:

Is there any reason why the *prima facie* entitlement to a hearing should be limited?

- express statutory exclusion;

- implied statutory exclusion;

- where a hearing, or disclosure of information, would be prejudicial to the public interest;

- in an emergency;

- where it is administratively impracticable to require a hearing;

- where the unfair decision has been 'cured' by a fair appeal;

- where the decision is only preliminary to a subsequent decision before which a hearing will be given;

- where the error made 'no difference' to the result, or where a hearing would be futile.

A 'menu' of possible procedural rights that the applicant can demand includes:

If a some sort of hearing is required, what procedural protection can the applicant actually demand?

(i) disclosure to the applicant of the case to be met;

(ii) written or oral representations, or consultation;

(iii) the right to call witnesses;

(iv) the right to legal representation and to cross examination of witnesses;

(v) the right to reasons for the decision.

What is appropriate in any given case is once again a matter of asking what 'fairness' requires. Broadly, the above list is in descending order of importance: while (i) and (ii) are fundamental to almost any case in which a fair hearing is required (and within (ii), the representations will more usually be required to be oral rather than written), (iii) and (iv) are more likely to be required only in 'formal' proceedings, such as disciplinary hearings or other hearings of an adversarial nature. (v) has traditionally been seen (where it has been recognised at all) as only available in 'exceptional' circumstances, but its rapid development may mean that it must be promoted up the list – we may be seeing the development of a general duty on public bodies to give reasons for decisions.

Chapter 15

The Grounds of Judicial Review II: The Rule Against Bias

A decision may be challenged on grounds of procedural impropriety if it can be established that there was 'bias' on the part of the decision-maker. Bias can take many forms. At one extreme, there are blatant cases which break the rule that nobody may be a judge in his or her own cause (*nemo judex in causa sua*) – where, for example, the decision-maker knowingly has a financial interest in the outcome of the case. At the other end of the spectrum are cases where people may disagree as to whether 'bias' exists, and if so, whether it matters; where, for example, a decision-maker has strong views about the subject-matter of the case before him.

In considering what constitutes bias, we need to look not only at public law cases but also at criminal cases, because here too the same considerations of 'natural justice' and the need to maintain public confidence in decision-making processes apply. The modern leading case on bias is in fact a criminal one, *R v Gough* (1993), and in his judgment Lord Goff confirmed that it was:

> 'possible, and desirable, that the same test should be applicable in all cases of apparent bias, whether concerned with justices or members of other inferior tribunals, or with jurors, or with arbitrators.'

What a court is usually looking for when it reviews a decision for bias is whether the *appearance* of bias is sufficient to justify intervention, rather than whether there was *in fact* any bias (although if it is shown that there was *in fact* bias, this will also justify intervention). This distinction might appear inconsistent with the notion that the rule against bias is a facet of 'natural justice', which is normally concerned with what the decision-maker actually did; it might be argued that a mere appearance of bias does not mean that a biased decision is inevitable, or even likely, because it is perfectly possible for a decision-maker with an interest in the outcome of a case to decide purely on the merits of the case. There are, however, sound reasons of policy why the law should ordinarily take apparent bias as a sufficient reason for intervention:

- it is often extremely difficult to determine the actual state of mind of an individual who is alleged to be biased;

- bias can operate even though the individual concerned is unaware of its effect;

- even where no bias has in fact occurred, it is important that public confidence in the integrity of a decision-making process is maintained, such that, in the often-quoted words of Lord Hewart CJ in *R v Sussex Justices ex p McCarthy* (1924), 'justice should not only be done, but should manifestly and undoubtedly be seen to be done'.

- If a court was obliged to investigate the actual state of mind of a decision-maker, the confidentiality of the decision-making process might be prejudiced (see *R v Gough, per* Lord Woolf at p 672; although you may question how serious this would be in many cases).

Accordingly, a decision may be quashed merely if there is found to be a sufficient degree of possibility of bias, even if there is no suggestion that actual bias occurred. It is rare, therefore, for actual bias to be shown to exist, but if it is proved, relief will, of course, be granted too.

On the other hand, if the court can be satisfied on the facts that there was *no possibility* of actual bias, then the court may be willing to disregard allegations of 'apparent bias'. In a recent case in which relatives of some of the victims of a collision involving the *Marchioness* passenger launch on the River Thames sought to have the coroner at the inquest removed on the ground of apparent bias, the Court of Appeal appeared to set limits on the extent to which courts should consider allegations of apparent bias. It was suggested that where it has to consider allegations of unconscious bias, the court is not strictly concerned with the appearance of bias, but rather with establishing the possibility that there was actual bias. The term 'apparent bias' was even considered by one of the judges (Sir Thomas Bingham MR) to be a unhelpful term, because:

> '... if despite the appearance of bias the court is able to ... satisfy itself that there was no danger of the alleged bias having in fact caused injustice, the impugned decision will be allowed to stand.' (*R v Inner West London Coroner ex p Dallaglio* (1994)).

The position today, in summary, is therefore that:

- actual bias will almost inevitably provide good grounds for challenging a decision;

- apparent bias, if sufficiently serious, will also provide grounds for challenge; unless

- it can be proved that, despite the appearance of bias, there was in fact no actual bias; in that case, the decision will be allowed to stand (on the authority of *Dallaglio*).

When it can be shown that a decision was actually affected by bias then, as we have seen, the court will intervene. In cases where the appearance of bias is alleged, however, the court must determine whether the appearance of partiality is sufficiently serious to justify intervention. Two different tests have traditionally been employed to assess this, and although the confusion this caused has seemingly been cleared up by a recent decision of the House of Lords, it is worth considering both approaches briefly, because they are revealing about the kind of apparent bias that the law has set out to prevent.

The first test was whether the facts, as assessed by the court, gave rise to a 'real likelihood' of bias. This approach was often applied in cases where the possibility that actual bias had occurred seemed remote. Under the second test, the court considered whether a reasonable person would have a 'reasonable suspicion' of bias. This test inevitably begged the question of how much knowledge of the facts the hypothetical reasonable person had. In practice, courts chose whichever terminology best suited the particular case, according to whether they believed the decision under review ought to be quashed or not.

In *R v Gough* (1993), the House of Lords decisively came down in favour of the first of the two competing approaches, but preferred the phrase *'real danger'* to 'real likelihood' of bias, so as 'to ensure that the court is thinking in terms of possibility rather than probability of bias'. The requirement for the court to postulate the view of a 'reasonable person' was expressly discarded in favour of a test relying on the opinion of the court, which 'personifies the reasonable man'. Lord Woolf emphasised the universal nature of this 'real danger' test, stating that it could 'ensure that the purity of justice is maintained across the range of situations where bias may exist'. The recent decision of the Court of Appeal in *R v Inner West London Coroner ex p Dallaglio* (1994) (the *Marchioness* case) is consistent with *Gough*, although it adds the explanation that 'real danger' can be interpreted as 'not without substance' and as involving 'more than a minimal risk, less than a probability'.

Cases where a person acting in a judicial capacity has a financial interest in the outcome of proceedings are sometimes regarded as being in a special category. These circumstances are treated as being conclusive of apparent bias and therefore of justifying intervention, regardless of the extent of the interest (unless negligible) and regardless of whether the interest has actually had an effect on the decision in question (see eg *Dimes v Proprietors of Grand Junction Canal* (1852)). In

15.3 The test for the appearance of bias

15.4 Direct pecuniary interest

such situations, there is no need to apply the usual test of whether there was a 'real danger' of bias; instead, the nature of the interest is such that public confidence in the administration of justice requires that the person be disqualified from acting as decision-maker in the matter, and that the decision should not stand.

You may feel that it is not necessary to place cases such as these in a special category of 'conclusive' apparent bias. It may simply be that in such a case, the 'real danger' test is almost inevitably made out on the facts. Indeed, in rare cases it might still be that even a direct financial interest would not be sufficient to establish bias; for example, where it is demonstrably clear that a decision-maker was not aware at the date of his decision that he possessed the financial interest. On the other hand, Lord Goff in *Gough* re-stated the traditional view that where direct pecuniary interest can be shown, it is unnecessary to inquire whether there was any real likelihood of bias.

15.5   Different manifestations of bias

One common cause of objectionable bias is where a decision-maker has previously been involved with the case in some other capacity. In one such example, an individual who had already supported a measure in his capacity as a member of the local authority was disqualified from adjudicating on it as a magistrate (*R v Gaisford* (1892)). In another case, a conviction for dangerous driving was invalidated because the clerk to the justices was also a solicitor in the firm which was acting against the defendant in a civil action (*R v Sussex Justices ex p McCarthy* (1924)). In another example, a decision of a local council to grant planning permission was quashed because one of the councillors was the estate agent of the owner of the property to whom permission was granted (*R v Hendon Rural District Council ex p Chorley* (1933)).

An individual will not necessarily be barred from adjudicating if he is a member of an organisation which is one of the parties in an action, provided he has himself been inactive in the matter. Thus a magistrate was allowed to hear a prosecution brought by the Council of the Law Society even though he was himself a solicitor (*R v Burton ex p Young* (1897)).

'Bias by predetermination' may occur where it can be shown that a person acting in a judicial capacity has committed himself to one outcome before hearing part or all of a case. For example, bias was established where a magistrate was found to have prepared a statement of the sentence halfway through a trial (*R v Romsey Justices ex p Green* (1992)).

However, the mere fact that an adjudicator is known to have strong personal beliefs or ideas on a relevant matter need not mean that he will be disqualified. In such cases it is a question of degree as to what extent the decision-maker is to be credited with the ability to act impartially despite his or her views, and thus, for example, a licensing magistrate's ruling was allowed to stand although he was a teetotaller (*R v Nailsworth Licensing Justices ex p Bird* (1953)).

The rule against bias is often enforced very strictly, going well beyond the original principle that what is to be avoided is for a person to decide in their own cause. Sometimes, mere contact between the adjudicator and one of the parties can amount to bias. For example, a disciplinary committee was overruled because it had consulted privately with the chief fire officer who had reported a fireman for lack of discipline (*R v Leicestershire Fire Authority ex p Thompson* (1978)).

It is common for a government department to initiate a particular proposal and for the relevant minister also to be given the power to confirm that proposal after hearing objections to it. A ministerial decision of this kind cannot be objected to on the ground that the minister was biased simply because the decision was made in accordance with government policy, since the whole purpose of Parliament giving the deciding power to a political body is so that the power may be exercised politically.	**15.6 Ministerial bias**

In *Franklin v Minister of Town and Country Planning* (1948), it was alleged that the minister's political support for the establishment of a new town had prevented him from giving impartial consideration to objections made at a public inquiry, and therefore, it was suggested, he should be disqualified from ruling on whether or not the proposal should be adopted. However, it was held that provided that the minister fulfilled his statutory duty of considering the objections, his decision could not be impugned on the ground of bias.

On the other hand, the suggestion in *Franklin* and other early cases that the rule against bias did not apply (or fully apply) to 'administrative cases' has been firmly rejected; as with the right to a fair hearing, the distinction between 'judicial' and 'administrative' functions is no longer part of the test for bias (see Chapter 14, paras 14.4.1 and 14.4.2). Thus the requirement that a decision-maker should not be biased applies to all decision-makers – unless exceptional circumstances exist.

In three types of situation, bias has been held not to constitute a vitiating factor:	**15.7 Exceptions: when bias will not invalidate a decision**

- A party may waive its right to object to a biased adjudicator. This rule can operate harshly; if a party fails to object as soon as the fact of the alleged bias is known, it may be held to have waived its right to do so.

- The rule against bias will also cease to take effect in cases of necessity, such as where no replacement can be found for an adjudicator who is allegedly biased. One situation in which this can arise is where the case concerns one or more members of the judiciary – for example, where a Canadian court had to determine the tax status of judges' salaries (*The Judges v Attorney-General for Saskatchewan* (1937)). More commonly, if a statute empowers only one particular minister or other official to decide on a particular issue, the courts will not allow that decision to be frustrated by disqualifying the individual for bias.

  However, even in a case where all the available qualified adjudicators could appear to be biased, a decision would probably be quashed if actual bias was proved.

- In some cases, Parliament has deliberately acted to prevent the operation of the rule against bias by granting specific exemptions. Statutory dispensation can be effective to exclude the rule, but clear words of enactment must be used, and any ambiguity is likely to be interpreted narrowly so as to minimise the circumstances in which the decision-maker is exempted from disqualification. By statute, for example, a liquor licensing justice is permitted to hear the appeal from a refused application, even if he was also a member of the licensing committee which decided on the original application (see *R v Bristol Crown Court ex p Cooper* (1990)).

The Grounds of Judicial Review II: The Rule Against Bias

A decision may be quashed for bias if it can be shown either:

- that the decision-maker in fact had an interest in the decision which he reached, either financially or otherwise ('actual bias'); or

- even if there is no proof of actual bias, that the facts, as assessed by the court, disclose a 'real danger' of bias (*R v Gough* (1993)) – by which the court means a danger which is more than a minimal risk, if less than a probability (*Dallaglio* (1994)).

This latter test for bias – what has been known as 'apparent bias' – is important, principally because (in Lord Hewart's words) 'justice should not only be done, but should manifestly and undoubtedly be seen to be done'.

However, if it can be established that, on the facts, there was no actual bias, then the decision will be allowed to stand even if the facts would otherwise disclose apparent bias (*Dallaglio*). On the other hand, if a person acting in a judicial capacity has a financial interest in the outcome of the case, then this will normally be treated as conclusive of apparent bias.

Bias may be held not to invalidate a decision if it can be shown:

- that a party (with knowledge of the facts) has waived its right to object to a biased adjudicator;

- that the situation is one of 'necessity'; in other words, there is no realistic alternative to an adjudicator who appears biased;

- that the rule against bias has been excluded, either expressly or (very unusually) impliedly, by legislation (eg *R v Bristol Crown Court ex p Cooper*).

Chapter 16

The Grounds of Judicial Review II: The Doctrine of Legitimate Expectation

The doctrine of legitimate expectation is a recent development, even by fast-moving public law standards. The term was first mentioned in an English case in 1969 (in *Schmidt v Secretary of State for Home Affairs*), but it was not until the early to mid 1980s that the doctrine had settled into anything like a clear body of law. Partly because it is such a recent development, the doctrine is still perhaps rather skimpily treated in some of the major textbooks. But it is extremely likely to make an appearance in exams in problem questions (and perhaps essay questions), and in practice, it is a common and increasingly used ground of review.

16.1   Introduction

The basic principle behind the doctrine is rather like the idea behind estoppel in private law; that, if possible, the law ought to require people to keep to their promises or representations, even where the promise does not constitute a contract. More specifically, where a public body has represented to an individual that it will or will not do something, then (even though the body has not bound itself to follow that representation), it ought not to be allowed to disappoint the representation, at least unless it gives the individual a hearing first.

There are, however, a number of complications, and a host of recent reported cases, which make it necessary to spend a fair amount of time considering the doctrine.

The most useful definition of the legitimate expectation can be found is in the *GCHQ* case (*Council of Civil Service Unions v Minister for the Civil Service* (1985)). It is worth quoting from two of the judgments. First, Lord Diplock stated that for a legitimate expectation to arise, the decision:

16.2   The doctrine

> '... must affect [the individual] ... by depriving him of some benefit or advantage which either (i) he had in the past been permitted by the decision-maker to enjoy and which he can legitimately expect to be permitted to continue to do until there has been communicated to him some rational grounds for withdrawing it on which he has been given an opportunity to comment; or (ii) he has received assurance from the decision-maker will not be withdrawn without giving him first an opportunity of advancing reasons for contending that they should not be withdrawn.' (pp 408-9).

Lord Frazer put it rather more simply:

'Legitimate ... expectation may arise either from an express promise given on behalf of a public authority or from the existence of a regular practice which the claimant can reasonably expect to continue.' (p 401)

Drawing on these two passages, we can summarise the basic doctrine of legitimate expectation in a number of propositions:

- A legitimate expectation always arises from the *conduct of the decision-maker*. It is always something which the decision-maker does which gives rise to expectation.

- The expectation may arise in one of two ways. First, it may arise from an express promise given by the decision-maker that, for example, a benefit will be continued, or not withdrawn.

- Second, it may arise from conduct on the part of the decision-maker, such as a past regular practice or pattern of settled conduct by the decision-maker, which the individual can reasonably or legitimately expect will continue.

- The legitimate expectation (from the quotation from Lord Diplock, above) appears to be only an expectation of having an *opportunity to make representations* before the benefit is withdrawn (ie before the expectation is disappointed). Thus, on this view, it is only a 'procedural' concept, because all that one can obtain if one can establish a legitimate expectation is an opportunity to put one's case at a hearing. We will consider later whether there is more to the doctrine: whether (and when) one can claim a legitimate expectation of a 'substantive benefit', and not just of a hearing.

We can illustrate the doctrine by reference to our example.

The MTLB issues a policy statement, which it sends to all applicants, in which it states that 'if we decide to grant you a licence, then the licence will run for at least a year, and will be renewable thereafter'. Paul applies for a licence, and the MTLB grants him one for six months only.

Paul has a legitimate expectation (based on the express promise contained in the MTLB's policy statement) that if he is granted a licence, it will have a term of at least a year. The MTLB cannot withdraw this 'benefit' without first giving Paul an opportunity to make representations on why the MTLB ought not to depart from its policy. Since it has not given him such an opportunity, Paul would have a good case for quashing the decision on judicial review. (We reserve for now the question of whether Paul could claim not simply an opportunity to make representations, but rather the substantive benefit: a year-long licence.)

Let us look at some examples of legitimate expectation in practice. First, examples of the 'express promise' type of case.

In *Attorney General of Hong Kong v Ng Yuen Shiu* (1983) a senior immigration officer made an announcement of government policy that in future, before illegal immigrants were repatriated, they would be interviewed, and further, that each case would be 'treated on its merits'. The Privy Council held that this announcement gave the applicant, who was an illegal immigrant, a legitimate expectation that he would be able, before the decision to repatriate him was taken, to state his case as to why he should not be repatriated.

In *R v Liverpool Corporation ex p Liverpool Taxi Operators' Association* (1972). Liverpool Corporation was responsible for issuing taxi licences in the Liverpool area. It promised the LTOA that it would be consulted before a decision was taken to grant new taxi licences (the LTOA was worried that to increase the total number of licences would have an adverse impact on its members). When the Corporation went ahead and increased the number of licences without giving the LTOA a hearing, the Court of Appeal quashed the decision, effectively on the basis that the Corporation could not depart from its promise (in fact, the reasoning in the case is not entirely clear – but note the early date of this case relative to the age of the doctrine).

The best example of the 'past practice' limb of the doctrine is the *GCHQ* case itself (1985). The government had for many years consulted the Civil Service Unions which represented employees at GCHQ, Cheltenham, about proposed changes to employees' terms and conditions of employment. Although there had never been any formal agreement as to this consultation, this was 'the way things were done'. The government decided to change the employees' conditions by removing their right to trade union membership, and purported to do so without consulting the unions first. The unions challenged the government's action, and the House of Lords held that the unions did indeed have a legitimate expectation, based on the past practice of consultation, that they would be consulted before any major change to employees' conditions, such as the removal of the right to trade union membership. However, on the facts it was held that this entitlement to consultation was defeated by national security considerations.

Identifying a past practice which gives rise to a legitimate expectation is not always easy. It is important to resist the temptation to conclude that a legitimate expectation exists merely because something has occurred more than once in the past. In *GCHQ*, it was not merely the fact that the unions had been consulted in the past that gave rise to the expectation, but rather the practice combined with the general expectation of all involved that that was the 'way things were done'. In contrast, in *R v Secretary of State for the Environment ex p Kent* (1988), a past practice did not give rise to a legitimate expectation. There, a person who was affected by someone else's planning application was not notified of either the hearing of the application, or of the subsequent appeal to the Secretary of State. The Council had in the past notified people of hearings and appeals relating to applications affecting them. The court held, however, that there was no legitimate expectation of such notification; the mere fact that the Council had notified people in the past was not sufficient.

These examples demonstrate some further characteristics of legitimate expectations which we can summarise:

- The express assurance or conduct which gives rise to the expectation does not need to be *personally directed* at the individual applicant. It is enough that the expectation is directed at a class of people of whom the applicant is one. Thus, for example, in *Shiu* the applicant was one of a group (alleged illegal immigrants) at whom the circular was directed. In each case, the question is: was it reasonable, or legitimate, for the individual applicant to rely on the representation?

- In the ordinary case, it is not necessary for the individual applicant to demonstrate that he has relied upon the representation or assurance to his detriment before he can demonstrate that he has a legitimate expectation. In *Shiu*, for example, there was no evidence that the applicant had done, or had not done, anything in reliance upon the announcement of government policy; similarly in the other cases. This is an important difference between the doctrine of legitimate expectation and the private law concept of estoppel.

16.3   Distinguishing legitimate expectations from the right to a fair hearing

We have now looked at two different ways by which a person may become entitled to a hearing before a decision adverse to him or her is taken. Firstly, an entitlement may arise by virtue of the rules of natural justice/fairness, (examined in Chapter 14). Secondly, the person may be entitled to a hearing by virtue of a legitimate expectation which they hold.

Both these routes to a fair hearing depend, in the final analysis, upon the concept of 'fairness'. The doctrine of legitimate expectation is often described as being a facet of the public decision-maker's general duty of fairness; 'the doctrine is rooted in the ideal of fairness' (*per* Laws J in *R v Secretary of State for Transport ex p Richmond-upon-Thames London Borough Council* (1994)). It is for this reason that we have included it as a ground of review under the head of 'procedural impropriety'.

However, it is very important to distinguish between these two different routes to a fair hearing, because within the general concept of fairness they are based on quite different arguments. A hearing flowing from the rules of natural justice arises because the right or interest which the applicant seeks, or may lose, is considered so important that it merits protection (in the form of a hearing) before it is taken away or not granted (for example, in *Ridge v Baldwin*, Ridge was entitled to a hearing because of the effect of the decision on his livelihood and reputation). What is crucial is that the hearing is granted because of the *importance of the interest affected*. By contrast, the doctrine of legitimate expectation does not generate an entitlement to a hearing because of the importance of the interest, but simply because of the *way in which the decision-maker has acted* – because he has encouraged the expectation.

The best way to appreciate this distinction is to look at a case which involves both natural justice and a legitimate expectation. In *R v Great Yarmouth Borough Council ex p Botton Brothers* (1987), the applicants were amusement arcade owners. They claimed that they should have been permitted to make representations to the Council before it granted planning permission for a new amusement arcade – they feared that the new arcade would reduce their own custom. The Divisional Court held, firstly, that the applicants did not have a legitimate expectation to a hearing. The Council had never made an express promise of a hearing, and there was no past practice as understood in the *GCHQ* case. Thus there was nothing upon which a legitimate expectation could be founded. However, the court went on to find that the Council was in breach of its duty to give the arcade owners an opportunity to make representations. It reasoned that because they would be substantially prejudiced by the new arcade, which would have a potentially serious effect on their livelihoods, they were entitled, in the unusual circumstances of the case, to a fair hearing before the decision was taken. The hearing thus arose from the rules of natural justice, not from the doctrine of legitimate expectation.

16.4   Substantive protection of legitimate expectations?

We must now return to the question which we postponed when considering the example of Paul and the MTLB (in para 16.2): can an individual ever rely upon a legitimate expectation to claim not simply an opportunity to make representations, but rather to claim the substantive 'thing' that was promised? In some cases, this question simply does not arise, because the individual was never promised more than a hearing. For example, in *Attorney General of Hong Kong v Ng Yuen Shiu* (1983) (above), the promise was simply that illegal immigrants would be *interviewed* before they were repatriated; in the *GCHQ* case the past practice upon which the unions relied was that there had always been *consultation* before changes were made to employees' conditions of employment. In such cases, the legitimate expectation is only of a hearing or of consultation, and so, if successful, the individual will obviously only be entitled to a hearing.

Sometimes, however, the assurance or promise upon which the alleged legitimate expectation is based is not of a hearing, but of a 'substantive benefit'. For example, in *R v Secretary of State for the Home Department ex p Khan* (1984), the Home Secretary had issued a circular specifying the criteria upon which he would exercise his discretion to allow parents to bring a foreign child to the UK for adoption. The circular specified four conditions which intending adoptive parents would have to satisfy. The Khans fulfilled all the four conditions, but were still refused permission to bring a child to the UK for adoption, the Home Secretary turning them down for a reason which was not contained in the circular. The Court of Appeal held that the circular gave the Khans a legitimate expectation that entry decisions for such children would be made in accordance with the circular; ie that the Home Secretary would not refuse entry for a reason not contained in the circular.

But the court was then faced with the question of what remedy it could grant. If the doctrine of legitimate expectation was merely procedural, then it would follow that the Khans would only be entitled to a *hearing* before the Home Secretary disappointed their expectation; ie they would get a chance to persuade him not to refuse their application for a reason not contained in the circular (but he could go on to do just that if he was not persuaded). The Khans argued, however, that they were entitled to a *substantive* remedy; in other words, to an order from the court forbidding the Home Secretary from refusing their application for a reason *not* contained in the circular. This would be, in effect, to force the Home Secretary to apply the circular.

You might think that there is a major difficulty with the Khans' argument. If the Home Secretary was forced by the Court to apply his own circular, without the power to depart from it in exceptional cases, would he not have unlawfully fettered his own discretion (see Chapter 13, para 13.4)? The Home Secretary might appear to be in an impossible position; accused of fettering his discretion if he automatically followed his policy; accused of breaching a legitimate expectation if he did not! If right, this might make it impossible for any public decision-maker to adopt a policy.

The Court of Appeal in *Khan* adopted a middle course. It held, by a majority, that the Home Secretary ought not to have disappointed the Khans' legitimate expectation as he did, and quashed the decision refusing entry. In an important passage, Parker LJ stated:

> '... the Secretary of State, if he undertakes to allow in persons if certain conditions are satisfied, should not in my view be entitled to resile from that undertaking *without affording interested persons a hearing, and then only if the overriding public interest demands it* ... The Secretary of State is, of course, at liberty to change the policy but, in my view, vis-à-vis the [holder of an existing legitimate expectation], the new policy can only be implemented after such a recipient has been given a full and serious consideration whether there is some overriding public interest which justifies a departure from the procedures stated in the letter.' (Emphasis added.)

The decision in *Khan* therefore did two things:

- It allowed a measure of protection to substantive legitimate expectations: it held that a decision-maker cannot depart from an assurance previously given (whether in a policy or otherwise) unless he can point to overriding public interest reasons for doing so;

- It avoided conflict with the rule against the fettering of discretion by ensuring that a decision-maker can in exceptional cases depart from the legitimate expectation.

It is important to remember that the decision in *Khan* is not entirely settled law; in the case itself, Watkins LJ dissented, and Dunn LJ's judgment was not so clear as that of Parker LJ. Nevertheless, there are other cases which may be cited as examples of the enforcement of substantive legitimate expectations.

In *R v Home Secretary ex p Ruddock* (1987) various officers of the Campaign for Nuclear Disarmament had discovered that their telephones had been tapped by the security services. They contended that the interceptions were ordered by the

Home Secretary in breach of their legitimate expectation that interceptions would only be ordered when certain criteria published in a government circular were met. The Divisional Court held (i) that the doctrine of legitimate expectation was not restricted to cases where the expectation was merely of a hearing, or of consultation; (ii) that the applicants did have a legitimate expectation that the Home Secretary would only authorise interceptions where the criteria set out in the published circular had been met; but (iii) that on the facts there was no evidence that the Home Secretary had deliberately flouted the criteria.

This is a case where obviously there could be no 'procedural' protection of the legitimate expectation: one could not imagine a court ordering the Home Secretary to consult with the applicants before he authorised the tapping of their telephones!

In *R v Inland Revenue Commissioners ex p Preston* (1985) the Revenue had agreed with Preston that it would not press certain tax demands against him if he abandoned certain claims for tax relief. Later, when it was too late for Preston to claim the reliefs, the Revenue changed its mind and sought to reinstate the claims against him. Preston challenged the claims as an 'abuse of power'. The House of Lords held that in principle, it would be an unfairness amounting to an abuse of power for the Revenue not to honour its undertaking – but that on the facts, Preston had not been entirely open with the Revenue at the time that the earlier agreement was made, and therefore the Revenue was justified in going back on its word.

It is important to note that the term 'legitimate expectation' is not mentioned at all in their Lordships' judgments; the ground of review is described as 'abuse of power'. Nevertheless, commentators have pointed out that in essence, Preston was arguing that he had a legitimate expectation (based on an express promise: the Revenue's agreement) that he would not be pursued for the claims (a substantive expectation), and the House of Lords in effect found that in principle such a claim was valid, but that on the facts his expectation was not 'legitimate' because of his non-disclosure. Thus in principle, *ex p Preston* would appear to support the case for the concept of a substantive legitimate expectation, even though the term was not mentioned in the case. Indeed, the decision was followed in *R v Inland Revenue Commissioners ex p MFK Underwriting Agencies Ltd* (1990), where the Divisional Court did use the language of 'legitimate expectations'. On the other hand, in a recent decision the House of Lords has upheld and followed *ex p Preston*, once again without mentioning the doctrine of legitimate expectation, and analysing the position solely in terms of 'abuse of power'! (*Matrix-Securities Ltd v Inland Revenue Commisioners* (1994)).

It has been necessary to spend some time looking at the cases on the substantive legitimate expectation because, as can be seen from the above, the existence of the concept is still to some extent uncertain. Two recent cases, both at first instance, show the depth of the present dispute as to the existence of the concept. In *R v Secretary of State for Transport ex p Richmond-upon-Thames London Borough Council* (1994), Laws J suggested that the distinction between 'procedural' and 'substantive' legitimate expectations was unhelpful, and cast doubt on the possibility of substantive protection, particularly in the *ex p Khan* context. However, in *R v Ministry of Agriculture, Fisheries and Foods ex p Hamble Fisheries (Offshore) Ltd* (1994), Sedley J disagreed with Laws J's analysis and reaffirmed the existence of the doctrine, pointing out that it did not involve any fettering of the discretion of public bodies because no individual could legitimately expect the discharge of public duties to stand still, or that policies might not change. This last point is an important one (and represents a refinement of the law as suggested by *ex p Khan*); it suggests the need to distinguish between:

- a public body which fails to apply an existing policy to an individual (in which case, the individual's expectation will be substantively protected unless the body can point to 'overriding public interest' reasons to the contrary); and

- a public body which decides to change its policy (in which case an individual will not normally have a legitimate expectation to be dealt with under the old policy).

The case of *ex p Hamble* itself fell into the latter category: fishermen who had purchased two small boats under the expectation that they could transfer the boats' fishing licences to one larger vessel did not have a legitimate expectation that the Minister would not change his policy in a way which prevented them doing so.

Any attempt to summarise the present position in relation to the substantive legitimate expectation is fraught with difficulty, and can only be tentative. Nevertheless, the following position is suggested as representing the present law:

- Where a public body has created a legitimate expectation of a substantive benefit, by express promise or past practice, then in principle it appears that (subject to what follows), that expectation may be 'substantively protected' (*ex p Khan; ex p Ruddock; Preston*) – ie the public body can be compelled to fulfil that expectation.

- Where a public decision-maker has adopted a policy, then a person affected by that policy has a legitimate expectation that while the policy remains in existence, he or she will be treated in accordance with the policy, and this expectation will be substantively enforced (*ex p Ruddock*), unless:

  (i)   the decision-maker can demonstrate that there is an 'overriding public interest' that it be allowed depart from the policy; and

  (ii) the affected person(s) have first been consulted about the departure from the policy (*ex p Khan*).

- However, a public body is ordinarily allowed to change its policy; normally an individual cannot have a legitimate expectation that a policy will not change (*ex p Hamble*). It may occasionally be, however, that fairness will require that an individual who holds a legitimate expectation under an existing policy should be consulted before the policy is changed (*ex p Richmond* (1994), at p 596b-c).

- The existence of the entire doctrine is, however, still, in principle, vulnerable to challenge in the House of Lords.

Grounds of Judicial Review II:
The Doctrine of Legitimate Expectation

A legitimate expectation always arises from the conduct of the decision-maker, and is thus quite distinct from the fair hearing considered in Chapter 14, which is based upon an individual's protectable rights or interests (see para 16.3). The legitimate expectation arises (per Lord Frazer in *GCHQ*) either from:

- an *express promise* given by the decision-maker; or from

- the *existence of a regular past practice which the claimant can reasonably expect to continue* (this does not mean any past practice, but one which is sufficiently well established).

If such a legitimate expectation exists, then general principles of fairness will ordinarily mean that a decision-maker cannot disappoint the expectation – at least without offering the applicant a hearing (*'a procedural expectation'*), and sometimes (it appears) even then (*'substantive protection'*).

The legitimate expectation does not depend for its enforcement upon the applicant proving:

- that the express assurance or conduct which gave rise to the expectation was 'personally directed' at him or her (ie a general policy is sufficient);

- that he or she has relied upon the representation to his or her detriment.

If a person has a legitimate expectation of a *substantive benefit* (ie if the public body promises the person not simply 'a hearing' but rather that he or she will receive a benefit), then the court may offer *substantive protection* of the legitimate expectation by restraining the public body from acting otherwise than in accordance with that expectation. However:

- the public body will be entitled to disappoint the expectation if it can demonstrate that there is an 'overriding public interest' that it be allowed to do so, and that the affected person(s) have first been consulted (*ex p Khan*);

- a public body is ordinarily allowed to change its policy; normally an individual cannot have a legitimate expectation that a policy will not change (*ex p Hamble*). It may occasionally be, however, that fairness will require that an individual who holds a legitimate expectation under an existing policy should be consulted before the policy is changed (*ex p Richmond* (1994), at p 596b-c);

- this is a new development, and is still potentially vulnerable to a reconsideration of the law by the House of Lords.

Chapter 17

Grounds of Judicial Review III: Irrationality

In this chapter we examine the principles governing the ground of review which Lord Diplock in the *GCHQ* case called 'irrationality'. In the broadest of terms, we can characterise review under this head as review of the *substance of the decision (or rule) challenged*. Judges have, in the past, been very reluctant to concede that this ground of review does involve a judgment of the merits of the decision; indeed, to a cynic's eye the courts appear sometimes to have almost deliberately declined to clarify the basis upon which they do or do not intervene. As we shall see, one important task in this chapter is to distinguish what judges say from what they actually do.

It is helpful to highlight at the outset two fundamental issues which run throughout this chapter. The first concerns the *level of scrutiny* which the courts exercise when reviewing for irrationality: *what degree of irrationality or unreasonableness must be shown before the court will quash a decision?* As we shall see, it is not enough that a judge thinks that he would have come to a different conclusion if he, rather than the decision-maker, had taken the decision. Something 'more extreme' is required before the court will be prepared to intervene on the ground of irrationality. But how extreme? Is there any way of defining it, or at least, is there any agreed formulation against which one can measure the rationality of the decision? And is the standard always the same, or is scrutiny more 'intense' in some circumstances than others (eg where fundamental human rights are at stake)?

The second issue is even more basic: *what does an applicant have to show is irrational or unreasonable in order to establish grounds for judicial review?* The most usual answer is simply 'the decision' or 'the result' itself: the court may decide that the conclusion which the decision-maker reached (or the rule which the authority has enacted) is so unreasonable or irrational that it must be quashed. But there is another possible route by which an applicant may establish irrationality. If the *process* by which the decision-maker has arrived at the decision is irrational (eg tossing a coin), then the court may quash the decision even if the decision itself is one which, if it had been reached by a normal process of decision-making, would not inherently be irrational or unreasonable.

17.1 Introduction

It is worth considering a little further the difference between these two types of irrationality at this early stage.

- A classic example of a decision which is of itself 'inherently' irrational or unreasonable was suggested by Warrington LJ in *Short v Poole Corporation* (1926) (quoted by Lord Greene MR in *Associated Provincial Picture Houses Ltd v Wednesbury Corporation* (1948)), namely, a decision to dismiss a red-haired teacher on the ground that she has red hair. But while Warrington LJ's example is relatively straightforward, it does give rise to some difficult questions. In particular, what are the principles upon which the courts act in holding certain decisions or rules to be 'irrational' or 'unreasonable'? At times, the courts simply appear to operate on an 'instinctive' basis: they 'know' when a decision is so perverse that they can strike it down for irrationality. We must try to identify principles upon which the judges act (even if they do not articulate them), and we will therefore need to look at principles such as proportionality and certainty.

- Irrationality of the 'process' by which a decision was reached may be established in a number of ways. We have already encountered some of them in earlier chapters. For example, the process by which a decision is reached may be held to be irrational if a decision-maker has taken into account a consideration which is so irrelevant that no reasonable decision-maker could have considered it (compare Chapter 13, para 13.2 on irrelevant considerations). In Chapter 13 we focussed on considerations which the courts found were irrelevant because they were contrary to the express or implied meaning of the legislation; the court may, on the other hand, conclude simply that the consideration taken into account is so unreasonable that no reasonable decision-maker could have entertained it. Again, a decision which is reached in bad faith is sometimes described as being irrational; this may overlap with review for bias, considered in Chapter 15. The dividing line between a challenge for irrationality and a challenge on other grounds may not, therefore, be as clear cut as first appears.

17.2 Judicial review of the 'merits'?

In Chapter 12, we contrasted judicial review, which is a supervisory jurisdiction ensuring the *legality* of public law decisions, with an appellate jurisdiction in which the court may be concerned with the *merits* of the decision under challenge (paras 12.5.1 to 12.5.3). It is frequently suggested that judicial review for irrationality infringes this distinction (or, more forceful critics would say, completely undermines it), because review for irrationality does involve a scrutiny of the merits of the decision.

As we noted earlier, defenders of the *ultra vires* theory do have an answer to this criticism. Review for irrationality, they would admit, may involve some scrutiny of the merits of the decision (although not, perhaps, in cases of challenges to the decision-making *process*). It is, in fact, only a 'light' degree of scrutiny, because as we shall see the court will *not* intervene simply because it would have come to a different decision; it will only intervene if the decision is irrational. But even this 'light' level of scrutiny is explicable, they would say; the court intervenes because there is a *presumption* that Parliament cannot have intended, in conferring the decision-making power or rule-making power upon the public body challenged, to have allowed that power to be exercised in an irrational or unreasonable way. Hence, if the judge comes to the conclusion that the decision or rule is irrational or unreasonable, then it is outside the powers conferred on the decision-maker by Parliament and can be quashed. The power to review for irrationality is therefore explicable in the terms of the *ultra vires* theory; it is part of a system of review.

We noted, in Chapter 12, that this explanation can be criticised for its artificiality (para 12.6). This is an issue to which you may want to return having read this chapter. However, for the present, what is important to note is that judges do take the 'traditional' explanation seriously. In cases with a high profile, particularly those with a political dimension, judges frequently emphasise that their view of the merits of the decision under challenge is quite irrelevant to the case before them; that they are simply charged with assessing the legality of the decision. But this will only remain true, at a practical level, for so long as review for irrationality remains a 'light touch' scrutiny. If the courts intervened every time they found a decision 'a little unreasonable', the judicial disclaimer would soon ring obviously hollow. The courts therefore have a strong interest in limiting the intrusiveness of review for irrationality; of restricting it to an 'extreme case' remedy. This, in general terms, is what happens. It is important to remember that in practice, it is rare for review for irrationality to succeed. And it is extremely rare for an applicant to succeed *purely* on the ground of irrationality; where irrationality succeeds, it is normally in conjunction with another ground of review. Whilst irrationality is an important ground of review, it is always worth bearing in mind its modest practical significance.

17.3 *Wednesbury* **unreasonableness**

The traditional starting place for a consideration of this ground of review is the judgment of Lord Greene MR in *Associated Provincial Picture Houses Ltd v Wednesbury Corporation* (1948). The case involved a challenge by APPH to a condition imposed by Wednesbury Corporation upon a cinema licence, that no children under 15 should be admitted to Sunday performances. The Corporation had a wide power to impose conditions upon licenses 'as the authority think fit'. APPH challenged the condition upon several grounds, one of which was that it was unreasonable. In his judgment, Lord Greene MR considered the nature of a challenge for unreasonableness:

> 'It is true to say that if a decision on a competent matter is *so unreasonable that no reasonable authority could ever have come to it*, then the courts can interfere. That, I think, is quite right, but to prove a case of that kind would require something overwhelming ...
> It may be possible to say that although the local authority have kept within the four corners of the matters which they ought to consider, *they have nevertheless come to a conclusion so unreasonable that no reasonable authority could ever have come to it*. In such a case ..., I think the court can interfere' (emphasis added).

This formulation describes what has come to be known as '*Wednesbury* unreasonableness', after the name of the case. It was for many years adopted as (and, some would argue, still is) the best characterisation of this ground of review. It is not enough, to succeed on this ground, to convince a judge that the decision under attack is unreasonable; instead, it must be shown that the decision is *so unreasonable that no reasonable decision-maker* could ever have come to it. Of course, as a definition of unreasonableness it is tautologous, because it defines unreasonableness in terms of itself. But it does, in practice, indicate that 'unreasonable' means 'extremely unreasonable', or, as Lord Greene said, 'overwhelming'. What it does not do is to give any indication of any principled basis of assessing whether a decision is so unreasonable that this high hurdle of '*Wednesbury* unreasonableness' has been met.

Two further points should be made about the *Wednesbury* case. Firstly, Lord Greene in his judgment also considered in general terms the different grounds of judicial review, setting out a list of different heads of challenge. This list is sometimes referred to as 'the *Wednesbury* catalogue', and the grounds of review are sometimes still referred to collectively as 'the *Wednesbury* principles'. It is important that you distinguish these general references from the concept of *Wednesbury* unreasonableness, with which we are dealing here.

Secondly, it's worth bearing in mind the actual decision in the *Wednesbury* case. The court decided that the condition imposed by the Corporation could *not* be said to be unreasonable in the sense set out by Lord Greene MR, and it therefore refused to overturn the condition. Whether the result of the case would be the same if the facts were repeated today is a different question; this is a useful reminder that caution is required in citing older cases as authority in this area. Standards of reasonableness, and even standards of 'overwhelming' unreasonableness, may change from generation to generation. Perhaps the best illustration of this is the even earlier decision of *Roberts v Hopwood* (1925), which involved a challenge to the decision of Poplar Borough Council to pay its employees, both male and female, an equal wage, and to set that wage at a rate above the 'normal' rate of pay. The House of Lords held that the decision was not reasonable; there was 'no rational proportion between the rates of wages ... and the rates at which they would be reasonably remunerated'. Lord Atkinson made his view of the merits clear, criticising the Council for 'allow[ing] themselves to be guided in preference by some eccentric principles of socialistic philanthropy, or by a feminist ambition to secure the equality of the sexes in the matter of wages in the world of labour'. You may well consider that the decision is of dubious authority today; indeed, compare *Pickwell v Camden London Borough Council* (1983), where Ormrod LJ was of the view that an allegedly over-generous wage settlement with striking employees by Camden was 'a matter for the electorate at the next election', and not a ground for review of the decision.

As we have seen, in the *GCHQ* case Lord Diplock preferred the term 'irrationality' to '*Wednesbury* unreasonableness'. He stated that irrationality:

17.4   Irrationality

> 'applies to a decision which is so outrageous in its defiance of logic or of accepted moral standards that no sensible person who had applied his mind to the question to be decided could have arrived at it. Whether a decision falls within this category is a question that judges by their training and experience would be well equipped to answer, or else there would be something badly wrong with our judicial system ... "Irrationality" can now stand upon its own feet as an accepted ground on which a decision may be attacked by judicial review.' (pp 410-11)

An important element of this definition is Lord Diplock's recognition that the test involves an assessment of both the *logic* which led to the decision, and the moral standards which it embodies. Some judges have, however, been less than welcoming as to the adoption of the word 'irrationality' itself. In *R v Devon County Council ex p G* (1988), Lord Donaldson MR expressed a preference the old term *'Wednesbury unreasonable'*:

> 'I eschew the synonym of "irrational", because, although it is attractive as being shorter than *"Wednesbury unreasonable"* and has the imprimatur of Lord Diplock in [the *GCHQ* case], it is widely misunderstood by politicians, both local and national, and even more by their constituents, as casting doubt on the mental capacity of the decision-maker, a matter which in practice is seldom, if ever, in issue ...'.

Lord Donaldson's point is that the term 'irrational' surely implies a lack, or absence, of rational justification for the decision under attack. This may be a good description of some unreasonable decisions – for example, it will cover the decision-maker who consults an astrologer, or spins a coin (examples given by Diplock LJ, as he then was, in *R v Deputy Industrial Injuries Commissioner ex p Moore* (1965)). But there are other decisions which might be described as unreasonable, even though the decision-maker has acted in a deliberate and 'coldly rational' manner. For example, in *Backhouse v Lambeth London Borough Council* (1972), the Council attempted to avoid a requirement that it increase rents generally in its area by loading the whole of the increase onto a single property (on which the rent was increased from £7 to £18,000 per week), while leaving all the other properties with unchanged rents. While such a decision may be held to be unreasonable, it is perhaps not accurate to describe it as irrational.

Thus the term 'irrational', while frequently used by judges, has by no means been universally adopted. The phrase *'Wednesbury* unreasonableness' is still in use, and has been joined by other formulations; it has been suggested that a decision is reviewable if, for example, it can be said that 'the public body, either consciously or unconsciously, are acting perversely' (per Lord Brightman in *R v Hillingdon London Borough Council ex p Pulhofer* (1986)), or (even) if the decision provokes the reaction, 'My goodness, that is certainly wrong!' (*per* May LJ in *Neale v Hereford & Worcester County Council* (1986)).

17.5 Substantive principles of review?

There have been a number of attempts to formulate 'substantive principles' which underlie and explain review for irrationality; see, for example, Jowell & Lester, 'Beyond *Wednesbury*: Substantive Principles of Administrative Law' [1987] Public Law 368, and Peiris, *'Wednesbury* Unreasonableness: The Expanding Canvass' (1987) CLJ 53.

Jowell and Lester have emphasised the advantages of developing such principles:

'... The recognition and application of substantive principles would satisfy the need in a fast developing area of law for clarity and coherence. Far from encouraging judges to meddle with the merits of official decisions, it would we believe promote consideration of the proper role of the courts in the growing common law of public administration. It would also enable the courts to strengthen the protection of fundamental human rights against the misuse of official discretion without usurping legislative or executive powers.' (pp 368-369)

In general, however, the courts have been reluctant to take up this invitation, perhaps because 'clarity and coherence' of reasoning, while desirable in principle, may in fact expose judges more readily to the charge that they are intervening in the merits of decisions. At any rate, in seeking to identify such principles, it is necessary to read between the lines of the cases, rather than looking for clear statements of principle.

Is a rule or decision more susceptible to review for irrationality if it impinges upon important rights of the individual affected? In such circumstances, is the decision subject to 'heightened scrutiny'? At present, no clear answer can be given to these questions from authority. But as a matter of common sense, it is surely right that in considering whether a decision or rule is unreasonable or not, it is inevitable that one of the factors that must be taken into account is the effects which that decision or rule is likely to have. We will explore this further when considering the concept of proportionality (below, para 17.6), but, if this is right, then it follows that a decision having a serious impact upon fundamental human rights may be more susceptible to challenge for irrationality/unreasonableness simply because such an important decision requires greater justification.

There are a number of decisions which support this line of reasoning. The old case of *Kruse v Johnson* (1898) involved a challenge to a bye-law which sought to prohibit singing 'in any public place or highway within fifty yards of any dwelling-house' (a measure clearly impinging upon what would now be described as freedom of speech or expression). Lord Russell CJ held that the courts had the power to strike down even a bye-law for unreasonableness 'if, for instance, they were found to be partial and unequal in their operation between different classes; if they were manifestly unjust; [or] ... if they involved such oppressive or gratuitous interference with the rights of those subject to them ...' – although, on the facts, the court

17.5.1   Decisions affecting fundamental human rights

found that the bye-law was not unreasonable. In *R v Secretary of State for Transport ex p de Rothschild* (1989), there was a challenge to the Secretary of State's decision to approve a recommendation of a planning inspector in favour of the compulsory purchase of the applicant's property. Slade LJ appeared to accept that increased judicial scrutiny was appropriate where property rights were affected:

> '[I]n cases where a compulsory purchase order is under challenge, the draconian nature of the order will itself render it more vulnerable to successful challenge on *Wednesbury* ... grounds unless sufficient reasons are adduced affirmatively to justify it on its merits ... Given the obvious importance and value to land owners of their property rights, the abrogation of those rights would, in the absence of what he perceived to be a sufficient justification on the merits, be a course which surely no reasonable Secretary of State would take' (pp 938-939).

And in the House of Lords' decision in *Bugdacay v Secretary of State for the Home Department* (1987), Lord Bridge stated that the courts are entitled, within limits:

> 'to subject an administrative decision to the more rigorous examination, to ensure that it is in no way flawed, according to the gravity of the issue which the decision determines. The most fundamental of all human rights is the individual's right to life and when an administrative decision under challenge is said to be one which may put the applicant's life at risk, the basis of the decision must surely call for the most anxious scrutiny' (Lord Templeman delivered a similar opinion on this point).

These decisions must, however, be read in the light of the decision of the House of Lords in *R v Secretary of State for the Home Department ex p Brind* (1991). This case concerned a directive by the Secretary of State requiring the British Broadcasting Corporation and Independent Broadcasting Authority not to broadcast any matter which included words spoken by persons representing certain organisations proscribed under the Prevention of Terrorism (Temporary Provisions) Act 1984 (such as the IRA and Sinn Fein). The directive was challenged by journalists who argued (inter alia) that it involved a significant infringement of the right of freedom of expression, and that it was *Wednesbury* unreasonable and disproportionate. One question which arose was as to the 'intensity' of scrutiny appropriate in a case where fundamental human rights were at issue. It is not at all easy to derive a clear ratio from the five speeches of their lordships. On the one hand, Lord Ackner appeared to deny that the fact that a decision impinged upon fundamental human rights would alter the degree of scrutiny appropriate on a challenge for unreasonableness; he denied that Slade LJ in the *Rothschild* case was in any sense 'increasing the severity of the *Wednesbury* test' (p 757), although Lord Ackner did accept that 'in a field which concerns a fundamental human right – namely that of free speech – close scrutiny must be given to the reasons provided as justification for interference with that right'. On the other hand, Lord Bridge (with whom Lord Roskill agreed) appeared to take a more interventionist line:

> 'I do not accept that ... the courts are powerless to prevent the exercise by the executive of administrative discretions, even when conferred, as in the instant case, in terms which are on their face unlimited, in a way which infringes fundamental human rights ... We are ... perfectly entitled to start from the premise that any restriction of the right to freedom of expression requires to be justified and that nothing less than an important competing public interest will be sufficient to justify it ... We are entitled [to ask] whether a reasonable Secretary of State, on the material before him, could reasonably make [that decision]' (pp 748-749).

Lord Templeman, the 'swing' member of the House of Lords on this issue, did not come to a clear conclusion on the question, but did appear to have regard to the fact that human rights were affected by the decision; he stated that 'the courts cannot escape from asking themselves whether a reasonable Secretary of State ... could reasonably conclude that the interference with freedom of expression which he determined to impose was justifiable' (p 751). On the facts, none of the members of the House of Lords thought that the broadcasting ban *was* a significant infringement of freedom of speech or expression, because there was nothing to prevent the words of the 'banned' person being spoken by an actor.

In summary, therefore, it is clear that the courts do continue to apply the *Wednesbury* test where fundamental human rights are affected; they ask whether the decision-maker could reasonably conclude that the infringement of human rights was justifiable. Although it is not entirely clear whether this involves a 'heightened degree' of scrutiny, it would appear that this is in practice so, simply because the court will not accept that the decision-maker could reasonably have concluded that the measure was justifiable unless it can point to some 'important competing public interest'.

At the other extreme, there appear to be types of decision which the courts are reluctant to scrutinise even on the *Wednesbury* test. In general terms, the courts are particularly

17.5.2 Decisions subject to reduced scrutiny?

chary of involvement in decisions involving questions of resource-distribution, and 'high policy'. Normally, the courts will simply dismiss irrationality challenges to such decisions with the minimum of analysis, but on occasions the courts have gone further and held that the *Wednesbury* test should not even be applied. In *R v Secretary of State for the Environment ex p Nottinghamshire County Council* (1986), the House of Lords had to consider a challenge to a decision of the Secretary of State to reduce the grant paid by central government to Nottinghamshire (because of overspending by the Council). The decision to reduce the grant had been approved (as the legislation required) by an affirmative resolution of the House of Commons, and was not only highly 'party political', but was part of a very complex settlement of grants with local authorities throughout the country. Nottinghamshire's submission that the Secretary of State's decision was *Wednesbury* unreasonable was not even entertained by the House of Lords; Lord Scarman (with whom the rest of the House agreed) held that where a decision concerned matters of public expenditure, and where it had been approved by resolution of House of Commons, then it was constitutionally improper for the Court to entertain a challenge on *Wednesbury* grounds. Instead, a challenge could only succeed if 'the consequences of the [decision] were so absurd that he must have taken leave of his senses'. It is almost inconceivable that a decision which the House of Commons had approved by resolution could fail to pass such a test (see also the later decision of the House of Lords in *Hammersmith and Fulham London Borough Council v Secretary of State for the Environment* (1990), approving *Nottinghamshire*).

17.5.3 Other substantive principles of review

Commentators have drawn on European legal principles to put forward other substantive principles of review which, it is suggested, underlie review for *Wednesbury* unreasonableness or irrationality. Jowell and Lester, in the article cited above, suggest that both the *principle of legal certainty* and the *principle of consistency* are nascent in our administrative law. The latter principle underlies the concept of the substantive legitimate expectation, which we have already considered in Chapter 16 (see para 16.4 and, for example, *R v Inland Revenue Commissioners ex p Preston* (1985)). An example of the former principle, Jowell and Lester suggest, can be seen in the decision of the House of Lords in *Wheeler v Leicester City Council* (1985), which concerned a resolution of the Council to ban Leicester Rugby Football Club from continuing to use a Council-owned ground, because three members of the Club had participated in a tour of South Africa (the Council had a statutory power to grant permissions for the use of its grounds). The House of Lords quashed the resolution, at least in part on the basis that it was *Wednesbury* unreasonable; as Lord Templeman put it, 'the club having committed no wrong, the council could not use their statutory powers in the management of their property or any other statutory powers in order to punish the club'. Jowell and Lester suggest that the decision 'could be justified more convincingly than [it was] by spelling out more clearly the notion that legal certainty requires no punishment without the breach of established law' (at p 377). You may want to consider this in the context of subsequent cases such as *R v Lewisham London Borough Council ex p Shell UK Limited* (1988), (where Lewisham's decision not to contract with Shell as part of a South African sanctions campaign was held to be unlawful), and *R v Somerset County Council ex p Fewings* (1993) (where Somerset's ban on stag hunting on Council land was held to be unlawful – although in this case the judge preferred to base his decision on the ground that the Council had adopted an improper purpose, rather than on irrationality).

17.6 The doctrine of proportionality

As we have noted, Jowell and Lester draw on the jurisprudence of European Community law and the European Convention of Human Rights to suggest substantive principles underlying review for irrationality. It is important to remember, however, that the European Convention is not part of English law save by virtue of Treaty obligation (see Chapter 8, para 8.1.3), and European Community law is applicable only insofar as a Community law right is in issue (para 8.1.4). This has, without doubt, moderated the influence of European principles upon English law. Nowhere is this clearer than in relation to the doctrine of proportionality.

The doctrine of proportionality requires that the means employed by the decision-maker to achieve his legitimate aim must be no more than is reasonably necessary – no more than is *proportionate* - to achieve that aim. It is sometimes described as requiring that 'one must not use a sledgehammer to crack a nut'. The European principle allows a 'margin of appreciation' for the decision-maker, but would clearly require judicial intervention in circumstances where the decision would not, on English principles, be held to be *Wednesbury* unreasonable or irrational (see generally, Jowell and Lester, 'Proportionality: Neither Novel Nor Dangerous', in Jowell & Oliver (eds) *New Directions in Judicial Review* (1988)).

Although a well-established European legal principle, there was for a long time until the decision in *ex p Brind* a debate as to the status – or the very existence – of the principle in English law. There were, in essence, three different positions:

- that proportionality was a separate ground of review in English law (hinted at by Lord Diplock in the *GCHQ* case, where after enumerating his three grounds of review, he suggested that this is 'not to say that further development on a case by case basis may not in the course of time add further grounds. I have in mind particularly the possible adoption in the future of the principle of "proportionality" ...');

- that proportionality simply did not exist in English law (the view of Millett J in *Allied Dunbar v Frank Weisinger* (1987), where he called the principle 'novel and dangerous'); and

- that proportionality was not a separate ground of review, but was a part of the reasoning process that might lead a court to conclude that a decision was *Wednesbury* unreasonable or irrational.

The status of the principle fell to be finally resolved by the House of Lords in *R v Secretary of State for the Home Department ex p Brind* (1991) (see para 17.5.1 above). The journalists submitted that the directive banning the broadcasting of the voices of members of proscribed organisations was unlawful because it was disproportionate to the legitimate aims of the Secretary of State. Whilst all the members of the House of Lords rejected the argument based on proportionality (not least because they considered that, on the facts, the interference with freedom of speech and expression was minimal), there was a wide variation of approach between their Lordships. Any attempt to summarise the different speeches is difficult, given the ambiguities which exist, but the following propositions can be put forward:

- All the members of the House of Lords agreed that reference to the law of the European Convention on Human Rights was only permissible if there was an ambiguity in the relevant English legislation (*Garland v British Rail Engineering* (1983)), and agreed that no ambiguity existed where (as in *Brind*) the legislation simply conferred a wide discretion upon the Secretary of State.

- Hence, the applicants could not refer to the ECHR. The issue was simply whether proportionality existed in English law. Their lordships were unanimous that proportionality, as a separate doctrine, could not on the facts of *Brind* be invoked.

- Lords Ackner and Lowrie were of the view that proportionality was simply not part of English law: 'there appears to me to be at present no basis upon which the proportionality doctrine applied by the European Court can be followed by the courts of this country' (*per* Lord Ackner at p 763);

- On the other hand, Lords Bridge and Roskill expressly left open the possibility of the future adoption of the principle of proportionality in an appropriate case. What sort of case might be appropriate was not indicated.

- Lord Templeman expressed no views either way as to the possible future development of the doctrine.

- However, all the members of the House of Lords appeared to accept that the test of proportionality, as outlined above, had a role within the confines of *Wednesbury* unreasonableness; that it might be useful as a way of helping to decide whether a decision is irrational or *Wednesbury* unreasonable. Thus even Lord Ackner asked whether the Secretary of State had in issuing the directive 'used a sledgehammer to crack a nut' (the classic description of 'proportionality' reasoning); he commented that, 'Of course, that is a picturesque way of describing the *Wednesbury* "irrational" test. The Secretary of State has in my judgment used no sledgehammer' (p 759).

The use of proportionality in the limited sense envisaged by Lord Ackner and the other members of the House of Lords is clearly very different from the more interventionist test applicable under European law. We are therefore at present left with the position that where a European Community right is in issue (or where an ambiguity exists such that recourse can be had to the European Convention), then English judges must apply the European doctrine of proportionality (we saw an example of that use in para 8.4.3 above, in the case of *Stoke-on-Trent City Council v B & Q plc* (1991); see also *R v Intervention Board ex p E D & F Man (Sugar) Ltd* (1986)). Where, on the contrary, there is no such Community or Convention connection, the principle of proportionality must be foresworn by the courts, except as an 'aid to construction' in applying the test of *Wednesbury* unreasonableness or irrationality.

Whether this is a tenable position in the longer term, and whether the position can only now be altered by the incorporation of the European Convention on Human Rights or other legislative intervention, remains to be seen. It would appear that the majority of the House of Lords in *Brind* did leave the door at least a little ajar to further judicial development of the doctrine.

The Grounds of Judicial Review III: Irrationality

The ground of review known as irrationality involves (to a limited degree) review of the 'substance' of the decision or rule challenged. In the traditional formulation (as set out in the judgment of Lord Greene MR in *Associated Provincial Picture Houses Ltd v Wednesbury Corporation* (1948)), the applicant must show that *the decision is so unreasonable that no reasonable decision-maker could ever have come to it* ('*Wednesbury unreasonableness*').

Lord Diplock reformulated the test in the *GCHQ* case, preferring the term 'irrationality', and describing it as applying to 'a decision which is so outrageous in its defiance of logic or of accepted moral standards that no sensible person who had applied his mind to the question to be decided could have arrived at it'.

Both the terms 'irrationality' and '*Wednesbury* unreasonableness' are still in use – along with 'perversity' (*ex p Pulhofer* (1986)), and other terminological variations. In practice, it matters little which phrase is used; what is more significant is the 'level of scrutiny' which the courts require.

A decision may be flawed for irrationality *either* because the decision itself (the 'end result') is irrational or unreasonable (eg the dismissal of the red haired teacher), or because the process by which the decision is reached is irrational (tossing a coin or consulting an astrologer). Standards of irrationality may change between generations!

Lord Greene's definition of 'unreasonableness' was (intentionally) tautologous. Academics and judges have attempted to clarify the principles on which the courts act by developing 'substantive principles' of review. For example:

- Decisions impinging upon fundamental human rights may be susceptible to 'heightened' scrutiny for irrationality; see

  R v Secretary of State for Transport ex p de Rothschild (1989)

  Bugdacay v Secretary of State for the Home Department (1987)

  R v Secretary of State for the Home Department ex p Brind (1991) – where the House of Lords was divided on the issue.

See also, Jowell & Lester, 'Beyond *Wednesbury:* Substantive Principles of Administrative Law' [1987] *Public Law* 368.

- The principle of legal certainty (the law must be accessible and foreseeable; no one should be punished except for breach of an established law); see *Wheeler v Leicester City Council* (1985).

- The principle of consistency: compare the doctrine of substantive legitimate expectation, Chapter 16 (para 16.4) and *R v Inland Revenue Commissioners ex p Preston* (1985));

- The doctrine of proportionality (the means employed by the decision-maker to achieve his legitimate aim must be no more than is reasonably necessary – no more than is proportionate – to achieve that aim). The status of the doctrine is uncertain in English law even after the decision of the House of Lords in *R v Secretary of State for the Home Department ex p Brind* (1991):

  (i) it is clear that the European doctrine has not been incorporated into English law (although the better view is that the majority of the House of Lords left open the possibility that this could happen by judicial intervention in a future suitable case), but

  (ii) it would appear that the doctrine is of relevance in assessing whether a decision is *Wednesbury* unreasonable or irrational; if a decision-maker uses an excessively large sledgehammer, then the decision may be unreasonable/irrational.

The doctrine must be applied by the English courts with full rigour when they are dealing with a European Community law right (or where an ambiguity in English law permits reference to the ECHR); see eg *Stoke-on-Trent City Council v B & Q plc* (1991).

Chapter 18

Restrictions on Review: Ouster Clauses

Government may want to protect public decision-makers from judicial review of their decisions for a number of reasons. In some cases there may be a pressing need for 'finality in administration'; for example, where a large public project such as the construction of a motorway is at risk of being held up by uncertainty during the period in which a person could ordinarily apply for judicial review. In such a case, even the three month time period within which applications for leave to apply for judicial review should normally be brought (see Chapter 10, para 10.5 above) may be considered too long to leave such a project 'in the air'. Another reason that government may be 'anti-' judicial review may be simply that it believes that the public body would be better-off without the interference of the courts in its decision-making process. Bearing in mind that the government is the most frequent respondent to judicial review applications, we might expect this latter train of reasoning not to be uncommon!

One way in which the opportunities to challenge a decision by way of judicial review may be reduced is by providing the applicant with an alternative remedy. Where, for example, there is an appeal from a decision to a tribunal or other 'appellate' body, then in the ordinary course of events, a person wishing to challenge the decision must avail him or herself of that statutory appeal rather than seeking judicial review. Alternatively, it may be possible to 'divert' people from making a formal challenge to the decision at all, by providing alternative means of redress, such as the Ombudsmen (Chapter 9).

A more radical way of limiting the scope of judicial review is by means of a statutory provision which attempts either to limit or to exclude entirely the right to challenge the decision in the courts. It is these types of provision, often called ouster clauses, with which we are concerned in this chapter.

The history of the courts' attitude towards ouster clauses is a complex one, and even today the law on the subject is far from straightforward. On the one hand, the courts in dealing with such clauses are faced with what is often a fairly obvious intention of Parliament – to exclude or limit their power to intervene. On the other hand, the courts often feel that ouster clauses present a challenge to the rule of law, because they

18.1   Introduction

displace the courts' proper constitutional role of scrutinising and regulating the actions of public bodies. There is therefore a general presumption that such clauses have as narrow an ambit as possible. Indeed, the courts' restrictive interpretation of some ouster clauses has limited their effect almost to nothing.

The difficulty has been that in their attempts to avoid the apparent intention of such clauses (ie that the courts' jurisdiction is to be limited or excluded), the courts have developed principles of statutory construction which, if consistently applied, would have *too great* an effect, because they would logically lead the courts to by-pass most or all ouster clauses *entirely*. The courts have shied away from such a radical result, which would so obviously flout the intentions of Parliament. There has thus been an uneasy attempt to walk a fine line between the theory and the practice; the result has been apparent, and real, conflicts between different authorities, and distinctions of almost excruciating complexity. Students often have great difficulty with this topic; indeed, some courses avoid the subject altogether. There is some sense in doing so, because in practice, cases on ouster clauses are comparatively rare; no more than a very few every year, if that. On the other hand, for those who do have to deal with the topic, some path through the minefield is required.

In what follows, we seek to give an overview of the subject, although it not possible in the space available to discuss the full intricities of even the major decisions. We have divided ouster clauses into two types.

18.2   Two types of ouster clauses

Although ouster clauses come in a number of different formulations, there is a broad distinction between two types of clause, which the courts treat in very different ways. On the one hand, there are clauses which do not try to exclude the courts' jurisdiction completely, but only seek to time-limit it by providing for a specified period of time (almost always six weeks) within which any challenge to the decision must be brought; after that time, any challenge is excluded. On the other hand, there are the so-called *total ouster clauses*, which seek to exclude the courts' powers entirely, by providing that 'the decision shall not be challenged in any court of law', or some similar formulation.

The history of the two types of ouster clause is very different. Whilst total ousters, often known as 'no certiorari clauses', have a statutory pedigree going back centuries, six week ousters are a more recent invention. The first such clause was enacted in s 11 of the Housing Act 1930, and dealt with slum clearance orders; indeed, many early six week ouster clauses were enacted in the context of public works schemes, and were framed to combat difficulties which had arisen following a series of cases in which successful applications *certiorari* had been made to quash orders of local authorities, when the schemes concerned had been brought almost into operation, and after considerable expense had been incurred. Since that time, six week ouster clauses have been enacted in a wide variety of statutory contexts; some modern examples of their use being:

• Petroleum Act 1987 s 14

• Airports Act 1986 s 49

• Telecommunications Act 1984 s 18

• Town and Country Planning Act 1990 ss 287, 288

• Ancient Monuments and Archaeological Areas Act 1979 s 55

• Highways Act 1990 Schedule 2

We will have to look in some detail at how the courts respond to the two different types of ouster clause, and examine how they distinguish between them. It is worth summarising straight away, however, the end result of the discussion:

• The courts will almost invariably give effect to a six week ouster clause. If such a clause provides that a decision may not be challenged in any way after a six week period, then the courts will not entertain a challenge after that period – even, apparently, if the applicant claims that the reason that he or she did not bring a challenge within six weeks was due to bad faith on the part of the decision-maker (see *R v Secretary of State for the Environment ex p Ostler* (1976), discussed below).

• By contrast, the courts are very unwilling to give effect to a total ouster clause – although there are occasions where the courts have accepted that judicial review is barred by such a clause.

The courts' 'respectful' attitude to ouster clauses is best illustrated by a classic decision of the House of Lords which concerned a six week ouster clause. In *Smith v East Elloe Regional District Council* (1956), Mrs Smith wished to challenge a compulsory purchase order made by the Council in respect of her property. She had various grounds of challenge, including an allegation that the Order had been procured in

18.3   General principles; the courts' attitude to ouster clauses

bad faith by the clerk of the Council. Unfortunately, she did not bring her challenge until almost six years after Order was made; indeed, until after a house on her land had been demolished and new houses had been built. She was therefore met with the argument that her claim could not succeed, because the Acquisition of Land (Authorisation Procedure) Act 1946 (Part IV of Schedule 1) provided that:

> '15(1) If any person aggrieved by a compulsory purchase order desires to question the validity thereof ... on the ground that the authorisation of a compulsory purchase thereby granted is not empowered to be granted under this Act ... he may, *within six weeks* from the date on which notice of the confirmation or making of the order ... is first published ... make an application to the High Court ...
>
> 16.   Subject to the [above], a compulsory purchase order ... shall not ... be questioned in any legal proceedings whatsoever.'

The House of Lords unanimously held that this six week ouster clause precluded any challenge after the six week period had expired – even a challenge on a ground such as bad faith. As Viscount Simonds put it:

> 'I think that anyone bred in the tradition of the law is likely to regard with little sympathy legislative provisions for ousting the jurisdiction of the court ... But it is our plain duty to give the words of an Act their proper meaning and, for my part, I find it quite impossible to qualify the words of paragraph [16] ... What is abundantly clear is that words are used which are wide enough to cover any kind of challenge which any aggrieved person may think fit to make. I cannot think of any wider words.'

It is important to note that the House of Lords did not suggest in *East Elloe* that their decision was dependent upon the fact that para 15 of the Schedule allowed a challenge within a six week period. If you read Lord Simonds words quoted above, it appears that he would have come to the same conclusion if the legislation had contained a *total* ouster clause, framed as in para 16.

However, the decision in *East Elloe* was called into question by another decision of the House of Lords, in the landmark case of *Anisminic v Foreign Compensation Commission* (1969). This case involved a 'total' ouster clause: the Foreign Compensation Act 1950 provided that determinations of the FCC 'shall not be called into question in any court of law'. Anisminic wished to challenge a determination of the FCC on the ground that the FCC had misconstrued the legal effect of the statutory framework under which it operated, and had therefore reached a decision which was a nullity. Could Anisminic avoid the ouster clause? Or did the reasoning of *East Elloe* apply, so that the statutory words were wide enough to exclude 'any kind of challenge'?

The House of Lords held, by a majority, that the ouster clause did not prevent Anisminic from challenging the decision of the FCC. The leading speech of Lord Reid is well worth reading in full, but its essential reasoning can be summarised in a series of propositions. He held:

(i) Anisminic's challenge involved a claim that the FCC had, by misconstruing the statutory framework, acted beyond its powers (ie 'outside its jurisdiction').

(ii) The FCC's decision was therefore a 'nullity' - the determination had no legal effect.

(iii) Although the ouster clause provided that determinations of the FCC 'shall not be called into question in any court of law', this could have no effect because *the FCC had never made a determination* – it simply made a purported determination, which was a nullity. Thus Lord Reid did not *ignore* the statutory wording; rather, he found a way round it, by holding that *there never was a valid determination in respect of which the courts' powers could be ousted*. The court was not 'calling into question' a determination; instead, it was pointing out that a determination had never been made.

The reasoning in (iii) is clearly the crucial step which enabled the House of Lords to avoid the total ouster clause without simply defying the words of Parliament. But the case left at least two important questions unanswered:

• Which grounds of judicial review, if established, mean that the public body as acted 'outside its jurisdiction' in the sense of (i) above? All errors? Only misconstructions of law?

• What was the status of *East Elloe* after *Anisminic*? The House of Lords in the latter case did not overrule *East Elloe*; instead, it purported to distinguish it. But surely the reasoning of Lord Reid at (iii) above applies with equal force to the *East Elloe* ouster contained in para 16 of the Schedule of the Acquisition of Land Act: it could be said that the compulsory purchase order was a nullity, and that the court could therefore quash the purported purchase order even after the six week period without infringing the ouster's prohibition on 'questioning' any determination. Was *East Elloe* therefore impliedly overruled by *Anisminic*?

It is easier to examine these two questions in reverse order.

18.4   Six week ouster clauses

The answer to the second question is quite clear: *East Elloe* has survived *Anisminic*, and the former decision remains good law in respect of six week ouster clauses. The Court of Appeal was given the opportunity to choose between (or to attempt to reconcile) the two decisions in *R v Secretary of State for the Environment ex p Ostler* (1976). Here, Mr Ostler asked the courts to quash an order authorising the construction of a new road, and associated compulsory purchase orders, on the basis that they were vitiated by a breach of natural justice and by bad faith on the part of the Secretary of State or his Department. As in *East Elloe*, the legislation in question contained a six week ouster clause providing that after the six week period, the scheme 'shall ... not be questioned in any legal proceedings whatsoever'. And like Mrs Smith, Mr Ostler had failed to challenge the scheme within six weeks. However, he submitted that at least part of the reason why he had not brought his challenge earlier was that he had been unaware of a secret agreement between the Department and a particular firm. In other words, he blamed the Secretary of State for the fact that he had not brought his challenge within the statutory time limit.

The Court of Appeal rejected the argument that *East Elloe* was inconsistent with *Anisminic*. Lord Denning MR (with whom Shaw LJ agreed) advanced a number of distinctions between the two cases, not all of which are totally convincing (indeed, Lord Denning himself later 'recanted' in his book, *The Discipline of Law* (1979)). Perhaps his most important distinction was that whereas *Anisminic* concerned a total ouster clause, in *East Elloe* (and in *Ostler*):

> 'the statutory provision has given the court jurisdiction to inquire into complaints so long as the applicant comes within six weeks. *The provision is more in the nature of a limitation period than of a complete ouster.*'

It may be objected that while this provides a *practical* reason for distinguishing the two types of case, it does not provide a *principled* answer to the question posed above: why is it that Lord Reid's reasoning does not apply to ouster clauses where a six week 'grace period' is allowed? There is no simple answer to this objection. In one sense, Lord Reid's reasoning is just too strong: its logic impels the conclusion that *all* ouster clauses providing that decisions 'shall not be questioned' or 'are conclusive' are of no effect (as long as the decision in question is a nullity) – whether or not an applicant is afforded a six week period in which to bring a challenge.

Still, *East Elloe* and *Ostler* have, however, been followed in a number of more recent cases. Thus in *R v Secretary of State for the Environment ex p Kent* (1988), the applicant was frustrated by a six week ouster clause, even though the reason that he had not challenged the decision in question (a grant of planning permission) within six weeks was that the local council had mistakenly failed to notify him of the application for planning permission! (See also *R v Cornwall County Council ex p Huntingdon* (1992)).

The absence of principle in the case law can be illustrated by asking a simple question: what would happen if legislation included a 'one week' ouster clause? Or a 'one day' ouster clause? Presumably, at some point the courts would conclude that such a provision was no longer 'more in the nature of a limitation period than of a complete ouster', to quote Lord Denning's words – and when that dividing line had been crossed, the court would treat the provision according to the principles governing total ouster clauses (see below). But at present, the basis upon which such a dividing line could be drawn is not clear.

In relation to total ouster clauses, the reasoning of Lord Reid in *Anisminic* remained undisturbed by *Ostler* and the other six week ouster clauses cases. We therefore need to return to the first of the two questions which we asked at the end of para 18.3. Which grounds of judicial review will, if established, lead the court to conclude that the decision in question is a 'nullity', such that Lord Reid's reasoning that 'there never was a decision' can operate?

18.5   Total ouster clauses

Lord Reid himself did not in *Anisminic* provide a formal answer to the question. But he made it clear that his answer would have been a wide one, from the range of examples which he gave:

'There are many cases where, although the tribunal had jurisdiction to enter into the inquiry, it has done or failed to do something in the course of the inquiry which is of such a nature that its decision is a nullity. It may have given its decision in bad faith. It may have made a decision which it had no power to make. It may have failed in the course of the inquiry to comply with the requirements of natural justice. It may in perfect good faith have misconstrued the provision giving it power to act so that it failed to deal with the question remitted to it and decided some question which was not remitted to it. It may have refused to take into account something which it was required to take into account. Or it may have based its decision on some matter which, under the provisions setting it up, it had no right to take into account. I do not intend this list to be exhaustive.'

Lord Reid may not have meant the list to be exhaustive, but in fact, with the exception of irrationality, it is difficult to think of any head of review which does not fall within Lord Reid's catalogue. He clearly did not think that all errors which a body might make would lead to the decision being a nullity, because he continued the above passage as follows:

'But if [a body] decides a question remitted to it for decision without committing any of these errors it is as much entitled to decide that question wrongly as it is to decide it rightly.'

The difficulty, post-*Anisminic*, has been to identify *any* errors which fall within this latter category; ie errors which do *not* take the body outside its powers (which are not 'jurisdictional errors'). Without going through the subsequent case law in enormous detail, the following different (and contradictory) views of the law can be suggested:

- *View 1*: All errors of law are jurisdictional; any public law decision which is judicially reviewable takes the decision-maker outside its powers.

  You may remember that we suggested that this is the everyday working assumption of the courts in cases where an ouster clause is not involved (Chapter 13, para 13.7 above). It was also the view taken by Lord Denning MR in *Pearlman v Governors of Harrow School* (1978). There the question was whether a challenge to the decision of a county court judge that a central heating system was not a 'structural alteration' for the purposes of the Housing Act 1974 was barred by a provision that 'any determination [of the judge] shall be final and conclusive'. Lord Denning (in the minority of the Court of Appeal on this point) held that the distinction between jurisdictional and non-jurisdictional errors of law was so fine that it could now be 'discarded'; all errors of law were jurisdictional, and since the judge had (he thought) made an error of law, the Court of Appeal could avoid the ouster clause and quash the decision by holding that there never was a valid 'determination' for the ouster clause to protect.

- *View 2:* There is still, for all public decision-makers, a distinction between 'jurisdictional' and 'non-jurisdictional' errors of law.

  This was the view of the other two members of the Court of Appeal in *Pearlman*, Lane and Everleigh LJJ. Unfortunately, the two judges then disagreed as to whether the particular decision before them was or was not jurisdictional! Everleigh LJ held that the error *did* take the county court judge outside his powers, and the decision could therefore be quashed (thereby agreeing with Lord Denning in the result), while Lane LJ, dissenting, held that the decision was one on which Parliament had given the judge the power to decide wrongly as well as rightly – and that his decision therefore could not be questioned. Lane LJ's dissenting view has been supported by the Privy Council in *South East Asia Fire Bricks v Non-Metallic Mineral Products Manufacturing Employees Union* (1981), and by the High Court of Australia.

- *View 3:* The compromise position of Lord Diplock in *Re Racal Communications Ltd* (1981).

In the decision of the House of Lords in *Re Racal*, Lord Diplock (with whom Lord Keith agreed), set out a position mid-way between Lord Denning and Lane LJ's views in *Pearlman*. He held:

(i)   That as respects *administrative tribunals and authorities*, the effect of *Anisminic* is effectively (as Lord Denning said) that any error of law takes such a body outside its powers; there is no longer any distinction between jurisdictional and non-jurisdictional errors of law.

(ii) However, as regards *inferior courts of law* (such as county courts), there was 'no similar presumption'; Parliament may have given an inferior court the power to decide questions of law wrongly. The 'subtle distinctions' between jurisdictional and non-jurisdictional errors of law thus survive in this context. Since *Pearlman* concerned the decision of a county court judge, Lane LJ's dissenting judgment was, on the facts, correct.

The practical reasoning behind Lord Diplock's distinction between administrative bodies and inferior courts is that Parliament is more likely to have intended to leave the ultimate power to adjudicate upon questions of law to a court than to an administrative body which may not be legally qualified. This has been translated by Lord Diplock into a 'presumption' about the intention of Parliament.

Many students find the above distinctions not only of great complexity theoretically, but confusing practically, because the present state of the law is so uncertain. However, strictly in point of authority, it is now becoming clear that neither view 1 (Lord Denning's view in *Pearlman*) nor view 2 (Lane LJ's approach) have been followed by later decisions. Instead, Lord Diplock's view in *Re Racal* now represents the law. Even though only Lord Keith of the House of Lords explicitly agreed with him in that case (and even though Slade LJ did not accept Lord Diplock's view in the later case of *R v Registrar of Companies ex p Central Bank of India* (1986)), Lord Diplock's view appears to have been approved (obiter) by the House of Lords in *R v Hull University Visitor ex p Page* (1992), followed in *R v Visitors to the Inns of Court ex p Calder* (1993).

One is still left, at the end of the day, with no clear answer to the question of *how* one identifies those errors of law which an inferior court has the power to decide rightly or wrongly. Lord Diplock in *Re Racal* suggested that where the question at issue is 'an interrelated question of law, fact and degree' (for example, 'does the installation of central heating count as a 'structural alteration'?), the courts should be slow to hold that Parliament did not intend a county court judge to have the power ultimately to decide the question. Nevertheless, it is difficult not to have some sympathy with the view of Lord Denning in *Pearlman*:

> 'So fine is the distinction [between errors within and without jurisdiction] that in truth the High Court has a choice before it whether to interfere with an inferior court on a point of law. If it chooses to interfere, it can formulate its decision in the words: 'The court below had no jurisdiction to decide this point wrongly as it did.' If it chooses not to interfere, it can say: 'The court had jurisdiction to decide it wrongly, and did so.' Softly be it stated, but that is the reason for the difference between the decision of the Court of Appeal in *Anisminic* and the House of Lords.'

18.6 'Super-ouster clauses'?

In this chapter, we have not, for reasons of simplicity, distinguished between different types of total ouster clause. On the whole, this is justifiable because Lord Reid's basic *Anisminic* reasoning applies to all such clauses, however worded. Thus, the courts have found that review for jurisdictional error is not excluded notwithstanding a provision that:

- the decision 'shall not be questioned' (*Anisminic* itself);

- the decision is 'final and conclusive': *R v Medical Appeal Tribunal ex p Gilmore* (1957);

- the decision 'shall not be removed by *certiorari*': *per* Lord Denning, *obiter*, in *Gilmore*.

However, it should not be assumed that this will necessarily always be the case. It is at least possible that a super-ouster clause could be framed so as to defeat Lord Reid's reasoning, thereby excluding judicial review entirely.

For example, consider a clause providing that:

> 'any decision or purported decision made *or purported to be made* under the authority of [the statutory power] shall not be called into question in any proceedings whatsoever.'

It could not be argued that because the decision was a nullity, there was no *purported* (as opposed to actual) decision; thus it might be that a court would hold that such an ouster was effective to exclude judicial review. The question is largely theoretical, because no ouster clause in such terms has been enacted; however, you might want to consider the effect of s 4 of the Local Government Act 1987, which provides that:

> 'Anything done by the Secretary of State before the passing of this Act for the purposes of the relevant provisions ... shall be deemed to have been done in compliance with those provisions.'

Whilst there is no reported case dealing with s 4, it may be that the courts would still seek to resist the 'deeming' effect of the provision by holding that anything done by the Secretary of State which was in fact *not* for the purposes of the relevant provisions is not, by the terms of the provision, to be the subject of the 'deeming' clause. In that way, the court would preserve, at least in a limited measure, the ability to scrutinise by way of judicial review decisions taken under the relevant provisions.

Restrictions on Review:
Ouster Clauses

An ouster clause is a legislative provision which purports to limit or exclude the power of the courts to review a decision.

The courts interpret ouster clauses as restrictively as possible; there is a presumption that Parliament did not intend to prevent the courts from exercising their constitutional role of scrutinising the exercise of power by public bodies, and of quashing decisions flawed by errors of law. However, there is a clear distinction between the courts' attitude to two types of ouster clauses:

- *Six week ouster clauses* (providing that a decision may not be challenged in any way after a six week period); and

- *Total ouster clauses* (which purport to exclude the jurisdiction of the court completely by providing, for example, that a decision 'shall not be questioned' in any court of law).

The courts will almost invariably respect a *six week ouster clause*. An applicant may not challenge a decision after the six week period, even if it is alleged that the delay is the responsibility of the respondent:

> *Smith v East Elloe Regional District Council* (1956)

> *R v Secretary of State for the Environment ex p Ostler* (1976)

> *R v Secretary of State for the Environment ex p Kent* (1988)

There is a far greater reluctance to accept that the court's jurisdiction has been excluded by a *total ouster clause*. In *Anisminic v Foreign Compensation Commission* (1969), the House of Lords held that if the error of law allegedly committed by the decision-maker takes the body outside its powers (ie if it is a 'jurisdictional error'), then the courts' ability to intervene is *not* excluded by a 'shall not be questioned' clause, because the court in reviewing the decision is not 'calling into question' the decision, but rather finding that a valid decision was never made.

Anisminic left open the question of *which* errors of law are 'jurisdictional errors' such that the court can avoid the effect of a total ouster clause and intervene. This generated great confusion in the subsequent case law. The position now appears to be that enunciated by Lord Diplock in *Re Racal Communications Ltd* (1981):

- as regards administrative tribunals and authorities, *all* errors of law are jurisdictional errors, so that the court, if it finds that the decision-maker has made an error of law, can always evade the ouster clause and intervene to quash the decision (approving, in this context, the view of Lord Denning MR in *Pearlman v Governors of Harrow School* (1978));

- as regards inferior courts of law, it may be that in particular circumstances Parliament did intend to give an inferior court the power to decide questions of law wrongly as well as rightly – ie in this context, an error of law may be 'non-jurisdictional' (approving, in this context, the dissenting opinion of Lane LJ in *Pearlman*).

This distinction was approved by the House of Lords in *R v Hull University Visitor ex p Page* (1992). It is not, however, very clear how one identifies which errors of law are non-jurisdictional, beyond the point that 'interrelated question of law, fact and degree' are more likely, insofar as they are treated as questions of law, to be non-jurisdictional. As Lord Denning has suggested, in practice the tail appears to wag the dog; if the court wishes to intervene, then it will label the error of law as going to jurisdiction.

Index